Helmut
Laßmann
Juli '80

Feeding and the Feeding Apparatus in Waders

Feeding and the feeding apparatus in waders: a study of anatomy and adaptations in the Charadrii

Philip J. K. Burton

Trustees of The British Museum (Natural History)
London: 1974

First edition 1974.

Publication no. 719
ISBN 0 565 00719 X

British Museum (Natural History)
Cromwell Road
London
SW7 5BD

Abstract

This book presents detailed information on the anatomy of jaws, tongue and neck in the Charadrii, devoting most attention to the important superfamily Charadrioidea. The adaptive significance of modifications encountered is assessed as far as possible, aided by studies of feeding behaviour and diet in five representative species – Golden Plover, Redshank, Curlew, Dunlin and Common Snipe. These five also receive special attention in the anatomical sections. The results of these studies are followed by a summary of available information on feeding behaviour for other members of the superfamily.

Environmental forces acting on the skull and jaws during feeding are analysed, and essential features of the morphology and mechanics of the skull are reviewed and discussed. Succeeding sections describe jaw musculature, tongue, the hyoid skeleton and hyoid musculature, salivary glands and epidermal structures, and cervical muscles inserting on the skull. In the descriptions of muscles, particular attention has been paid to the orientation and siting of raphes and aponeuroses. Quantitative data are given on tongue length relative to that of the bill. Throughout, descriptions of structures are followed by discussions of their functions.

Adaptive features in the representative species are surveyed and discussed, and other species of Charadrii are then reviewed from adaptive and taxonomic standpoints. The concluding discussion considers evolutionary implications of some aspects of this study, and some problems involved in interpreting the adaptive or phylogenetic significance of anatomical features.

Contents

Contents continued

Acknowledgements

For his help and encouragement during this investigation I owe a considerable debt to Sir Landsborough Thomson who acted as my adviser on behalf of the Scientific Research in Schools Committee of the Royal Society, and continued to assist after I had relinquished my teaching post to take up an appointment at the British Museum (Natural History). I am also deeply indebted to Dr. A. d'A. Bellairs for his valuable advice and criticism throughout this study.

A grant from the Royal Society was of much assistance during the early part of this study.

Mr. J. D. Macdonald, Dr. D. W. Snow and the staff of the Bird Section at the British Museum (Natural History) deserve thanks for the willing assistance given to me first as a visitor and now as a colleague. I should like to record my especial gratitude to Mr. G. Cowles for his help in connection with anatomical material and Miss E. Crawford for typing this manuscript.

Some of the specimens used in this study were loaned by the American Museum of Natural History, New York, the Smithsonian Institution, Washington D.C., the Yale Peabody Museum, New Haven, Connecticut, and the Zoological Institute of the Academy of Sciences of the U.S.S.R., Leningrad. My sincere thanks are due to the staffs of these institutions who made these loans possible. For the use of ciné films I am indebted to Professor N. Tinbergen and Mr. K. Watkins.

Permission to collect some protected species was granted by the Nature Conservancy. Mr. G. H. Fowler and the Rev. N. Motley gave permission to collect and make observations on their land, without which a great deal of this investigation could not have been carried out.

Many other people have helped with advice, information and translations. I would particularly like to thank Dr. J. S. Ash, Prof. W. J. Bock, Dr. J. Jehl, Mr. A. Kollator, Dr. D. Lack, Dr. G. L. Maclean, Mr. K. Morimoto, Dr. R. K. Murton, Mr. A. M. Suggate and Dr. R. L. Zusi.

This book is a modified version of a thesis accepted by the University of London for the degree of Doctor of Philosophy, 1969. Before undertaking this revision, the thesis was read and criticized by Prof. W. J. Bock and Dr. R. L. Zusi, and I am sincerely grateful to them for their comments and suggestions. Soon after completion of this thesis I was able to visit the American Museum of Natural History, New York, aided by the Frank M. Chapman Memorial Fund. This gave the opportunity for valuable discussion, and for further examination of anatomical material, prior to preparing this account for publication. I owe special thanks to Dr. Dean Amadon for the facilities placed at my disposal.

For her patience and forbearance, as well as for valuable criticism, I am deeply grateful to my wife.

Introduction

A striking feature of the avian order Charadriiformes is the wide range of feeding adaptations exhibited by its members. The order comprises three suborders; Charadrii (waders and allies); Lari (skuas, gulls, terns and skimmers) and Alcae (auks). By far the greatest diversity is shown by the first of these three, and in particular the superfamily Charadrioidea, with which this account is mainly concerned. The vernacular term "waders" is usually applied specifically to the Charadrioidea in Britain; the North American usage is "shorebirds". The diversity of this group, and the extremes of specialization reached by some species, have rendered them an attractive subject for studies of functional anatomy, and they are well represented in the literature. Previous accounts have, however, dealt principally with the skull and kinetic mechanism. The present investigation has been undertaken to gain a detailed knowledge of the anatomy of systems so far treated less fully or not at all; and to elucidate as far as possible the adaptive significance of the structural modifications encountered.

A thorough knowledge of feeding methods is obviously necessary for an understanding of feeding adaptations. The literature on the feeding behaviour of waders is extensive, but very rarely detailed or careful enough for the purposes of the present study. To remedy this, field observations, study of captive birds, examination of ciné film and analysis of stomach contents have all been carried out, in addition to the anatomical work. A comprehensive review of the waders is aimed at, since this approach makes it possible to view the various adaptations in an evolutionary perspective. However, only a small proportion of the species available for dissection could also be studied in life. Therefore, five species have been selected for intensive study, and information for the remainder is presented in more concise form. These five are Golden Plover (*Pluvialis apricaria*), Redshank (*Tringa totanus*), Curlew (*Numenius arquata*), Dunlin (*Calidris alpina*) and Common Snipe (*Gallinago gallinago*). They were chosen partly because they are common and relatively easily observed, and also because they illustrate important and distinctive types of feeding modification. Observations on the first four were all made in the same area, a region of coastal fresh marsh, salting and mudflats near Sales Point, Bradwell-on-Sea, Essex. This has facilitated comparison between the species. The fifth, Common Snipe, occurs only sporadically at Bradwell, and was watched at Beddington, Surrey. Throughout this account, the five are referred to as "the representative species", and the Bradwell area as "the study area".

The thesis is divided into two main parts followed by conclusions and discussion. The first part deals with feeding behaviour, and presents detailed information for the representative species, followed by a summary of available information for other waders. The second part is concerned with anatomy. Skull morphology and kinetics are reviewed, followed by descriptions of the musculature of jaws, tongue and the anterior part of the neck, and of epidermal features and salivary glands. In the myological sections, there is emphasis on muscle architecture, and the disposition of aponeuroses and the orientation of fibres are carefully described. Emphasis on the representative species is most marked in the jaw muscle accounts, since the complexity of these muscles has produced a wealth of detail; information on jaw myology for species other than the representative ones is given in condensed form, in small type. Species representing other superfamilies of the Charadrii have also been dissected, in the hope of shedding further light on the evolution of feeding mechanisms in the Charadrioidea. The chief results of these dissections are presented concisely at the end of the anatomical section; further information concerning feeding adaptations in these superfamilies is given by Yudin (1965). The conclusions consist of a comparison of adaptations in the representative species, followed by a review of the Charadrii as a whole in which taxonomic as well as adaptive problems are considered. The final discussion examines some general points emerging from these conclusions.

The classification and nomenclature followed are basically those of Peters (1934), but incorporate the modifications used by Thomson (1964). The chief of these are the adoption of Bock's (1958) proposals for the plovers, the inclusion of *Limosa* and *Limnodromus* with the Calidridinae, as in the A.O.U. Check-list (1957), and the inclusion of Peters' *Erolia* species in *Calidris*, in conformity with current European practice. The sequence used throughout for the representative species differs from that of Peters in placing *G. gallinago* last. This is done because of the five, the Snipe exhibits the most extreme condition of important morphological trends in the Charadrioidea. This sequence thus permits much of the subject-matter to be presented in a more logical order.

Literature concerning feeding behaviour and anatomy is reviewed or referred to in appropriate places in the text. Some sources of information of general importance may be mentioned here. A major part of the theoretical groundwork for this, as for many other studies of adaptation, is provided by Simpson (1953). In addition, an important and helpful discussion of adaptation is that of Bock & Von Wahlert (1965) ; in this paper, many important concepts are clarified and definitions formulated. The reviews by Bock (1959, 1963 and 1965) have also been found valuable.

Part 1: Feeding Methods

Detailed accounts are presented for the five representative species. The following methods have been used to provide information:

1. Field observations. Observations have been made with the aid of a ×60 telescope and ×8 binoculars, either from natural cover, or from a hide mounted on skis to enable it to be towed across a mudflat. Running commentaries made into a portable tape recorder have yielded abundant data in a form amenable to numerical treatment where required.

2. Examination of tracks. In the case of deep probe holes, injection with latex has been used to make casts for examination.

3. Observations on captive birds, carried out only for *G. gallinago*.

4. Film analysis. Frame by frame examination of the films "The Beachcombers" (Zoology Dept., Oxford University) and "Winter Meadow" (Mr. K. Watkins) has been used to supplement field observations on *Numenius arquata* and *G. gallinago*. As these films run at 24 f.p.s., it was not possible to use them to determine the speed of any but the slowest actions.

5. Analyses of stomach contents of birds collected in the study area, or nearby parts of the Essex coast. The primary aim of these analyses has been to discover as far as possible the prey obtained in the study area by the feeding methods observed. In the case of Redshank and Dunlin, this has been accomplished largely by collecting birds after they had been watched feeding. Golden Plover and Curlew could only be obtained while flighting at dawn or dusk, or with the tide. Common Snipe were watched in a different area from which an adequate sample could not be collected; information on diet for this species rests on material examined from other areas, and on the extensive survey by Sperry (1940).

The merits and demerits of various methods of assessing the food of birds have been discussed by Hartley (1948). In the present account, the total number of items for each type of prey are given, followed (in brackets) by the number of stomachs from which it was recorded. Empty, or nearly empty stomachs are not included in the total examined.

Special attention has been paid to the size and condition of major items; small prey, such as *Hydrobia*, have been measured with an eyepiece micrometer graticule.

Material obtained for several other species can only be presented very briefly here, but will form the basis of future papers on comparative feeding ecology. This includes observations made on the South East Caspian, Iran in autumn 1963, and in Texas during spring 1969. This material is combined with a review of feeding methods throughout the suborder, based on accounts in the literature. Only species examined anatomically are included. Valuable reference sources are Bent (1927–29), Stout (1967), Witherby *et al.* (1943), Kozlova (1962), and the detailed comparative survey compiled by Streefkerk (1960).

Golden Plover *(Pluvialis apricaria)*

The feeding behaviour of Golden Plovers has been investigated by field observation only. In the study area they feed principally inland, and leys are particularly favoured for much of the winter. Permanent pasture and plough are also used, and there is some preference for ley grown over stubble in autumn, and for fields of young wheat in early spring. Much feeding takes place at night.

Feeding Golden Plovers show great mobility. They move by repeated runs of a few yards at a time, interrupted by pauses in a very upright attitude. These pauses frequently lead to feeding movements, either directly, or after a further pause with the head lowered close to the ground and bill pointing ahead. This attitude is maintained for about a second, and a peck at the ground usually follows. Some feeding movements occur after short, swift runs. Fallett (1962) presents evidence from Golden Plovers in captivity that prey can be located by hearing, and she suggests that the two pauses enable this to be done. In any case, it is clear that many prey animals are also found entirely by visual hunting. The majority of feeding movements last only a fraction of a second, and are referred to as pecks. More prolonged movements may last for several seconds; for a few, an arbitrary element

* Feeding methods of *Turdus* spp. resemble those of pasture feeding plovers; it therefore seems relevant that Heppner (1965) has concluded from experiments on *Turdus migratorius* that earthworms are located only by visual means.

is involved in deciding whether to class them as pecks. Either may be accompanied by very rapid vibrations of the head, and longer ones frequently also include several slower but larger up and down movements. Prolonged movements often involve deep insertion of the bill into the ground. Pecks are sometimes arrested in mid-air, without contacting the ground ("abortive pecks"), and pauses with head lowered are sometimes not followed by a feeding movement ("abortive pauses"). The capture of some prey, particularly worms, can be clearly seen, but the consumption of many small items must escape notice. Numerical data summarized in Table I combine observations of 15 individuals feeding on pasture.

The 855 feeding movements were recorded in 217 minutes, a mean rate of 3·9 per minute (Maximum 9). Only a short sequence is available from the shore. The rate for 6 minutes averaged about 13 movements per minute (8 to 16) and all movements were pecks, only one (out of 80) preceded by a pause with head lowered. This recalls the behaviour of *P. squatarola* on the shore.

Table I shows that many prolonged movements are not preceded by a pause with head lowered, but they are more often preceded by a short run. Twenty-eight direct movements, and 15 preceded by a head lowered pause were seen to result in the capture of a worm. Evidently dashes to capture prey seen at the surface are an important

	Pecks	Prolonged	Abortive pecks	TOTAL	Preceded by run
Preceded by pause, head down	153 (17·9)	166 (19·4)	24 (2·8)	343 (40·1)	16 (1·9)
Not preceded by pause, head down	223 (26·1)	142 (16·6)	86 (10·0)	451 (52·7)	37 (4·3)
Abortive pauses				61 (7·1)	3 (0·4)
TOTAL	376 (44·0)	308 (36·0)	110 (12·9)	855	56 (6·6)

Table I.
Feeding movements of *P. apricaria* on pasture. (Percentages of total in brackets.)

hunting method as well as the postulated "listening" technique. The large number of pecks and abortive pecks not preceded by a pause suggests that this method results in a high proportion of failures. Approximately a third of the feeding movements recorded were made more or less to one side.

Once grasped in the bill, worms are pulled out nearly vertically by stretching the neck and tilting the body. The bill is inclined at *c.* 45° to the horizontal. Often, the worm slips, and is quickly seized again, and it also frequently breaks. Many objects are seized with the jaws widely open ("snatching"), so that a large piece of earth is grasped together with the prey.

Stomach contents of birds collected in the study area have been analysed, and results are given in Table II. Examination and measurement of the earthworm fragments in these stomachs indicate that a large proportion of the earthworms taken are incomplete, the anterior end having broken away from the rest. Many of these are large specimens of *Lumbricus terrestris;* this species is abundant in the study area, and is often found lying with the anterior end protruding from a burrow. Evidently this provides valuable opportunities for the plovers. Intact worms up to 75 mm. long have been found in Golden Plover stomachs.

Redshank *(Tringa totanus)*

A general account of the feeding behaviour of this species is given by Streefkerk. In the Essex study area, Redshanks feed on intertidal mud, saltmarsh creeks, by fresh or brackish dykes inland, and on rough pasture. On the mud there is a preference for pools or the tideline. Feeding takes place also by night.

Most observations have been carried out on the shore. The usual gait is a brisk walk, interspersed with occasional runs. Feeding movements can be classed as pecks, jabs, probes and "mowing". Pecks are swift, brief movements contacting only the mud surface, and are usually made on the move, either straight ahead, or to one side. Abortive pecks also occur. In shallow pools, pecks are made in the same manner, and usually appear to touch the bottom. In deeper water, pecks are made at the surface, and an attitude with neck stretched up and bill pointed steeply down is often adopted. The amount of opening involved in the pecks is slight, and usually scarcely visible. Probes are short, single movements, involving bill insertion into the mud. Most are to less than the full length of the bill, and slight up and down vibration is usual. "Mowing" is a prolonged action usually carried out while walking forward, in which the bill is held nearly vertical with its tip in contact with the mud while the lower jaw makes extremely rapid small vibrations. The head is usually moved

Food items	Total No. of items (Nos. of stomachs bracketed)
ANNELIDA (18 stomachs):	
Oligochaeta:	
Lumbricus	11 (7)
Allolobophora	> 68 (13)
INSECTA (23 stomachs):	
Lepidoptera (2 stomachs):	
Caterpillars	2 (2)
Coleoptera (22 stomachs):	
Carabidae, adults	37 (13)
,, larvae	14 (8)
Hydrophilidae, adults	9 (6)
Staphylinidae, adults	17 (9)
,, larvae	6 (6)
Silphidae, adults	3 (2)
Curculionidae, *Sitona* (ads.)	20 (11)
,, larvae	1 (1)
Diptera (16 stomachs):	
Orthorrhapha:	
Tipulidae, larvae	11 (4)
Bibio, larvae	>350 (15)
Cyclorrhapha: larvae	27 (11)
ARACHNIDA (2 stomachs):	
Aranoida: Lycosidae	2 (2)
MOLLUSCA (8 stomachs):	
Prosobranchia:	
Littorina neritoides	2 (2)
Hydrobia ulvae	>100 (3)
Pulmonata:	
Helicidae	3 (2)
Limacidae, *Agriolimax*	94 (4)
Undetermined eggs	8 (1)
PLANT MATERIAL:	
Wheat grains	23 (2)
Grass	(25)
Miscellaneous	(11)
Stones and shell fragments, 2–9 mm.	255 (26)

Table II.
Pluvialis apricaria: contents of 28 stomachs from Bradwell-on-Sea, Essex.

from side to side while "mowing", and the mean length of 100 timed sweeping movements is 2·8 secs (Maximum 10·4). Possibly "mowing" is intended to cause prey to move and reveal themselves. Most prey are swallowed swiftly with only small head and mandible movements; small crabs may require more violent head jerking to raise them from bill tip to mouth. Prey are sometimes washed in pools or the tideline, as in many other waders.

Goss-Custard (1967) has shown a relationship between feeding rate and climatic factors, especially mud temperature, in a population of Redshanks feeding largely on *Corophium*. Data obtained in the present study are less extensive, but serve to indicate the relative frequency of different feeding actions. Table III combines details from 16 individuals during the period September to March in three winters.

Table III.
Feeding movements of *Tringa totanus*.

Movement	Total		Mean No. per minute	Max. No. per minute
Pecks	922	79·8	22·6	46
Abortive pecks	16	1·4	0·4	4
"Mowing"	146	12·6	3·6	29
Probes	71	6·1	1·7	7
TOTAL	1155		28·3	49

Insufficient information is available to demonstrate variation in these ratios with conditions, but it is clear that pecks are of great importance in most circumstances.

Analyses of stomach contents for birds collected in the study area and neighbouring districts are presented in Table IV. It is clear from these that *Hydrobia* is a major item, and probably many of the high proportion of pecks observed are made to obtain this prey. This is not always the case, however; two birds shot after long sequences of pecks had been observed had stomachs containing entirely crustacea, mainly shrimps (Decapoda, Caridea). The proportion of captures seen to follow those pecks was under 10%, although the capture of such large prey could hardly escape detection. Presumably most were failures, due perhaps, to the darting escape movements of the prey.

Nereidae, *Macoma* and *Cardium* are nearly certain to have been obtained by probing; probably many *Corophium* are obtained in this way, although this amphipod may also be taken from shallow pools.

The swiftness and shallowness of most probes indicates that these prey are generally obtained near the surface; their position is presumably indicated by visual clues.

Food items	Total No. of items (Nos. of stomachs bracketed) Littoral (31)	Pasture (4)
ANNELIDA (16 stomachs):		
Polychasta, Nereidae	> 281 (15)	
Oligochaeta, *Lumbricus*		1 (1)
CRUSTACEA (17 stomachs):		
Isopoda, undetermined	1 (1)	
Amphipoda, *Corophium*	> 26 (4)	
Decapoda, Caridea	> 41 (8)	
,, Brachyura, *Carcinus*	> 16 (10)	
INSECTA (4 stomachs):		
Coleoptera; adults		3 (2)
Diptera, Tipulidae; larvae		2 (2)
,, Cyclorrhapha; larvae		3 (2)
,, ,, adults		30 (2)
MOLLUSCA (22 stomachs):		
Gastropoda (19 stomachs):		
Littorina rudis	6 (1)	
Hydrobia ulvae	>1050 (19)	
Lamellibranchia (8 stomachs):		
Mytilus edulis	1 (1)	
Cardium edule	1 (1)	
Macoma balthica	> 23 (7)	
CHORDATA (1 stomach):		
Pisces, *Gobius*	11 (1)	
Grass scraps (3 stomachs)		(3)
Stones, 2–5 mm. (2 stomachs)		65 (2)

Table IV.
Tringa totanus: Contents of 32 stomachs from Bradwell-on-Sea and neighbouring parts of Essex.

The lengths of 392 *Hydrobia* from these guts have been measured, giving a mean of $2{\cdot}53 \pm 0{\cdot}123$ mm. ($P=0{\cdot}99$). *Macoma* and *Cardium* specimens taken did not exceed 7 mm. in length. Three hundred and forty-two Nereid mandibles were also measured; mean and confidence limits after adjustment to the minimum number of individuals represented (177; based on individual stomach totals) is $1{\cdot}51 \pm 0{\cdot}041$ mm. ($P>0{\cdot}99$). Observation of feeding methods suggests that only a fragment of the worm is captured in many cases, but the remains in the guts were too digested to shed any light on this. The largest prey item recorded was a shrimp (*Crangon*) measuring approximately 70 mm., and swallowed whole. Other shrimps found were in the size range 25–35 mm. Crabs (*Carcinus*) are also swallowed whole; the largest specimens measured 12 mm. across the carapace.

Curlew *(Numenius arquata)*

Field observations

Curlews appear to feed almost entirely by day. In the study area they feed at all levels of intertidal mud, but especially exposed mud, well away from the tideline, and also on saltings and pasture (permanent or ley). Seasonal variations of diet are partly reflected in habitat use.

Streefkerk (1960) assigned the feeding movements of Curlews to three categories: pecks, in which only the bill tip touches the substrate; jabs, in which about half the bill is inserted; and probes, in which it is fully inserted. He suggests that jabs are trial probes, intended to locate prey, and this is probably true, although the difference is not clear cut. Prolonged, and successful, probes, often involve quite shallow insertion. Jabs are perhaps best characterized by their brevity; most are too swift for accurate timing with a stopwatch. Pecks form a large proportion of feeding movements under all circumstances, but their significance is not always easy to assess. When small crabs are abundant, they are of course captured by pecks; most pecks, however, do not result in any obvious capture, and possibly they, too, permit tactile detection of prey lying near the surface.

The proportions of these movements vary considerably with conditions; the greatest amount of observations have been made on tidal mud in midwinter, and these are summarized in Table V.

Jabs are used least often on the lower shore, and when crab hunting. On the flat smooth mud below mid-tide level, Curlews may be seen to

Movement	Total	%	Mean No. per minute	Max. No. per minute
Peck	819	48·7	7·0	16
Jab	503	29·9	4·3	27
Probe	361	21·4	3·1	8
TOTAL	1683		14·4	36

Table V.
Feeding movements of *Numenius arquata* on intertidal mud.

walk with head held high, making frequent runs, sometimes of several yards, ending in a probe for prey that has presumably been seen. Hunting by sight is also used for catching crabs, which are an important prey on the upper shore in autumn.

Probes may commence directly in front or diagonally to one side. They involve a great deal of movement of head and neck, and of legs and feet, as the bill is inserted. Side to side, forward and back, and up and down head movements are all used. Slower raising and lowering of the head over a wide range is also seen during a probe, apparently connected with changes of bill angle at depth. Turning the bill around its long axis normally takes place with a comparatively short length inserted; if the bill is already deeply in, it is usually raised before turning or taken out and reinserted. However, turns of up to half a circle have been seen with the bill full length in the mud. Groups of two to four probes close together normally occur in the course of pursuing or consuming a single prey organism. On pasture, the bill may be inserted just under the surface beneath grass tussocks. To accomplish this, the head is turned nearly upside down, so that its decurved tip lies nearly horizontal. Among the ridges of inshore mud, the bill may be inserted horizontally ahead, into the side of a ridge. Probe depths could be observed only on flat open mud; about half were to the full length of the bill, and occasionally the head entered the probe hole. The mean for 80 probes timed on intertidal mud is 5·0 secs. (Maximum 25·0). At the rate shown in Table V this suggests that as much as 25% of the time spent feeding on the shore may be occupied in probing.

With the exception of lamellibranchs, subterranean prey are extracted before being swallowed. They emerge gripped usually only by the bill tip, and can often be identified. Small earthworms and polychaetes are removed piecemeal in the course of several grouped probes. Washing of prey in a tidal pool is sometimes seen. The passage of small prey up the bill is effected by rapid, small opening and shutting movements of the mandible, accompanied by backward jerks of the head as it is gradually raised. Large worms are conveyed to the mouth and swallowed by fewer and more violent movements, with the bill nearer horizontal. Large specimens of *Macoma* and *Cardium* are difficult to grip owing to their shape and hardness. They appear to be swallowed without complete withdrawal of the bill, the mud presumably stopping the mollusc from slipping as it is raised by successive movements. A freak incident of a Curlew attempting, and failing, to swallow *Littorina* is reported by Fenton (1953). Small crabs are rapidly consumed in the same way as most small prey; larger ones are sometimes held by the legs of one side as they are raised. They are frequently dropped, and crab consumption may be a slow process. Twenty timed captures gave a mean of 6·3 secs. (Maximum 14·0). Apparently crabs are swallowed whole (see below) and presumably alive. An incident witnessed once suggests that this is not without hazard! A large crab (20 to 25 mm.) was swallowed, and about a minute later the curlew ran sideways across the mud for some 30 yards, sank down, and lay on its tarsi for several seconds with the bill widely open. It then stood up, apparently recovered. It is hard to resist the conclusion that the crab had gripped the oesophagus wall with a chela, and that the bird's extraordinary behaviour was a result of pain.

A distinctive method of crab capture has been observed at Foulness, where the inshore mud is covered with the leaves of *Zostera noltii*. The technique was to walk slowly across the mud with the bill tip in contact with the *Zostera*, and the mandible making rapid, small movements very similar to the "mowing" of *T. totanus*. This was often sustained for several minutes, and every now and then a small crab was picked out of the *Zostera* leaves and eaten.

Analyses of guts collected in Essex are summarized in Table VI. These analyses do not indicate the importance of polychaetes, especially *Nereis;* this is because birds from all situations have not been equally easy to collect. The extensive use of *Nereis* is nevertheless clear from field observations, and examination of fresh probe holes, which frequently still have live pieces of *Nereis* at the bottom. *Scoloplos armiger* may also be a common item, as its capture has frequently been witnessed.

The remains of up to 70 earthworms have been found in a single gut. A greater proportion than in *P. apricaria* are small, and it appears that fewer *L. terrestris* are taken. However, measurements of fragments

Food items	Total No. of items (Nos. of stomachs bracketed)	
	Littoral (22)	Pasture (20)
ANNELIDA (15 stomachs):		
Polychaeta (4 stomachs):		
Nereidae	> 6 (3)	
Arenicola	2 (1)	
Oligochaeta (11 stomachs):		
Lumbricus		> 20 (8)
Allolobophora		>219 (10)
CRUSTACEA (17 stomachs):		
Carcinus	>85 (17)	
INSECTA (18 stomachs):		
Lepidoptera:		
Hepialus, caterpillars		44 (9)
Coleoptera (12 stomachs):		
Carabidae, adults		12 (7)
,, larvae		31 (6)
Staphylinidae, adults		6 (5)
,, larvae		2 (2)
Scarabeidae, *Geotrupes* (ads.)		2 (2)
Elateridae, larvae		1 (1)
Diptera (10 stomachs):		
Orthorrhapha:		
Tipulidae, pupae		>130 (6)
,, larvae		12 (4)
Cyclorrhapha:		
Adults		1 (1)
Larvae		13 (4)
MOLLUSCA (8 stomachs):		
Gastropoda (2 stomachs):		
Prosobranchia, *Hydrobia*	9 (1)	
Pulmonata, *Helicella*		1 (1)
Lamellibranchia (6 stomachs):		
Cardium edule	>22 (6)	
Macoma balthica	> 7 (2)	
Grass scraps (11 stomachs)		(11)
Stones, 2–11 mm. (16 stomachs)		173 (16)

Table VI.
Numenius arquata: Contents of 39 stomachs from Bradwell-on-Sea and neighbouring parts of Essex.

indicate that on average, a greater proportion of the length of each worm is obtained. These differences reflect the use of probing, as opposed to surface snatching. Intact crabs measuring up to 26 mm. across the carapace (length 21 mm., depth 11·5 mm.) have been found in guts examined. *Cardium* and *Macoma* are swallowed whole, and the largest recorded (*Cardium*) was 13 mm. broad.

Film analysis

a. *Crab capture.* A sequence in "The Beachcombers" shows a crab measuring 20 to 25 mm. across the carapace being captured. The Curlew's efforts to swallow it do not meet with success during this short sequence.

The crab is raised up the bill principally by head jerking, synchronized with jaw movements. In one particularly violent jerk, the crab is seen to have travelled about 8 cm. up the bill in the space of one frame. Most frames give evidence of mandible movement. Movements of the upper jaw can also be detected in some cases, either by blurring – sometimes to the point of invisibility – or by straightening. These are mostly seen either when the crab is at the bill tip, or when it is at the mouth. In one case, the crab is picked up after being dropped, the jaw opening being almost entirely confined to the upper jaw. Several following frames show intense blurring of the upper jaw tip, suggesting that it is being used in pushing the crab up the bill. The upper jaw movements while the crab is at the gape are accompanied by the most extreme mandible depression in the sequence, the gap between the jaw tips reaching an estimated maximum of 45 mm. It is this stage which appears to give the bird greatest difficulty. The crab is moved up the bill held dorso-ventrally, but appears to require reorientation and precise positioning near the gape.

b. *Probing.* Probing sequences occur in "The Beachcombers" and "Winter Meadow". Jabs and full probes are seen, and the great mobility of the head and neck is well demonstrated. Changes of probe direction particularly involve the head and section I* of the neck, and in several cases these are made during insertion. An extreme case, in "The Beachcombers" shows a probe which starts directly ahead, but from about half insertion onwards is altered in direction by turning the head to the right, and rotating the bill about its long axis so that its tip travels slightly upwards.

* See p. 114 for an explanation of the sections of the neck.

Shallow probes are often made with the weight on one foot, but the legs are brought together for deep probes, and for withdrawal. In removal of the bill, sections II and III are flexed, hunching the neck back against the body; lateral flexion is seen in one case.

Dunlin *(Calidris alpina)*

Descriptions of the feeding behaviour of Dunlin have been given by several workers, including Dewar (1909), Streefkerk (1960), Ehlert (1964) and Holmes (1966).

Dunlin in the Essex study area feed on intertidal mud and in smaller numbers in saltmarsh creeks. At high tide they gather on shell beaches and spits to rest, though some feeding may take place. Some birds roost inland, especially during spring tides. Feeding takes place by night as well as by day. On the shore there is a general preference for wet mud near the tide edge, or at the mouths of creeks.

Three types of feeding action used by Dunlin are referred to here: 1. Pecks, in which the bill touches only the mud surface. 2. Probes, in which the bill is inserted into the mud. 3. "Stitching", a very rapid series of probes, usually very shallow, made close together. Each series of "stitching" is counted as one movement, as was done by Holmes. He includes "stitching" in the broader category of "jabs", together with isolated probes penetrating less than 1 cm.

Pecks are the most frequent action in most situations. They are often preceded by runs, as are many isolated probes. The high feeding rate and frequent runs give an impression of bustling activity. Location of prey is obviously largely by sight; "stitching" is presumably a method of test probing for prey location by touch. Dewar suggested that gastropods are ignored unless seen to move, and that worms may be found by looking for casts in the moment of extrusion. Many pecks are abortive, not making contact with the mud. The great majority of probes, even full length ones, are mostly too rapid for accurate timing, though probes lasting up to 20 seconds have been recorded. Rapid up and down vibration of the head ("quivering") accompanies most probes. Two or three probes are sometimes grouped in one place. Turning the bill around its axis is unusual, though turns up to a full circle, accomplished by walking round the bill, have been seen. "Stitching" generally takes place while walking forward, and may follow a straight or a zig-zag course, involving side to side head movements. The mean length of 80 "stitching" sequences is 3·9 seconds (Maximum 25·7).

Data available show a significant difference in the proportions of feeding movements between flood and ebb. Figures summarized in Table VII cover the period September to March. Although these data are not sufficiently extensive to rule out other factors, it seems likely that the differences between flood and ebb arise from the extent of saturation of the substrate. The chief differences are the greater incidence of "stitching" on the ebb, and the greater proportion of probes relative to pecks on the ebb. This is consistent with Ehlert's observation that water saturated substrates are favoured for probing, as they are less firm, and prey lie nearer the surface. This is manifested in the greater frequency of probes and "stitching" on the ebb, since for more than half the ebb, the mud in the study area is largely covered by a film of water running out of saltmarsh creeks.

Many captures are betrayed by swallowing movements and occasionally the prey is seen. Apparently the majority of prey are swallowed as the bill is extracted from the mud. At the moment of extraction, it is often possible to glimpse considerable downward deflection of the tip of the upper jaw, with daylight visible between the jaws further back. The capture of small prey by pecking must often go undetected. Worms are occasionally washed before swallowing; Ehlert comments that the "cleanness" of the worm appears unrelated to the incidence of washing.

Table VII.
Feeding movements of *Calidris alpina*. Numbers of the four categories of feeding movement were tested for association with tide direction by the use of χ^2. $P<0{\cdot}001$.

	Flood				**Ebb**			
Movement	**Number**	%	**Mean No. per min.**	**Max. No. per min.**	**Number**	%	**Mean No. per min.**	**Max. No. per min.**
Pecks	1360	70·8	27·1	54	573	54·1	15·7	61
Abortive pecks	30	1·6	0·6	5	2	0·2	< 0·1	1
Stitching	170	8·8	3·4	28	298	28·1	8·2	22
Probes	361	18·8	7·2	15	186	17·6	5·1	27
TOTAL	1921		38·3	68	1059		29·0	89

Dewar remarks on the association between Dunlin and Ringed Plovers (*Charadrius hiaticula*), and speaks of them following and feeding in the tracks of the plover.

The tracks left by feeding Dunlin have been examined, and some probe marks have been studied by making latex casts. "Stitching" tracks are characteristic. They consist of closely spaced bill marks, usually in pairs, forming straight or wavy lines across the mud. The marks show separation of 1 to 2 mm. between the jaws at the tip. Ehlert states that "stitching" tracks are most regular and closely spaced when made at night. Dewar claims that even deep probes are made with the bill slightly open. Latex casts do not, in general, support this, though in a

Food items	Total No. of items (Nos. of stomachs bracketed)
ANNELIDA (7 stomachs):	
Polychaeta, Nereidae	40 (7)
CRUSTACEA (5 stomachs):	
Amphipoda, *Talitrus saltator*	200 (4)
,, *Corophium volutator*	tr. (1)
Decapoda, Caridea	2 (1)
INSECTA (5 stomachs):	
Coleoptera:	
Hydrophilidae, *Cercyon*, ad.	1 (1)
Staphylinidae, adults	4 (4)
Diptera, Cyclorrhapha:	
Larvae	2 (2)
Adult	1 (1)
MOLLUSCA (22 stomachs):	
Gastropoda:	
Littorina neritoides	1 (1)
Crepidula fornicata	1 (1)
Hydrobia	600 (22)
Lamellibranchia:	
Cardium edule	1 (1)
Macoma balthica	1 (1)
CHORDATA (1 stomach):	
Undetermined fish	1 (1)
Plant fragments (2 stomachs):	(2)

Table VIII.
Calidris alpina: Contents of 26 stomachs from Bradwell-on-Sea and neighbouring parts of Essex.

few showing protraction of the upper jaw, a gap between the two jaws is visible. Perhaps in these cases, raising the upper jaw tip started before completion of the probe, and the jaws retraced the same path on removal, the probe having not met with success. The upper part of probe holes often shows widening, presumably by slight changes of direction while "quivering".

Dewar suggests that probes made at a shallow angle to the mud indicate attempts to follow crustaceans along their burrows. Ehlert considers this unlikely, though he suggests that shallow angled probes would stand more chance of discovering vertically oriented prey. One particularly interesting latex cast shows clearly a series of probes made along the course of a *Corophium* burrow; the final one, involving wide bill opening, was probably successful. There is, however, no indication of any attempt to insert the bill along the burrow.

The contents of 26 stomachs from birds collected in the study area were analysed. The results, presented in Table VIII, make an interesting comparison with those for Redshank (Table IV), since birds of both species were collected largely in the same situations and at the same times. *Hydrobia* is clearly a prey of great importance, and was abundant in the stomachs of all birds collected after observation; presumably a large proportion of the pecks witnessed were made to obtain this prey. A greater proportion than in Redshank were crushed and uncountable; hence, the total of 600 is a considerable underestimate. Thirteen of the Dunlin stomachs contained nothing else but *Hydrobia* (compared with only one of the Redshanks). Two hundred and eighty-eight *Hydrobia* taken by Dunlin have been measured, giving a mean of $2{\cdot}08 \pm 0{\cdot}030$ mm. ($P > 0{\cdot}99$), which is significantly lower than that for Redshank ($P > 0{\cdot}01$, Fisher-Behrens test).*

* Measurements from a larger sample of individuals would be desirable. Further investigation of partition by size of *Hydrobia* among competing waders would be rewarding, and should consider not only other species, but also the size range of prey available in different areas and at different times. (For a similar study of *Littorina* utilization, see Gibb, 1956.)

Nereids (probably mainly *Nereis diversicolor*) are also important, though less prominent in the present sample than in the larger one of Ehlert (1964). As in Redshank, no intact bodies were found. Only 64 mandibles (representing a minimum of 36 individuals) could be measured. The mean of 0·90 mm. is considerably below that for Redshank, but as with *Hydrobia*, a sample from a larger number of individuals would be desirable. The *Macoma* and *Cardium* specimens found would also have been obtained by probing; both were very small (as was the individual of *Crepidula*).

Corophium is abundant in many areas where Dunlin feed, and is probably more important than either this analysis or Ehlert's indicate. The large number of *Talitrus* and the few insects taken had been obtained on the upper shore by birds feeding on the beginning of the ebb.

Common Snipe *(Gallinago gallinago)*

Captive bird

Notes on the feeding methods of a tame snipe are given by Wormald (1909); the bird he describes had been hatched in an incubator and hand reared. The bird used in this investigation was a wild adult, captured by mist-netting, and retained in an aviary for two weeks. The aviary was provided with a small concrete floored pool, and the remaining space was covered with about an inch of fresh soil.

Earthworms and maggots were given as food. The earthworms included a wide size range, the largest being individuals of *Lumbricus terrestris* measuring about 25 cm. The bird was fed at 0900 and 1600 hours; a short spell of activity followed the morning feed, but it remained inactive for most of the day. More consistent activity followed the afternoon feed, increasing towards dusk. The overnight consumption of worms was considerably greater than during the day. Most prolonged observations were made between 1600 hours and dusk.

Most worms taken were small (under 10 cm.). These, and maggots were captured and consumed rapidly. Small worms were captured in the following manner. The bill was opened just enough to grasp the worm, apparently usually by depression of the mandible; brief protraction of the upper jaw was also seen occasionally. They were grasped initially by the tips of the jaws only, with the upper visibly deflected down, and were held at approximately right angles to the bill axis. Most were taken to the pool and washed, unless captured there in the first place. They were then transferred to about the midpoint of the bill either by one or more upward jerks of the head (sometimes a more rapid vibration), or by rapid, small, mandible movements, or both. The bill remained pointing downwards throughout at about 70° to the ground. Retraction of the upper jaw tip sometimes appeared instrumental in pushing the worm up. The worm was occasionally dropped during this stage. After reaching about the midpoint of the bill, the worm proceeded extremely rapidly to the gape and was swallowed. The gap between the jaw tips did not exceed 1 cm. during these captures, and usually seemed less. Occasionally the orientation of the worm was changed during the first part of the movement, so that it lay along the bill axis; it is not clear how this was accomplished. A sideways flick of the bill was noticed in a few of these cases only. Maggots were normally swallowed oriented along the bill.

Large worms gave more difficulty, but even the largest *Lumbricus* individuals were swallowed whole. They were usually first "hammered", with blows from the bill tip, delivered nearly vertically. The blows were given in short bursts. The most sustained attacks were made on a 10 cm. worm which received 83 blows in 7 bursts. In one case, the bill was seen to be slightly open during hammering. Wormald says that his tame snipe "hammered and pinched" large worms until they were broken up, but in the present case, the hammering did not appear to damage the worms at all. Large worms were much more often dropped than small, and from any point along the bill. The force of retraction used in holding large worms was often revealed by downward deflection of the whole bill tip, including the tip of the lower jaw. They were not washed.

Some special techniques were used in dealing with large worms. One was to retract the upper jaw strongly, and place its downward deflected tip in opposition to the mandible tip, leaving a wide gap behind recalling that of the Openbill Storks, *Anastomus* spp. The worm was held crossways in this gap, and jerked up by head movements, the opposed tips of the jaws ensuring that it could not slip forward and be dropped. Sometimes, worms were aligned with the bill axis by first stretching them. This was done by placing a foot on the worm, grasping it near one end, and stretching the neck as far up as possible. parallel with the bill axis. The grip was then momentarily relaxed, and the head plunged swiftly down in an attempt to seize it again nearer the mouth. Several such efforts were usually made in succession, and the worm was sometimes shifted more than half the bill length in one movement by this means. A variant seen once may have been fortuitous. A worm was grasped some way behind the head, with the jaws in the "open bill" position; the worm was then allowed to extend itself along the bill before a renewed grasp was taken higher up.

Once a large worm was securely in the mouth, the rest of its body was allowed to hang from one side of the gape, often still writhing. Very large worms took up to 4 minutes to swallow. Swallowing movements were repeated at about five-second intervals, and consisted of three or four upward jerks of the head, during which the floor of the mouth was pulled down, the upper jaw strongly retracted, and the mandible depressed. The gap between the jaw tips during these movements reached about 2 cm., the most ever observed. Brief retractions of the upper jaw tip were also seen unaccompanied by other movements during and just after swallowing. The tongue base could sometimes be seen being raised and lowered after swallowing, but its tip was never seen at this or any other time.

On several occasions, all at dusk, the snipe was seen "mowing" in the shallow water of its pool in the same manner as a Redshank.

Field observations

Snipe were watched at Beddington Sewage Farm, Surrey. When a field has been newly flooded, huge quantities of earthworms are brought to the surface, and Snipe gather in large numbers to feed on them (see Milne, 1956).

Snipe appear inactive by comparison with other waders, and spells of feeding are not long sustained. As with the captive bird, there is evidently more activity at night, and parties of snipe which have passed the day resting in other fields, flight in at dusk to the feeding areas. While feeding, minimal time is spent walking. Feeding movements tend to be concentrated in small areas, and groups of four to twelve probes are often made in a semicircle around the bird with little other movement than pivoting at the pelvis and sometimes a slight shift of one foot. Most probes appear to be to the full length of the bill, and the front of the head is sometimes immersed.

Most probes are made with slight vibration, and frequently several up and down movements occur without completely withdrawing the bill. Three hundred and seven probes (25 individuals watched) were counted in a total time of 37 minutes, an average of just over 8 probes per minute, with a maximum of 17. About half this time was spent actively probing the remainder walking or occasionally preening. The great majority of probes (240 out of 307) were too brief for accurate timing; the remainder averaged 7·7 seconds, the longest being 32·0 seconds. It may be assumed that most brief probes are trials, though the capture of prey is extremely difficult to detect. Worms are most often seen when the "stretch" technique is employed. This is very similar to the method used by the captive bird, except that a foot is not needed to anchor the worm since part remains in the ground. It is infrequently used, however, and the swallowing of prey otherwise is largely completed with the bill in the ground; the end of a worm is sometimes glimpsed for an instant as the bill is removed. Evidently worms travel up the bill oriented along its axis when obtained by probing, principally by tongue action rather than head jerking.

Groups of probes in a small area often show an obvious increase of force and tempo after the initial probe, presumably an indication that prey has been detected. Sudden lunges at an acute angle and short runs are sometimes seen, suggesting pursuit of an active prey discovered by sight. Turning around the bill axis while probing is infrequently seen, and little change of orientation occurs during the course of a single probe.

Film analysis

"Winter Meadow" contains sequences of a party of snipe feeding, and close ups of a single bird feeding. Frame by frame scrutiny served principally to confirm the results of direct observation. The "stretch" technique is used several times by the birds in the party, and it can be seen that at the top of the stretch, the bill lies in contact with segment III of the neck.

Food

Only three guts were available from Beddington, and these were almost empty. There can be little doubt, however, that the vast numbers of earthworms present in the area are the principal food. Stomach contents examined from other areas give a similar picture to the extensive North American survey carried out by Sperry (1940), in which insects, especially Dipteran larvae, are of special importance.

Other Species

Rostratulidae. There is little information on the feeding habits of *Rostratula*. Kobayashi (1954) records it as sometimes probing, but also feeding directly on grass seeds, which formed a high proportion of the contents of 10 stomachs he examined. A variety of invertebrates found in and around the swampy pools where it feeds have been recorded by other writers.

Haematopodidae. The ability of Oystercatchers to gain access to the meat of large molluscs has attracted the attention of many workers. e.g., Dewar (1908, 1910, 1913), Tomkins (1947), Drinnan (1957, 1958a & b) Tinbergen & Norton-Griffiths (1964) and Norton-Griffiths (1967).

Attacks on mussels (*Mytilus*) have been described in particular detail. Mussels which are under water and slightly agape may be incapacitated by a stab through the posterior adductor, and subsequently opened widely by "gaping", i.e., inserting the closed bill and then opening it. Closed mussels are placed ventral side uppermost, and blows are struck perpendicularly, with neck stiff, pivoting from the pelvis. Once a hole is made, the bill is thrust in to cut the adductor. Cockles (*Cardium*) are located by sight, or by test probing. They are levered out by lateral head movements with the bill inserted underneath, and opened by blows in the region of persistent gape. Accounts of feeding on other molluscs give a similar picture of powerful, vigorous and adaptable techniques.

Other invertebrates may also be important prey. Large crabs are killed by throwing them on their backs, and stabbing into the supraoesophageal ganglia. Polychaetes and earthworms are obtained by probing.

Charadriidae. Species occurring in the study area in addition to *P. apricaria* are *Vanellus vanellus*, *P. squatarola* and *Charadrius hiaticula*.

V. vanellus is frequently found in the same fields as *P. apricaria*, but spends proportionately more time on permanent pasture or plough rather than leys. It shows a liking for the vicinity of rain pools on pasture. Its feeding behaviour resembles that of *P. apricaria*, but the feeding rate averages slightly lower (approximately 3·3 per minute), bursts of rapid activity alternating with quiescent periods. Foot trembling frequently occurs during pauses. Pauses with head lowered, prolonged movements and abortive movements are recorded less frequently than in *P. apricaria*, and fewer are directly preceded by a run. Snatching of large pieces of earth with the prey as in Golden Plover has not been observed. However, the peck marks show evidence of "gaping" in rather more than half those examined, a feature not seen in Golden Plover tracks.

P. squatarola is found in the study area principally on intertidal mud, and salting creeks. The same feeding methods are seen as in *P. apricaria*, but the feeding rate is much higher (mean 23·2 movements per minute), and pecks are by far the most frequent movement, few preceded either by a pause with head lowered, or a run. A habit not seen in *P. apricaria* is a sideways flick combined with a peck, sending a piece of mud flying to one side; this occurred in 78 (12·8%) of 610 movements recorded. Its purpose is probably to expose prey, which is then consumed by several further movements. Despite their higher feeding rate, Grey Plovers are noticeably less mobile than Golden, and adopt a hunched posture, not an upright one for much of the time.

Charadrius hiaticula occurs on shingle banks and shingle over mud in the study area. The same components of feeding behaviour are exhibited as in the preceding species, and foot trembling is used frequently. The feeding rate is comparable with that of *P. squatarola*, and the usual carriage is similarly hunched.

Accounts in the literature for other plovers, though sparse, convey a clear impression of the uniformity of feeding behaviour throughout the group. Runs and pauses, either upright or with head lowered, appear to be normal features, and food thus obtained contains a high proportion of relatively large species, often active and mobile, such as crabs, amphipods and carabid beetles. Fallet (1962) concluded that auditory hunting was of general occurrence in the group. Some doubt on this interpretation of "head lowered" pauses is raised by the remarks of Ennion (quoted by Spencer, 1953). I have seen similar behaviour in *V. leucurus* in Iran, and since it was hunting prey submerged under water, auditory clues would not be expected. Foot trembling is probably used by all plovers, and is discussed by Simmons (1961), who considers its purpose is simply to make the prey move and thus reveal itself.

The habitats of *Vanellus* spp. are summarized by Bock (1958). *Charadrius* spp. occur mostly on hard bare substrates near water (inland or coast). Montane, steppe or plains areas are used by the group *C. mongolus, C. leschenaultii, C. asiaticus, C. modestus, C. montanus,* although the first two winter on the coast. *Eudromias* spp. inhabit similar areas, and *Phegornis* which is apparently related to them (Storer, personal communication; see systematic review) is a mountain torrent species, picking prey off aquatic plants (Goodall *et al.,* 1951, Johnson, 1964). *Pluvianellus* is briefly described by Crawshay (1907), who comments on its very high activity and fast running. He says it frequents lagoons not far from the shore, and feeds on crustaceans.

Tringinae. All *Tringa* species feed near shallow water, often while wading. Prey include a high proportion of actively swimming animals, e.g., shrimps and small fish for larger species, small water beetles and ostracods for smaller ones. Bottom living organisms, especially various dipteran larvae, are taken by species which probe.

The habits of *T. nebularia* and *T. erythropus* are described in some detail by Streefkerk. Both rely mainly on pecks or jabs, although *T. erythropus* has been seen probing vigorously (Wilkinson, 1951). Both also occasionally "mow" in a similar manner to *T. totanus*. A further technique described by Streefkerk is to thrust the bill forward through the water, partly open and half immersed; this is used most often by *T. nebularia*, invariably while running forward. These methods appear to be used for chasing shoals of fish, as described by Dittberner (1966), who has observed fishing in unison by two birds. A remarkable "high stepping" action is sometimes used by *T. nebularia* (cf. Simmons, 1951), possibly to cause fish to move, and I have seen this performed also by *T. flavipes*. *T. erythropus* is less mobile, and shows a preference for deeper water. *T. melanoleucos* frequently pursues small fish, using similar methods to *T. nebularia*. *T. stagnatilis* feeds largely in moderately deep water, displaying considerable activity. The habits of *T. flavipes* are similar. *T. ochropus* prefers feeding in sheltered situations, on aquatic or terrestrial prey at the water's edge. *T. glareola* spends more time in open water, and probes regularly.

Actitis spp. feed by water margins or rocky streams, and display considerable skill in catching winged insects. *Xenus* makes extensive use of probing. A pair watched in Iran used pecks in shallow water, and probed mainly on exposed mud. Another technique often used was a forward lunge at the mud surface with head held low, and bill almost horizontal, often preceded by a short rush. Aquatic larvae, especially dipteran, form the bulk of the contents in 3 guts examined.

Catoptrophorus feeds largely on open mud flats, but also on saltmarsh, in pools, and on sandy shores. Its feeding methods are also diverse, and include both surface pecks and probes. "Mowing" is often used. This is essentially similar to that of Redshank, but the mandible is more extensively depressed in the process, and there is an accompanying up and down head movement. Fiddler crabs (*Uca* spp.) are captured by stalking, ending with a sudden rush. I have also watched Willets feeding up to belly depth in water, making occasional swift jabs, and in at least some cases, capturing fish.

According to Streefkerk, *N. phaeopus* probes less often and less vigorously than *N. arquata*, but a trial probing technique apparently resembling the "stitching" of *C. alpina* is frequently employed. Beven

(1946) describes techniques used when feeding on crabs. The legs were broken off, and the prey crushed several times in the bill before being swallowed. A large crab (*c.* 3 in. across) was broken by blows to the carapace, part of the contents were eaten, and the remainder was swallowed whole.

Bartramia feeds in plover-like fashion on grasslands, swift runs being interspersed with sudden pauses. Surface invertebrates, especially grasshoppers and crickets, appear to be important prey. *Aechmorhynchus*, restricted to coral atolls of the Taumotu Archipelago, apparently feeds in a nimble manner on active insects (Greenway, 1958).

Calidridinae. Prey taken by *Calidris* spp. and *Crocethia* are principally small abundant animals, lying on the surface of soft substrates or buried just below. Small gastropods, small polychaetes and amphipods are important to shore feeders; by inland pools, free swimming or bottom living aquatic insects (especially dipteran larvae) are taken. Several species are efficient at catching small winged insects.

C. alpina typifies well the feeding methods of most of these species, though apparently utilizing probes more than most. Streefkerk compares *C. canutus*, *C. alpina*, *C. testacea*, *C. minutus* and *Crocethia* and comments on the inverse relation of activity and feeding rate to body size. (See also Ehlert, 1964.) "Stitching" was observed in all but *Crocethia*, though used by this species in other areas. In *C. testacea*, "stitching" is often carried out while standing still. *C. maritima* differs from the preceding species in its choice of rocky shores as a winter habitat. Its feeding methods are thus limited largely to pecking, although accounts from the breeding grounds mention probing. Notes made on *C. temmincki* in Iran, and the accounts quoted by Bent for the North American species of *Calidris* support the assumption that their feeding behaviour is essentially similar to other members of the genus.

Tryngites is an inland feeder, found on grasslands and sometimes more arid areas. It is said to feed in scattered flocks, and to move with a characteristic crouching posture. Coleoptera form a large proportion of its diet, as also for *Philomachus*, which feeds on wet grasslands or by inland waters. Accounts in the literature also mention capture of flying insects. *Micropalama* feeds principally while wading. It has a characteristic feeding attitude, with neck extended straight, allowing the bill to be jabbed perpendicularly into the water. In shallower water, "stitching" is frequent and prolonged. It frequently spends long periods feeding systematically within a small area. *Limicola* is recorded as taking both buried and surface prey, but there is little detailed information on its feeding behaviour.

Limosa spp. differ considerably from those preceding in their frequent use of prolonged and vigorous probing. Their food includes high proportions of moderate or large polychaetes and bivalves. *L. limosa* shows a strong preference for feeding in deep water, and its actions are generally leisurely. *L. lapponica* displays greater activity, feeding at the tideline or well up on the mud. The usual gait is a brisk walk, and a probing method frequently used is to insert the bill while walking, and to continue walking around it as it is inserted. Polychaetes are usually extracted before being swallowed. Shallow trial probes and "stitching" are used by both species for prey location, but *L. lapponica* evidently relies more on visual hunting than *L. limosa*. "Mowing" similar to that of *T. totanus* is used by *L. lapponica*. *L. haemastica* apparently shows more similarity to *L. lapponica*.

Limnodromus resembles the Scolopacinae in its great reliance on probing, but differs from them in its regular use of the shore for feeding. Probing techniques resemble those of *G. gallinago*, but probing rates are very high. Slight up and down quivering accompanies many probes. Pivoting around the bill and reorientation of probes are rare. Probing is regularly carried out while wading to belly depth. *Nereis* and gastropods are important foods on the shore, and dipteran larvae, particularly Chironomids, inland (Sperry, 1940).

Arenariinae. *Arenaria* is well known for its unique habit of overturning objects to reveal concealed prey. They are flipped over, or thrown in the air by a swift upward jerk of the head, after placing the bill under the object. Holes are often excavated in sand or mud, employing "gaping". *Enteromorpha* covering the inshore mud is habitually rolled up by moving briskly forward with the bill inserted under the weed. Major prey found by those means in winter quarters are amphipods such as *Gammarus* and *Talitrus*. *Hydrobia* is pecked from the mud surface and a wide range of other foods is obtained by scavenging.

Aphriza has received much less attention, but apparently does not turn over objects. An account quoted by Bent refers to active feeding on insects on the breeding grounds, and in the winter quarters it is described as feeding busily by the surf on a rocky island, apparently exclusively on tiny mussels.

Scolopacinae. Accounts in the literature give the impression that feeding methods similar to those of *G. gallinago* are used throughout the subfamily. *Scolopax* spp. inhabit woodlands, and substrates used for feeding are in many cases firmer than those used by *G. gallinago*. Sequences of *S. rusticola* in "Winter Meadow" show its highly refined method of trial probing. This is geared to leg movement, so that at each step, as the weight is transferred to the front foot, the bill is inserted for about a third of its length. The note on *Lymnocryptes* by Browne (1952) suggests that tapping the ground may have been employed in one feeding area to cause Collembola to emerge. Published diet analyses for the rest of the subfamily give a similar overall picture to *G. gallinago;* earthworms figure prominently, with dipteran and coleopterous larvae also important.

Phalaropodidae. Phalaropes obtain much of their food while swimming; it typically consists of very abundant and active small aquatic animals. Most feeding movements are swift pecks into the water surface. Feeding rate may be high; 300 pecks a minute are estimated for *Phalaropus fulicarius* in an account quoted by Bent. *Lobipes lobatus* is noted for its habit of spinning in circles on the water, presumably to stir up prey, and has been observed flying in pursuit of aerial insects. At sea, both show partiality for floating masses of seaweed, or the vicinity of whales, or shoals of fish. *P. fulicarius* is recorded as perching on the backs of whales to feed on crustacean parasites. *Steganopus tricolor* often feeds while wading in the shallows, where its actions are reminiscent of some Tringinae. While swimming, it often feeds in densely packed flocks, frequently upending, and keeping the head and neck immersed for several seconds at a time.

Recurvirostridae. Himantopus typically seizes active prey from the water-surface or below, by swift pecks. A wide variety of organisms is recorded, ranging in size up to small fish, dragonfly nymphs and grasshoppers. Streefkerk distinguishes two feeding actions in *Recurvirostra* – "scooping" and "scything". "Scooping", carried out mainly in deep water, is a modified pecking action with a forward and upward direction, made directly in front. "Scything" is used largely in shallow water or soft mud; the head is swung from side to side, so that the recurved end of the partly open bill contacts the water or mud at each swing. Prey are snapped up as encountered. Prey obtained by these means is varied and predominantly small for the size of the bird; the specialized feeding methods allow the capture of large numbers in a short time. *Ibidorhyncha* wades deeply in mountain streams, and obtains aquatic prey from amongst pebbles. Water beetles are stated to be a principal food. It has also been seen probing in sparse grass by a river (Kozlova, 1962).

Part 2: Anatomy

Materials and Methods

Specimens of the five representative species and others found in the study area have been expressly collected for this investigation. Some were examined fresh, for manipulation of the jaw apparatus, but most were injected in the field with 10% formalin, in which their fixation was later completed. This ensured excellent condition for dissection. Most of the remaining wide range of species examined were specimens in the British Museum (Natural History) and the majority were also in satisfactory condition.

The dissections were made using a stereoscopic dissecting microscope, and several specimens were frequently examined together for comparison. To elucidate the relationships of aponeuroses within some muscles, hand-cut sections or "steaks" were inspected. Each was cut with a new scalpel blade, and examined under water against a black background. By this method, even fine aponeuroses were revealed with great clarity, and its simplicity permits much more extensive use than histological sectioning techniques. Drawings were made with the aid of a Zeiss drawing apparatus. Adjustments of scale were facilitated by the use of pancratic objectives.

Descriptions

The statements made in the descriptions refer to the specimens dissected. The extent to which they may apply to species as a whole is considered in discussion sections. In order to keep lists of species as short as possible, group names (family, subfamily or genus) are used alone when a point applies to all the examined species of a group. Group names alone are also used:

a. For monotypic genera.

b. For polytypic genera or higher groups of which only one species was dissected.

The species dissected, and the number of specimens of each, are given below.

Species Dissected

Jacanidae: *Actophilornis africana* (2), *Irediparra gallinacea* (2), *Hydrophasianus chirurgus* (1), *Jacana spinosa* (2).

Rostratulidae: *Rostratula benghalensis* (4).

Haematopodidae: *Haematopus ostralegus* (4).

Charadriidae: *Pluvianellus socialis* (1), *Vanellus vanellus* (6), *V armatus* (2), *V. spinosus* (1), *V. tectus* (2), *V. malabaricus* (1), *V albiceps* (1), *V. coronatus* (3), *V. senegallus* (1), *V leucurus* (1), *V cayanus* (2), *V. chilensis* (2), *V. indicus* (2), *V tricolor* (3), *V. miles* (1), *Pluvialis apricaria* (15), *P. dominica* (3), *P. squatarola* (6), *Charadrius hiaticula* (3), *C. dubius* (2), *C. wilsonia* (2), *C vociferus* (2), *C. pecuarius* (2), *C. tricollaris* (2), *C. alexandrinus* (3), *C. peronii* (1), *C. bocinctus* (1), *C. falklandicus* (1), *C. mongolus* (3), *C leschenaultii* (1), *C. asiaticus* (1), *C. modestus* (3), *C. melanops* (3), *C. cinctus* (2), *Eudromias ruficollis* (2).

Scolopacidae:
Tringinae: *Aechmorhynchus cancellatus* (2), *Bartramia longicauda* (2), *Numenius phaeopus* (3), *N. arquata* (15), *Tringa erythropus* (2), *T. totanus* (15), *T. flavipes* (2), *T. stagnatilis* (3), *T. nebularia* (2), *T. melanoleuca* (1), *T. ochropus* (2), *T. solitaria* (1), *T. glareola* (2), *Xenus cinereus* (2), *Actitis hypoleucos* (2), *A. macularia* (2), *Catoptrophorus semipalmatus* (1), *Heteroscelus brevipes* (2), *H. incana* (2).

Arenariinae: *Aphriza virgata* (2), *Arenaria interpres* (6).

Scolopacinae: *Gallinago stenura* (1), *G. gallinago* (15), *G. paraguiae* (1), *Scolopax rusticola* (3), *S. saturata* (1), *Philohela minor* (1), *Lymnocryptes minima* (4).

Calidridinae: *Limosa limosa* (2), *L. haemastica* (2), *L. lapponica* (4), *Limnodromus griseus* (2), *Crocethia alba* (3), *Calidris canutus* (3), *C. tenuirostris* (1), *C. pusilla* (2), *C. ruficollis* (2), *C. minuta* (2), *C. temnincki* (2), *C. subminuta* (1), *C. minutilla* (1), *C. fuscicollis* (2), *C. bairdii* (1), *C. melanotos* (2), *C. acuminata* (3), *C. maritima* (2), *C. alpina* (15), *C. testacea* (2), *Limicola falcinellus* (2), *Micropalama himantopus* (3), *Tryngites subruficollis* (4), *Philomachus pugnax* (6).

Recurvirostridae: *Ibidorhyncha struthersii* (1), *Himantopus himantopus* (3), *Recurvirostra avosetta* (3), *R. novaehollandiae* (1).

Phalaropodidae: *Phalaropus fulicarius* (2), *Lobipes lobatus* (2), *Steganopus tricolor* (1).

Dromadidae: *Dromas ardeola* (2).

Burhinidae: *Burhinus oedicnemus* (2), *B. capensis* (1), *B. magnirostris* (2).

Glareolidae: *Pluvianus aegyptus* (2), *Cursorius cursor* (1), *C. temminckii* (2), *C. coromandelicus* (1), *Rhinoptilus africanus* (1), *R. cinctus* (1), *R. chalcopterus* (1), *Peltohyas australis* (3), *Stiltia isabella* (2), *Glareola pratincola* (1), *G. nuchalis* (2).

Thinocoridae: *Thinocorus orbignyianus* (2), *T rumicivorus* (2).

Chionidae: *Chionis alba* (2).

Environmental Forces

Forces arising by interaction between the bill and the substrate exercise an important influence on the evolution of the skull and jaw apparatus. Some of these forces are likely to be particularly severe in probing species, especially if probing is vigorous, and if the orientation of the bill is changed during probing. They will be greater, too, if probing is carried out in firm substrates, and if a concealed obstacle is encountered. Their effect on the mandible/quadrate articulation is especially pertinent to an understanding of the jaw musculature, which contributes importantly to the support of the lower jaw. Environmental forces may be conveniently grouped according to the direction of their lines of action:

1. *Forces acting parallel to the bill axis*

a. Forces directed posteriorly arise during pecking or probing. Their effect on the mandible will tend to cause backward disarticulation. During deep probing, these forces have a medial component with respect to the mandibular rami, tending to buckle them inwards. If the bill is pushed forward through the substrate with the jaws open, they will tend to increase protraction of the upper jaw and depression of the lower. In some highly rhynchokinetic species this may possibly contribute significantly to the force of protraction.

This would seem most likely in species such as *N. arquata* with the distal part of the bill heavily reinforced, and the tongue short; in the majority, pushing the open bill forwards for any distance while probing would force the substrate into its lumen.

b. Forces directed anteriorly arise when the bill is extracted after probing, assuming that changes of orientation have not greatly widened the probe hole. If the jaws are gripping prey, pressure on the culmen and gonys will tend to close them and to cause forward disruption of the mandible articulation. Pressure on the gonys alone may occur if the bill tip is strongly decurved, and on the culmen if recurved unless the path of the bill follows the line of its own curvature. Observation shows that in *N. arquata* a curved path is only followed if no prey is captured. When a capture does occur, the bill is removed along a straight path. Friction between bill and substrate will add to these forces, whatever the position of the jaws. Extraction of prey will increase forward acting forces without normally involving greater risk of damage, since grip on the prey may be expected to fail well before structure is endangered. Exceptions could perhaps occur if sudden tugs were exerted.

2. *Forces acting laterally across the bill axis*
Such forces will arise particularly when the orientation of a probe is changed without withdrawal of the bill. Their action on the jaw articulation will tend to cause forward disarticulation on one side and backward disarticulation on the other.

3. *Forces directed dorsally or ventrally across the bill axis*
These will occur through reorientation of the bill in the sagittal plane while probing, when they will act in a similar direction on both jaws; and when the jaws are opened underground, when they will act to oppose opening.

An experiment with a freshly killed Dunlin (*C. alpina*) showed that in the substrate where it had recently been probing pressure on the posteroventral end of the mandible, which causes raising of the upper jaw tip in the absence of other external forces, would only do so if the bill was inserted past the bending zone of the upper jaw. If only the tip was inserted, pressure on the mandible had the opposite effect, causing downward deflection of the upper jaw so that the "openbill" position (*v.* Common Snipe observations) was assumed. With larger species, and with *C. alpina* in very soft mud the upper jaw tip is raised in both circumstances. In life, this problem may be overcome by the hole widening resulting from the slight changes of direction during the "quivering" which accompanies most probes, even shallow ones.

4. *Twisting forces*
Forces arising when the bill is turned around its long axis while inserted. The inertia of the lower jaw relative to the skull and upper jaw will tend to cause downward disarticulation of the mandible on one side, and to exert upward pressure against the quadrate on the other. High twisting forces may be expected if the bill has a curved tip.

Skull, Jaws and Kinetics

The skulls of waders have attracted a great deal of interest, and have been the subject of a considerable volume of literature. Much work still remains to be done on the correlation of structural changes in the skull; however, the information already available provides a sufficient framework for this investigation. This section provides a short review of major features of their skull morphology as a background to the descriptions which follow; detailed accounts can be found in the important papers by Kozlova (1961, 1962) and Yudin (1961 and 1965), and in earlier work by Marinelli (1928), Von Kripp (1933a & b, 1935), and Feninger (1937). The morphology of the lower jaw has been surveyed by Lebedinsky (1918, 1920), who has also dealt with the ligaments of the avian jaw mechanism (1921).

Kinesis

This term refers to movement of the upper jaw relative to the braincase. This faculty is widespread in non-mammalian vertebrates, and reaches a high degree of refinement in birds; the system of bony levers involved is a feature of great interest in the avian skull. Important general reviews of this mechanism are those of Simonetta (1963) and Bock (1964a).

The essential feature of the kinetic mechanism of birds is the movable or streptostylic quadrate. This bone pivots at its articulation with the cranium, and is articulated with the jugal bar laterally, and with the pterygoid ventrally, the latter being attached to the palatine anteriorly. The upper jaw is flexibly attached to the skull. In raising the upper jaw, the quadrate rotates upwards, forwards and inwards, transmitting its push via the jugals and palatines. A system of this kind is known as a kinematic chain – an assembly of links joined in such

Plate 1.
Tringa totanus, chick.
To show bones of the skull, and important surface features referred to in the text.

Abbreviations:

an angular.
ar articular
bo basioccipital.
bp basitemporal plate.
d dentary.
ec ectethmoid.
ex exoccipital.
fr frontal.
hp hemipterygoid.
ip internal process.
ju jugal.
lc lacrymal.
ls laterosphenoid.
me mesethmoid.
mx maxilla.
mxp maxillo-palatine.
na nasal.
op opisthotic process.
or orbital process of quadrate.
ot otic process of quadrate
p palatine.
par parietal.
pp postorbital process.
pmx premaxilla.
ps parasphenoid.
pt pterygoid
qc articular condyles of quadrate.
qj quadrate-jugal.
rp retroarticular process.
sa surangular.
so supraoccipital.
sp suprameatic process.
sq squamosal.
vo vomer.
zp zygomatic process.

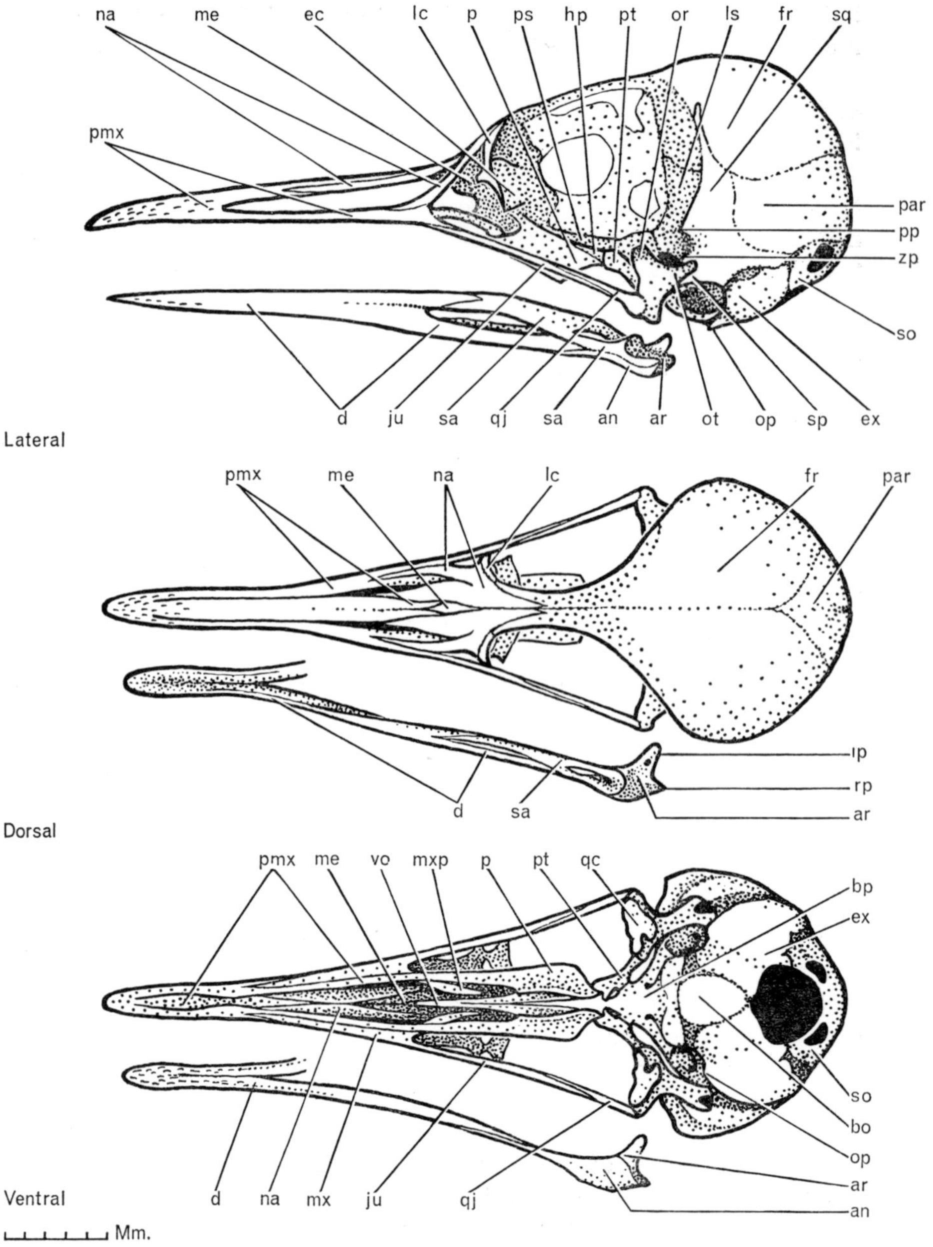

Tringa totanus, chick

a way that if one is fixed and another moved, all the rest must move in a predictable manner. The general properties of kinematic chains and their importance in animal mechanics are discussed by Alexander (1968).

Two principal modifications are found in present day birds. These are *prokinesis*, in which the upper jaw moves about a pivot formed by a narrow strip of flexible bone at the fronto-nasal hinge; and *rhynchokinesis*, in which bending occurs over a wider zone, some distance along the bill. Rhynchokinesis involves a change in bill shape, and occurs only in species with a schizorhinal upper jaw – that is, one in which the nasal bars are pivoted separately from the rest of the jaw so that a change of shape occurs automatically as it is raised* (see Zusi, 1962).

The Charadrioidea exhibit only rhynchokinesis, and its gradual refinement is a striking morphological trend in the group. This refinement consists principally of a forward shift in the zone of bending by progressive reinforcement of the proximal part of the bill; at the same time, the distance over which bending occurs is shortened. In the least specialized types (especially among the Charadriinae), bending occurs very close to the fronto-nasal hinge, emphasizing Bock's statement (1964a: 38) that there is no sharp division between the two forms of kinesis. Beecher (1962) states that bending occurs at the fronto-nasal hinge in plovers and sandpipers. This is not strictly correct, since to allow this, the nasal would have to lift off the mesethmoid. It is, in fact, possible to achieve this with prepared skulls, but not with freshly killed birds; it is doubtful if it happens in life. In this account it is found convenient to distinguish between *moderately rhynchokinetic* species in which bending occurs along the whole length of the upper jaw anterior to the internasal septum, and *highly rhynchokinetic* species in which reinforcement of the dorsal bar anterior to the nasal partition has moved the zone of bending much further forward. All species examined fall clearly into one or other category. Among the representative species, *P. apricaria* and *T. totanus* are moderately

* For convenience, this account employs the following short terms: Dorsal and Ventral bars, used by Bock (1964a) refer to the upper and lower parts of the schizorhinal bill. The dorsal bar includes elements of nasal and premaxilla, and the ventral bar includes elements of maxilla and premaxilla.
Nasal and Jugal bars have the same sense as nasal and jugal struts (Zusi 1962); "bar" is substituted because of the more restricted connotation of "strut" in mechanics. The jugal bar (= zygoma in many earlier accounts) includes jugal, quadrato-jugal and maxilla, and the nasal bar is the descending process of the nasal which makes contact with the maxilla (Plate 3). An excellent account of the bone elements of the avian skull is given by Jollie (1957).

rhynchokinetic, and *N. arquata, C. alpina* and *G. gallinago* highly rhynchokinetic.

The analyses by Von Kripp (1933a) of the lever systems involved in imparting forward movement to the maxillary bar include a section on two species of waders.* Unfortunately, however, the complex constructions involved have not proved helpful in the present survey.

Conditions affecting the amount of protraction possible have been discussed by Zusi (1962) for Lari. In waders, the forward shift of the zone of bending would appear to substantially reduce the extent of movement possible at the jaw tip as compared with a bill of equal length pivoted at the fronto-nasal hinge. In fact, however, the range is extensive, only a small forward movement of the ventral bar being necessary to produce a large deflection of the jaw tip.

Velocity ratio and mechanical advantage of the upper jaw have been studied for waterfowl by Goodman & Fisher (1962) and for a range of birds by Beecher (1962) employing measurements of skulls. Beecher gives a figure for velocity ratio of 0·18 for *Numenius americana* and 0·13 for *Philohela minor*, (low in comparison to his figures for prokinetic species). In fact, the determination of velocity ratios in rhynchokinetic birds by this method is extremely difficult. The fact that bending occurs over a wide curve, and includes also the ventral bar renders the system very different from the prokinetic arrangement. The form of the curve would require to be expressed mathematically, and allowance made for its change as protraction or retraction proceed. Experimental work on fresh material seems likely to be a more fruitful approach. Limited work of this kind already undertaken suggests that velocity ratio is, in fact, low in highly rhynchokinetic species.

Because the region of bending is relatively much broader than in the prokinetic condition, the likelihood of breakage is less. Histological changes have probably also played a part in reducing this risk. Hence, bony protraction stops such as those described by Fisher & Goodman (1955a) and Zusi (1962) are unnecessary. There are no obvious retraction stops either, although the suprameatic process may limit quadrate movement in extreme cases. The amount of bending which can safely occur is considerably more than that produced by normal

* It should be noted that Von Kripp's Fig. 7a, labelled as *Gallinago gallinago*, in fact depicts the skull of *Limosa limosa*. Fig. 7b is correctly labelled as *Scolopax rusticola*.

protraction, and may be most striking; in trials with freshly killed material I have bent the upper bill tip of a Knot (*Calidris canutus*) at 90° to the bill axis and allowed it to return with apparently no impairment of function. For this reason also measurements of kinetics using the apparatus devised by Fisher & Goodman (1955a) cannot be made on waders. The greatest deflection which can be produced by pressure on the posterior process of the mandible in fresh specimens could perhaps be used as a rough indication of the maximum protraction normally occurring.

An important feature of rhynchokinesis is that the pivots about which the two jaws move are relatively much further apart than in prokinetic species. The maximum pressure which can be exerted on prey by either jaw will be greatest near its pivot, and if these pivots are widely separated, the potential for pressure between the two jaws is much reduced. In many highly rhynchokinetic waders, e.g., *Numenius, Gallinago*, the dorsal and ventral bars are in contact or make contact under pressure, in much of the akinetic proximal part of the upper jaw. The pressure of the mandible must thus be opposed by the resistance to bending of the dorsal bar. In the majority of the Calidridinae, however, the dorsal and ventral bars are separated throughout the region proximal to the bending zone. Manipulation of fresh specimens shows that upward pressure on the flexible ventral bar tends to cause protraction; thus, the mandible in this case is presumably opposed by the retractor musculature, as in species with a bending zone at or near the fronto-nasal hinge.

A further consequence of the different positions of the pivots of upper and lower jaws in the avian skull has been pointed out by Yudin (1965); the two jaws are enabled to contact each other at varying angles, increasing the manipulative capabilities of the bill. If the bill is lengthened, without change in the position of the pivots, the capacity for varying the angle of contact between the jaws will be reduced. The forward position of the zone of bending in highly rhynchokinetic species compensates for this, and in fact enhances the manipulative ability of the bill considerably. The feeding techniques described for the captive Snipe illustrate this very well.

Some consideration is appropriate at this point of the theory of coupling between upper and lower jaws. Bock (1964a) discussed the role of the post-orbital ligament in enabling *M. depressor mandibulae* to assist protraction, and suggested that birds possessing either a well-developed post-orbital ligament or a bony clasp securing the mandible-quadrate articulation are unable to depress the lower jaw without raising the upper. Hence, depression of the upper jaw below the resting position would be impossible. Zusi (1967) has critically examined this suggestion in the light of experimental work, and proposes instead the recognition of a wider range of possibilities between strict coupling and complete independence. Since waders have well developed post-orbital ligaments, their ability nevertheless to oppose their jaws in a variety of ways provides strong support for Zusi's views.

Important accounts dealing with the lower jaw are those of Bock (1959 and 1960a), Yudin (1961) and Zusi (1962). Bock's papers are concerned with the secondary articulation between the medial process of the mandible and the basitemporal plate; the later of the two surveys the occurrence of this articulation throughout the avian orders. The present investigation confirms his findings. It is present in the Haematopodidae, Charadriidae, Recurvirostridae and *Numenius* and absent in other Scolopacidae and Phalaropodidae. Yudin and Zusi describe the movements of the lower jaw. In the course of normal depression, the articulating surfaces of the posterior ends of the mandibles slide backwards and outwards along the medial and posterior condyles of the quadrate. The distance between the mandibular rami is thus increased. Zusi has also found that in *Larus argentatus*, the possible range of lateral displacement of the mandible is reduced as the mandible is depressed. Further increase in the gap between the rami is possible by outward bowing. The mechanism by which this can take place is described for *Larus* by Yudin, and is considered further under M. pterygoideus. Retraction will in itself also slightly increase the gap between the rami. Yudin relates the capacity for bowing to structural features of the mandible, and reviews these in a wide range of birds, including the Charadrioidea. He shows modifications associated with bowing to be well developed in the Charadriinae and Recurvirostridae, less well developed in the Tringinae, and reduced or lost in the remaining families or subfamilies. Nevertheless it is probable that some capacity for bowing is retained by most members of the group; this would seem to be the most likely explanation of the retraction seen to accompany extreme depression in *G. gallinago* and *N. arquata* during swallowing.

Orientation of the Bill Axis

A further trend seen in the Charadrioidea is a progressive reduction in the angle between bill axis and basitemporal plate (*v.* Kozlova, 1961–62). Changes associated with this include:

1. A downward shift of the temporal fossa, post-orbital process and otic articulation of the quadrate relative to the bill axis.

2. Reduction in the angle between the otic process of the quadrate and the parasphenoid rostrum.

3. Increase of the angle between the jugal and nasal bars and reduction of the angles included ventrally between the jugal bar and the bill axis, and between the parasphenoid rostrum and the bill axis.

4. Reduction of the angle between the post-orbital ligament and the jugal bar.

5. Relative shortening of the ventral margin of the orbit, due to the forward shift of the quadrate, palatal mechanism and gape.

6. Increase of the angle, in the horizontal plane, of the jugal bars, pterygoids and posterior ends of the mandibular rami to the longitudinal axis of the cranium.

Bill Form

The Charadrioidea exhibit considerable diversity of bill form. This has been influenced to a great extent by feeding habits ; hence, the mechanical considerations discussed by Von Kripp (1935) and Bock (1966) are difficult to apply in this group. The significance of several major variants of form is briefly discussed below. Of the representative species, *N. arquata* shows strong decurvature, *C. alpina* moderate decurvature, and the remaining three have straight bills.

1. *Straightness*
Where pecks are the principal feeding action, a straight bill will have the advantage that external forces will be largely directed along the bill axis. Undesirable bending forces would be more likely if the bill were curved. Thus, straight bills are seen in, e.g., plovers, most *Tringa* species and *Himantopus*. Straight bills are efficient also for specialized probers, permitting the force of insertion to be exerted along the bill axis.

2. *Decurvature*
Many species exhibit slight downward curvature of the tomia only at the tip, possibly for mechanical reasons. Decurvature will aid in gripping prey, since no forwardly directed forces can act parallel with the whole length of the tomia. When species with decurved bills extract prey

from the ground, the pull is exerted along the line of the proximal part of the bill axis so that forward forces are opposed by the decurved distal region of the upper jaw. The tip of a decurved bill can explore a larger area during the course of a single probe if the bill is rotated about its long axis. Decurvature may aid some species in trial probing, since it facilitates perpendicular insertion of the bill tip, without involving the drastic skull modifications seen in very highly specialized probers. This will be of greatest significance for waders employing both trial probing and visual search (e.g., *N. arquata, C. alpina*), since the extent of movement necessary between the visual search and trial probe head positions is thereby reduced.

3. *Recurvature*
Upward curvature of the bill tip enables the distal part of the tomia to be more easily brought into a horizontal position. It is thus seen in species which frequently pursue active prey in shallow water (e.g., *Tringa nebularia*), since the escape path of these prey is horizontal; in species feeding from the surface of mud or water (e.g., *Xenus, Recurvirostra*); and in *Arenaria*, where it facilitates insertion of the bill beneath objects. Recurvature will enhance exploratory capacity and grip in probing species as does decurvature; this may be important to *Limosa lapponica*, which also occasionally uses active pursuit.

4. *Breadth*
Broadening of the bill as a whole may be related to consumption of prey which is relatively large or difficult to manipulate. Insufficient data on prey and prey size are available for *Limicola* and *Phalaropus fulicarius* in which this feature is prominent.

5. *Spatulate*
Broadening of the tip only is a feature of several highly rhynchokinetic species, e.g., *G. gallinago*. The extreme case is *Eurynorhynchus pygmeus* (not available for dissection during this study) for which there is little field information. Broadening may increase the effectiveness of the part of the bill tip which is not aided by tongue action, and will increase the area available for tactile receptors at the bill tip.

6. *Specialized rhamphotheca*
Striking hypertrophy of the rhamphotheca is shown by the chisel ended bill of *Haematopus*, the sickle bill of *Ibidorhyncha*, and to a less extent, by *Arenaria*. The rhamphotheca at the tip of the upper jaw forms a well developed notch, into which the lower jaw fits, in *Scolopax*. It is sharply hooked in *Rostratula*, and in *Catoptrophorus* and most *Tringa* species, both upper and lower jaws are slightly hooked at the tip

(downward and upward respectively). Presumably such notches and hooks serve to hinder prey from sliding forwards out of the bill.
In *Ibidorhyncha*, the rhamphotheca of both jaws is very finely serrated along the distal part of the tomium, perhaps aiding the grip of smooth hard prey such as water beetles.

Bill Length

A convenient measure of relative bill length is provided by the ratio of the bill length to skull length, each measured from the junction of nasal and jugal bars. This ratio has been determined for the representative species from the specimens used for tongue/bill ratio measurements (Table IX). The mean relative bill lengths for the five species are as follows:

P. apricaria	0·77
T. totanus	1·51
N. arquata	2·98
C. alpina	1·82
G. gallinago	2·94

Ligaments

The chief difference among the representative species is the absence in *C. alpina* and *G. gallinago* of L. jugomandibulare externus.

L. lacrymojugale
In many species there is no distinct ligament between the lacrymal and jugal, although it may be indicated as an ill-defined strengthened area of the sheet of connective tissue covering the nasal region. It is particularly clear and strong in the larger *Tringa* spp., *Xenus*, *Vanellus* spp. and the Recurvirostridae.

L. suboculare
The subocular ligament is strongly attached anteriorly to the ventral tip of the lacrymal. It is expanded caudally to surround the ventral and posterior edges of the eye, and has weak attachment to the posterior edge of the orbit. In the Scolopacinae dissected it is partially replaced by the bony suborbital bridge.

L. quadrati
This name is applied by Feninger (1937) to a weak ligament running from the suprameatic process to the lateral edge of the body of the

quadrate. It is strong in *Haematopus* and the Recurvirostridae, and moderately well developed in *Vanellus*, *Pluvialis* and most Tringinae. It is weak, often virtually undetectable, in most Calidridinae, the Phalaropodidae and *Arenaria*.

L. postorbitale

This ligament runs from the tip of the postorbital process to the external process of the mandible. The postorbital process is absent in *Limicola*, and in the Scolopacinae it arises from the caudal ventral edge of the suborbital bridge. In *Haematopus* and *Vanellus miles* a caudal branch runs from its dorsal end to the lateral edge of the zygomatic process; in several other species of *Vanellus* the ligament merges into tough connective tissue spanning this region, though there is no clearly defined fork.

L. occipitomandibulare

This extremely stout ligament is present in all the species examined. It runs from the exoccipital process of the skull to the posterior surface of the internal process of the mandible, where there is a raised facet to receive it. It is surrounded on all sides but the dorsal by fibres of M. depressor, whose dorsal medial edge it traverses.

L. jugomandibulare externus

A ligament running from the lateral caudal end of the jugal to the external process of the mandible, lateral to the internal jugomandibular and postorbital ligaments. It is absent in all Calidridinae, Arenariinae, Scolopacinae and Phalaropodidae examined, and among the Tringinae it is missing in *Aechmorhynchus*, *Actitis* and *Xenus*, and much reduced in *Catoptrophorus*.

L. jugomandibulare internus

A curved course is followed by this ligament which runs from the postero-ventral edge of the jugal around the posterior surface of the articular process of the quadrate, to the posterior dorsal edge of the mandible. A distinct sesamoid bone within the ligament is present in *Haematopus*, the larger Tringinae, *Philomachus* and *Limosa*.

Jaw Musculature

The terminology used is basically that employed in a survey of sauropsid groups by Lakjer (1926). Different nomenclature for a number of jaw and tongue muscles has been used in a wider survey by

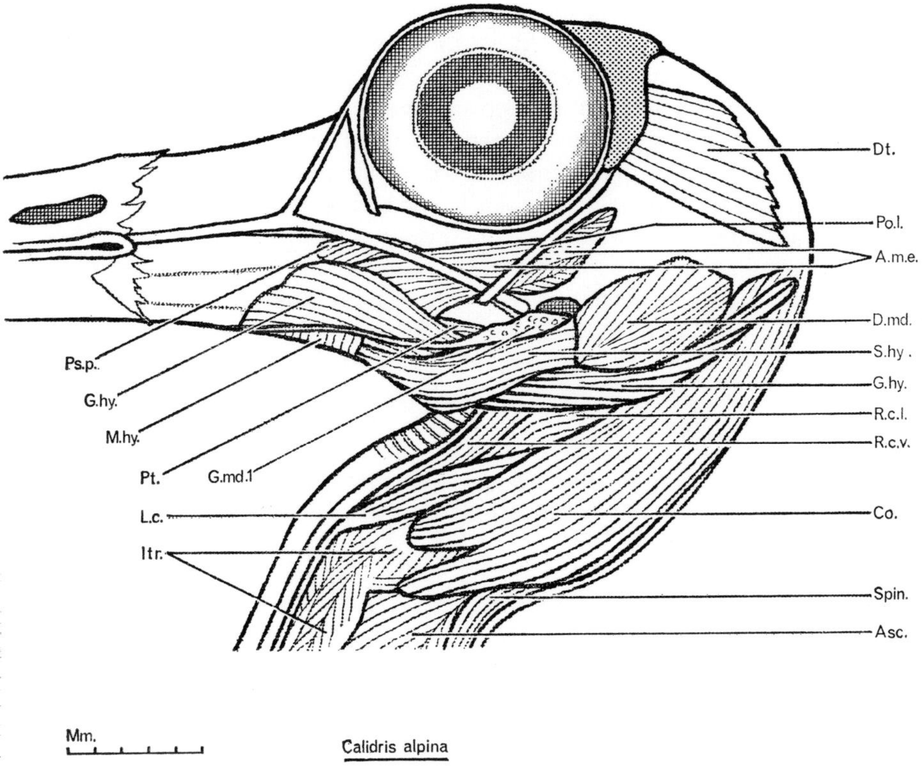

Plate 2.
Calidris alpina, head and anterior region of neck.
Abbreviations:
A.m.e. M. adductor mandibulae externus.
Asc. MM. ascendentes cervicis.
Co. M. complexus.
D.md. M. depressor mandibulae.
Dt. M. dermotemporalis (cut).
G.hy. M. geniohyoideus.
G.md.1 Gl. mandibularis 1.
Itr. MM. intertransversarii.
L.c. M. longus colli.
M.hy. M. mylohyoideus.
Po.l. Postorbital ligament.
Ps.p. M. pseudotemporalis profundus.
Pt. M. pterygoideus.
R.c.l. M. rectus capitis lateralis.
R.c.v. M. rectus capitis ventralis.
S.hy. M. serpihyoideus.
Spin. M. spinalis cervicis.

Edgworth (1935), but most later accounts have in general followed Lakjer. A more recent survey, of non-mammalian tetrapods, is that of Säve-Söderbergh (1944), and an important review of the avian jaw musculature is provided by Hofer (1950).

Interpretation of Lakjer's terms has, however, proved difficult in a number of later studies, and several workers have introduced modifications of their own. These, and inconsistencies of usage, have led to what Fisher & Goodman (1955b) call "a state of vast confusion". Progress towards resolving this confusion has been made by Barnikol (1953a and b, 1951), and Starck & Barnikol (1954), whose thorough approach has involved careful study of innervation and aponeuroses. Very detailed studies for a number of birds and other vertebrates have been made at the University of Leiden; references to these studies and general conclusions regarding muscle architecture based on them are given by Van der Klaauw (1963). The functional significance of muscle architecture is the subject of valuable discussions by Gans & Bock (1965) and Alexander (1968, pp. 15–19).

Zusi (1962) provides a clear account of the jaw musculature in four species of Lari. His analysis of M. adductor mandibulae externus based on that of Starck & Barnikol, and his treatment of M. pterygoideus have both been followed in this account; the recent study of grebes by Zusi & Storer (1969) differs in aponeurosis numbering, though similar in approach. Many of the aponeuroses described by Zusi (1962) can be recognized in the Charadrioidea, and in these cases, his lettering has been adopted. Letters are assigned only in muscles possessing more than one aponeurosis, and only to aponeuroses recognizable in a wide range of species. Aponeuroses of origin are numbered A, B, C *et seq.*, and of insertion, M, N, O *et seq.* Some aponeuroses not mentioned by Zusi receive new letters. The names of three muscles are shortened for discussion purposes; the shortened version is given in brackets after the heading.

Dorsal and lateral views of the jaw muscles are shown for the representative species and a number of others in Plates 3 to 19.

M. adductor mandibulae externus
(Short form: M. adductor externus)

Lakjer described this muscle as consisting of three parts, which he termed superficialis, medialis and profundus. These divisions have been widely used by later authors, and have been applied to the Charadrii by Feninger (1937), Kozlova (1961, 1962) and Yudin (1965). Inconsistencies in the usage of these terms have been demonstrated by Starck & Barnikol, who propose an analysis in terms of three major aponeuroses. This method of treatment was followed by Zusi, and is again used here.

Transverse sections have been found particularly helpful in clarifying the relationships of aponeuroses in this muscle, and are depicted for a number of species of Charadrii in Plates 21–25.

Part M. Following Barnikol, the region occupying the temporal fossa is called "external temporal", and that traversing the ventral caudal edge of the orbit is termed "rostral".

Aponeurosis M is generally expanded into a concave vertically orientated sheet within the external temporal region (where present). The edges of this sheet may reach the lateral surface. Ap. M narrows rostrally to insert on the surangular. The external temporal region is lined medially by Ap. C, which arises on the reduced temporal crest and extends a short way into the orbit; and laterally by Ap. E, which is frequently weak or absent.

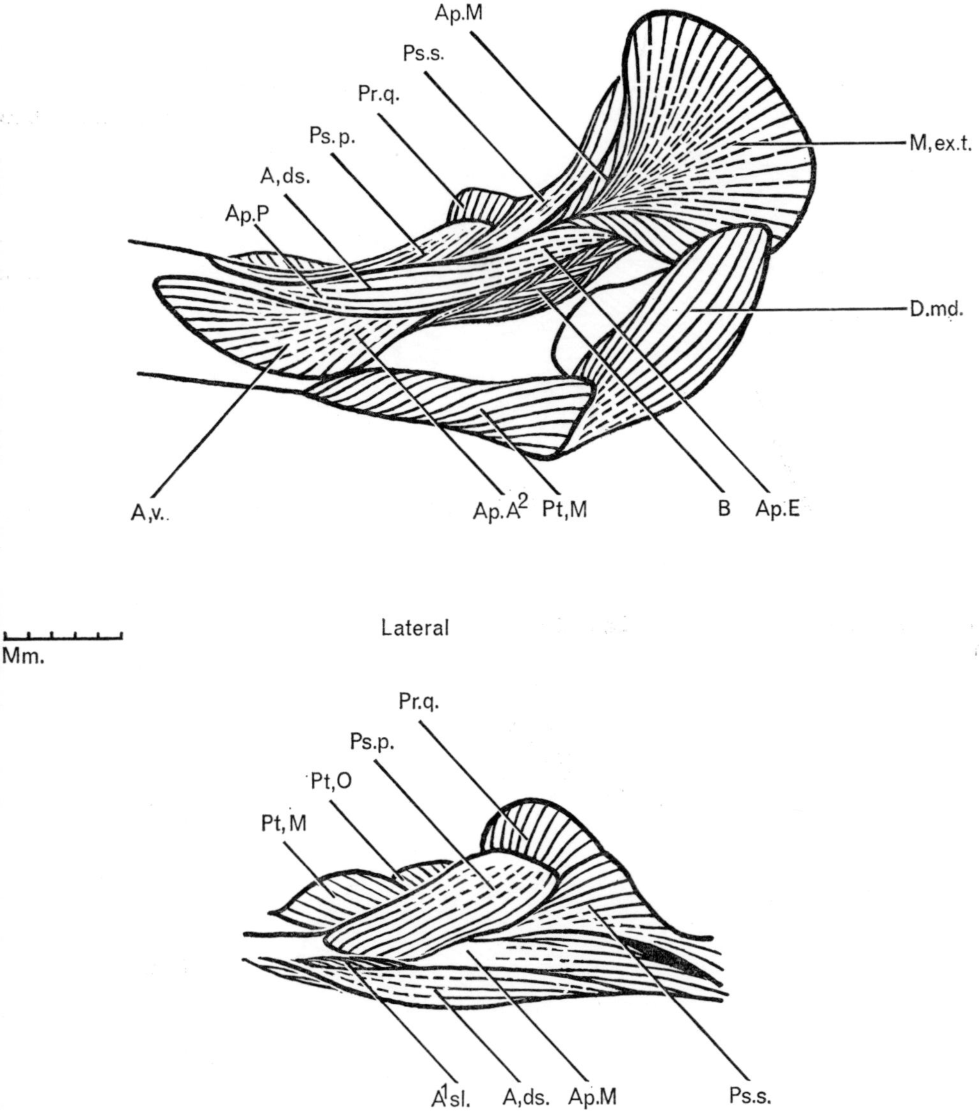

Dorsal

Pluvialis apricaria

Plate 3.
Pluvialis apricaria, jaw musculature, lateral and dorsal aspects.

Abbreviations, Plates 5 to 22.

A, ds. M. adductor mandibulae externus, part A, dorsal section.
A,v. M. adductor mandibulae externus, part A, ventral section.
A.m.p. M.adductor mandibulae posterior.
A'sl. Aponeurosis A' slip.
Ap.A Aponeurosis A; other aponeuroses similarly.
B M. adductor mandibulae externus, part B.
D.md. M. depressor mandibulae.
D sl. Aponeurosis D slip.
M,ex.t. M. adductor mandibulae externus, part M, external temporal region.
N.pt. N. pterygoideus.
Pr.q. M. protractor quadrati et pterygoidei.
Ps.p. M. pseudotemporalis profundus.
Ps.s. M. pseudotemporalis superficialis.
Ps.s.m. M. pseudotemporalis superficialis, medial slip.
Pt,M M. pterygoideus, part M.
Pt,O M. pterygoideus, part O.

Plate 4.
Tringa totanus: jaw musculature, lateral and dorsal aspects.

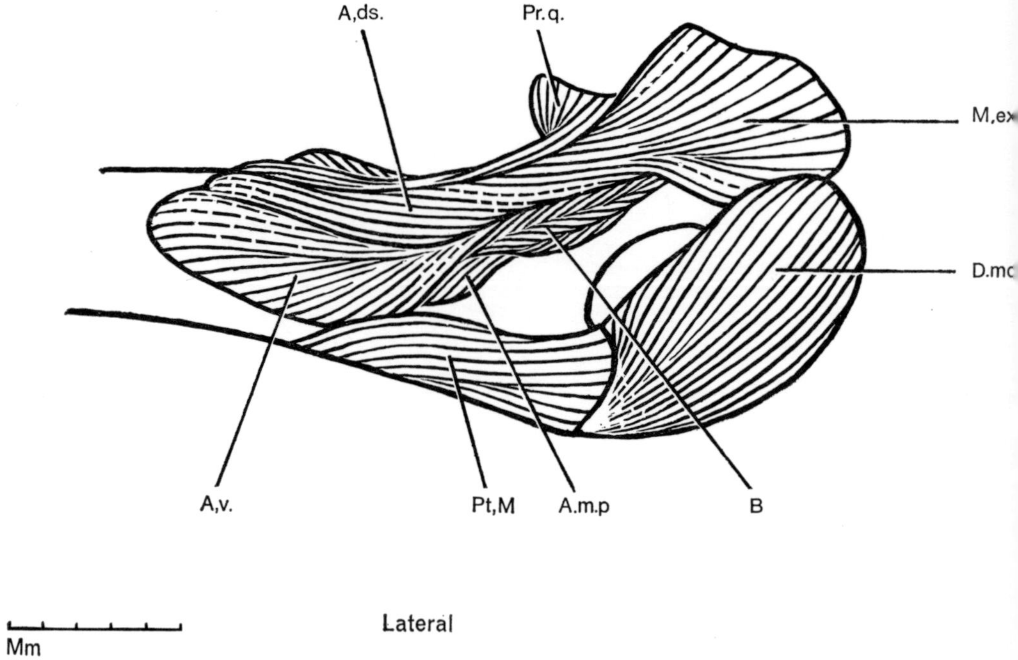

Lateral

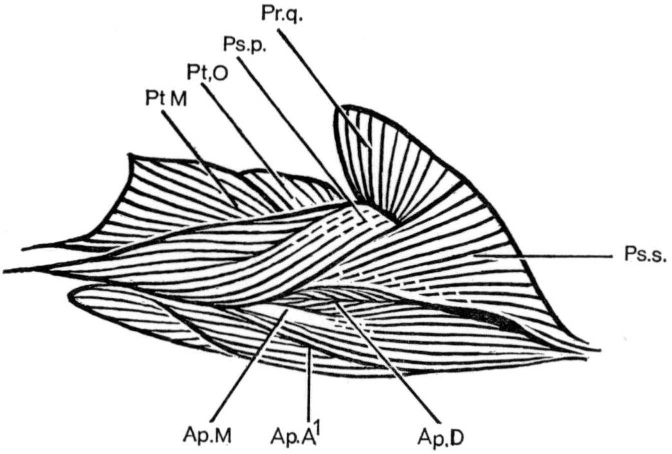

Dorsal

Tringa totanus

Plate 5.
Numenius arquata: jaw musculature, lateral and dorsal aspects.

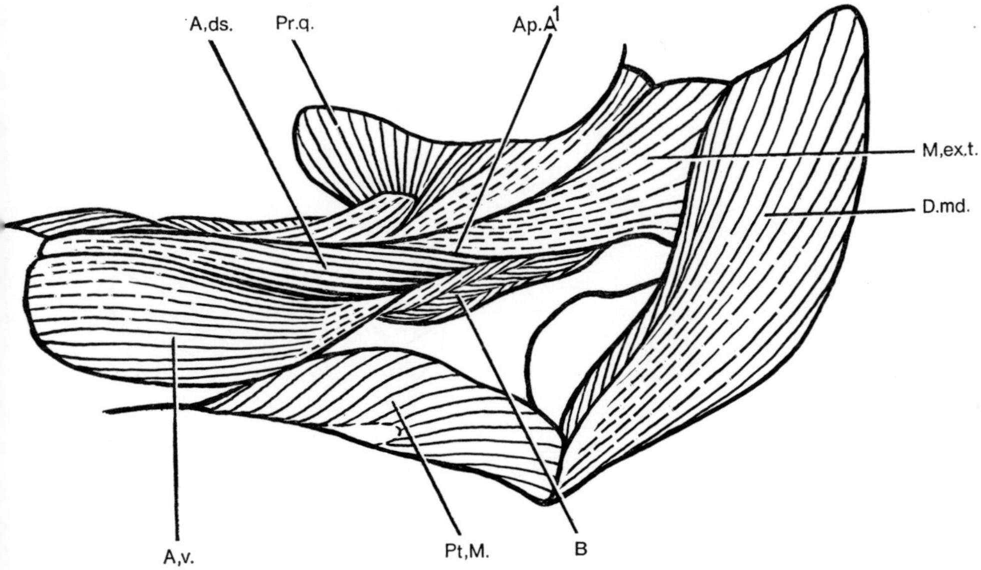

Lateral

m.

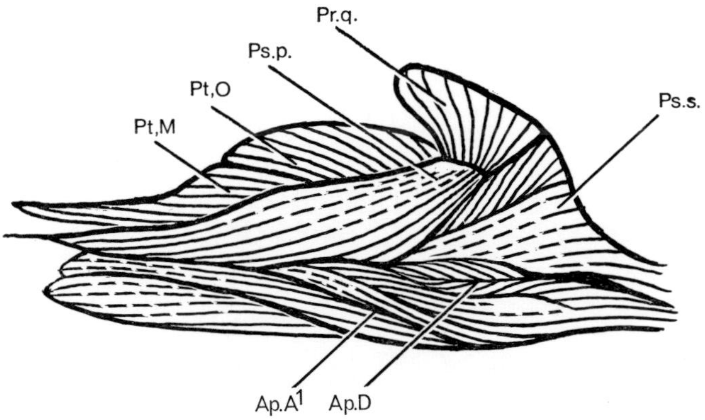

Dorsal

Numenius arquata

Plate 6.
Calidris alpina: jaw musculature, lateral and dorsal aspects.

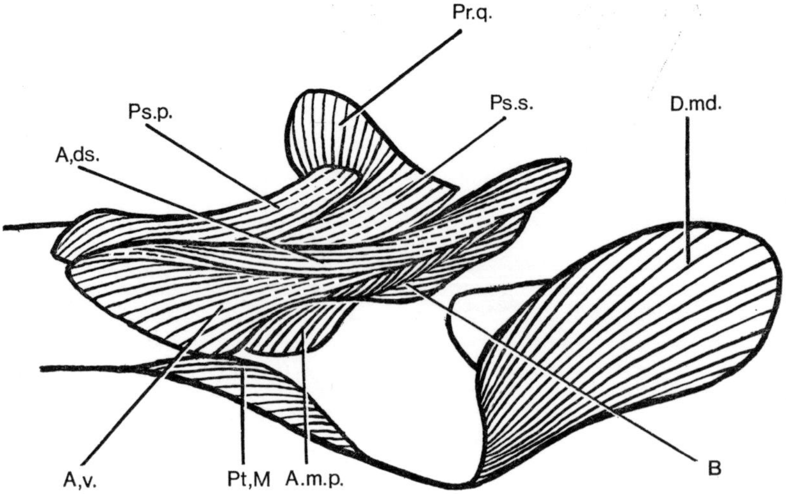

Mm.

Lateral

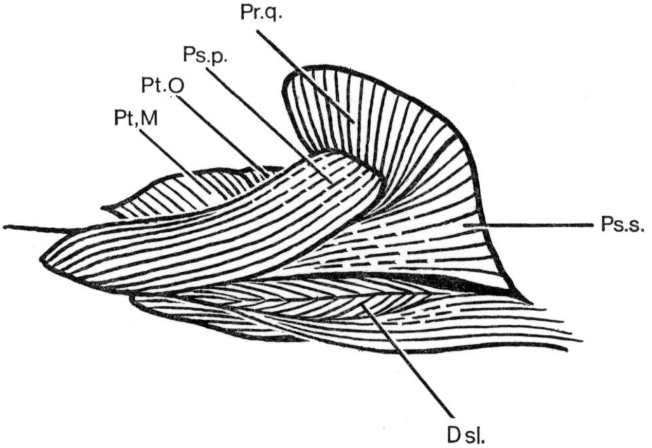

Dorsal

Calidris alpina

Plate 7.
Gallinago gallinago: jaw musculature, lateral and dorsal aspects.

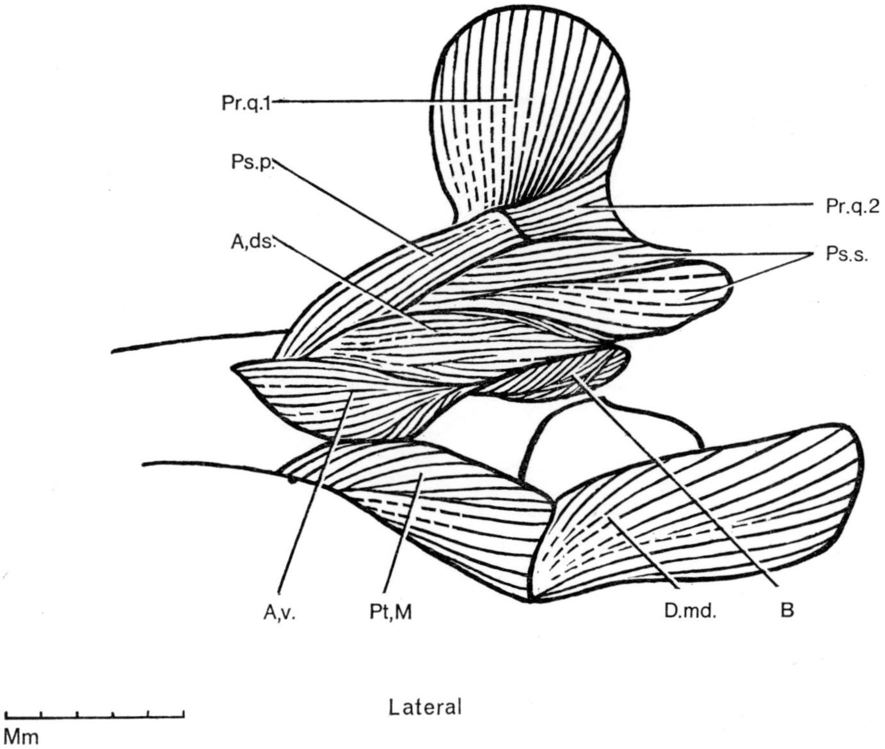

Lateral

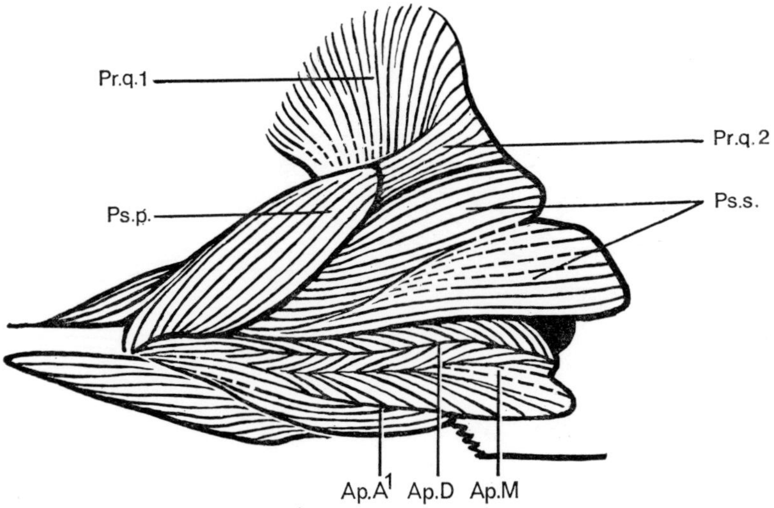

Dorsal

Gallinago gallinago

Plate 8.
Rostratula benghalensis:
jaw musculature, lateral and dorsal aspects.

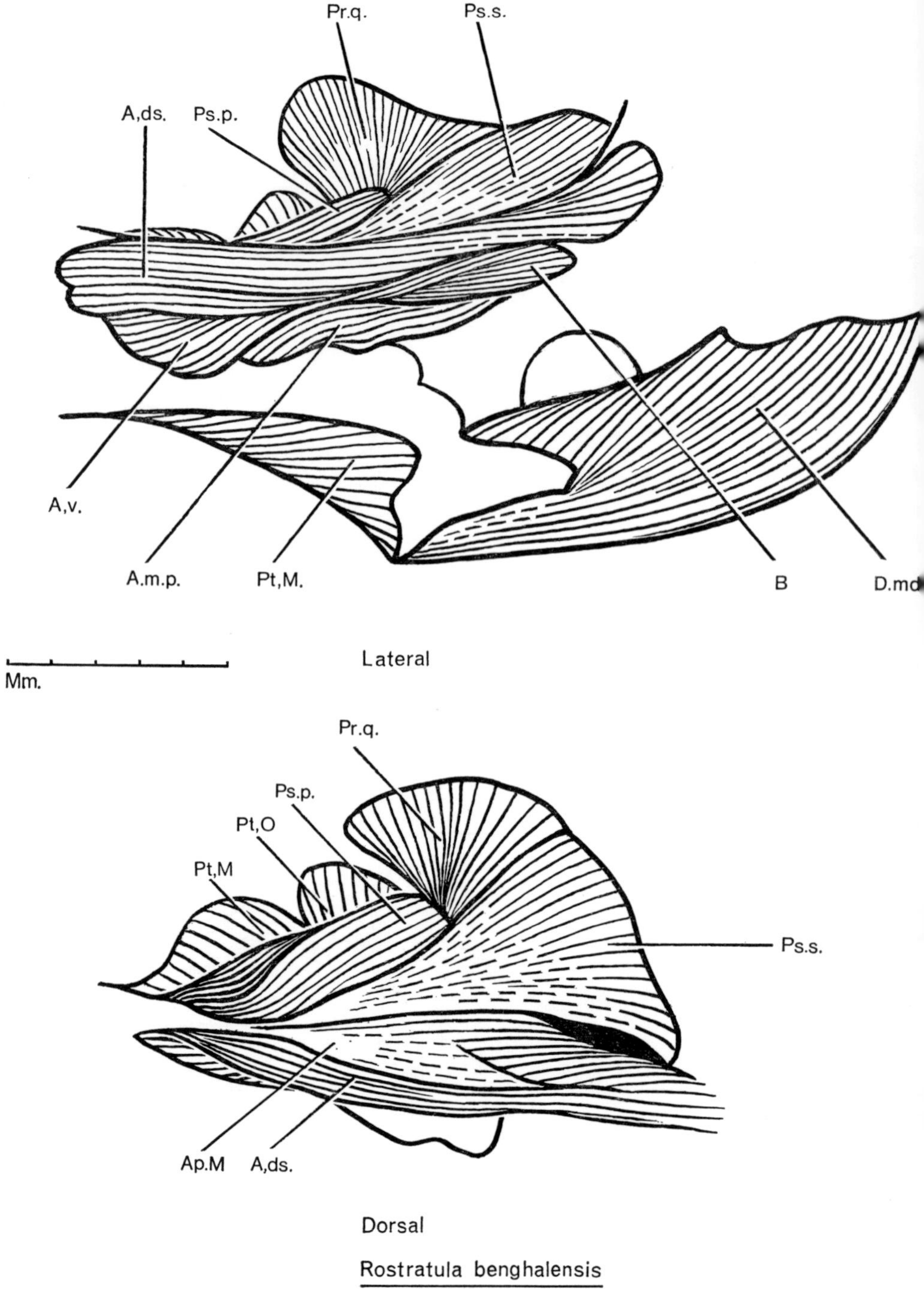

Plate 9.
Haematopus ostralegus:
jaw musculature, lateral and dorsal aspects.

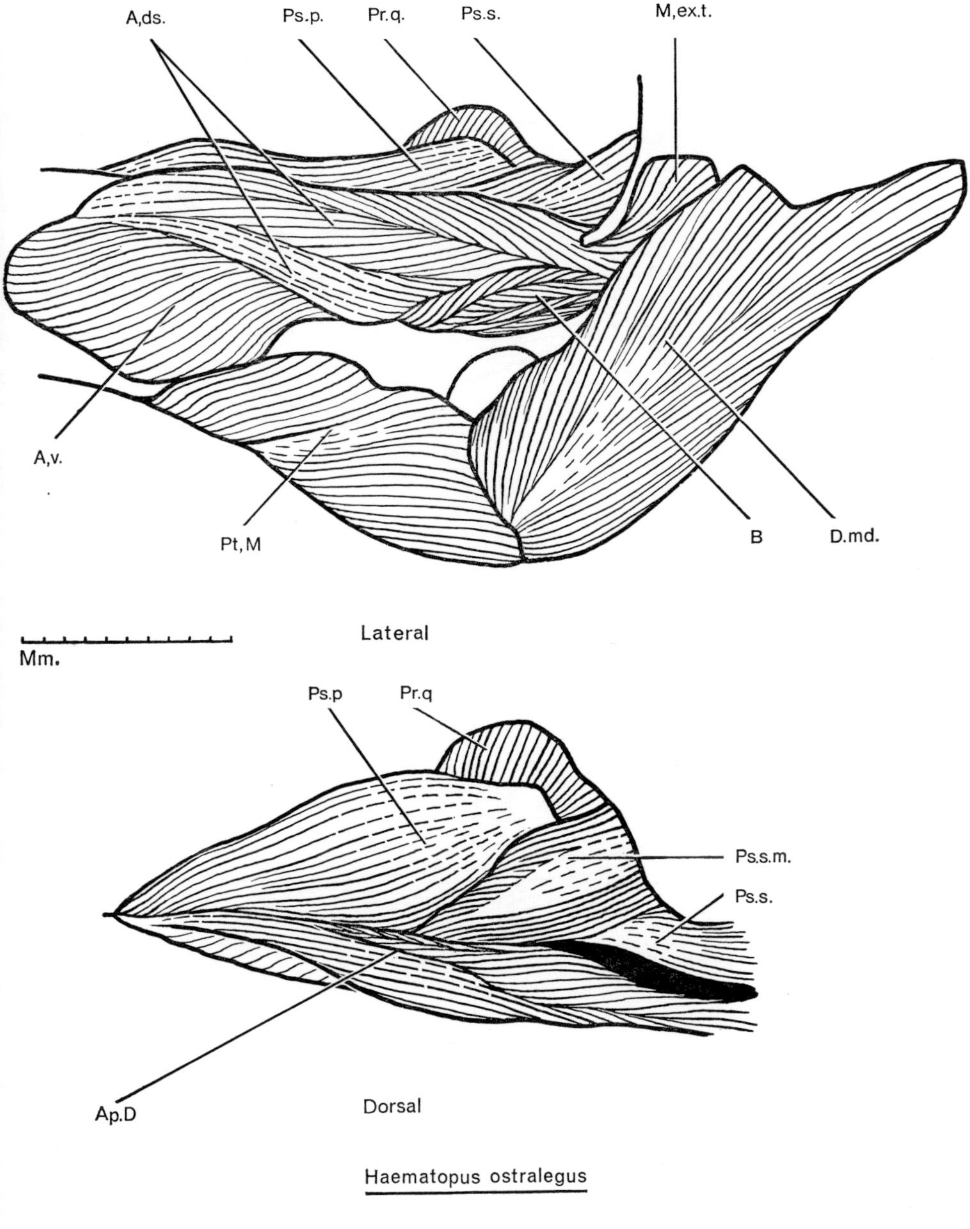

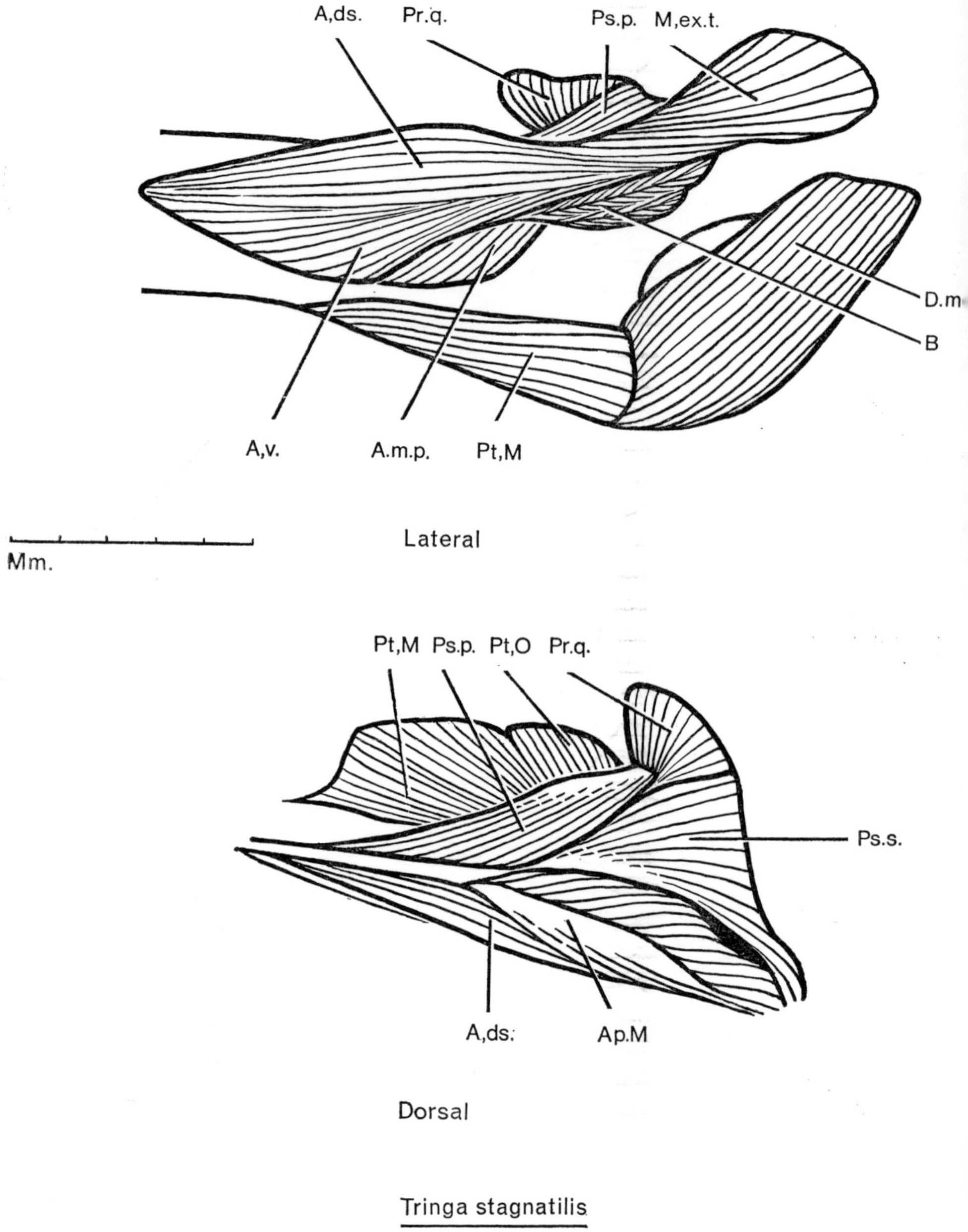

Plate 10.
Tringa stagnatilis: jaw musculature, lateral and dorsal aspects.

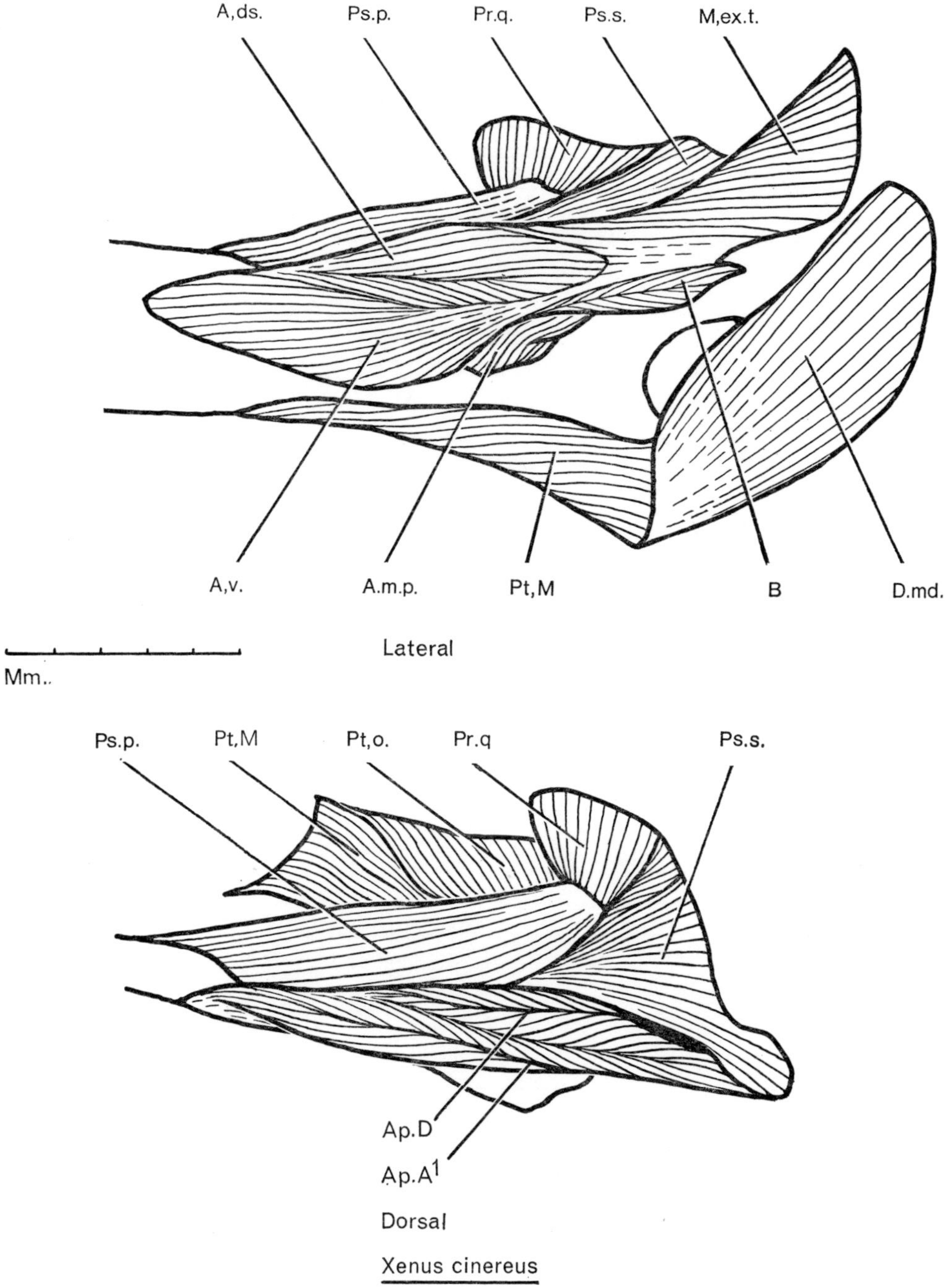

Plate 11.
Xenus cinereus: jaw musculature, lateral and dorsal aspects.

Plate 12.
Arenaria interpres: jaw musculature, lateral and dorsal aspects.

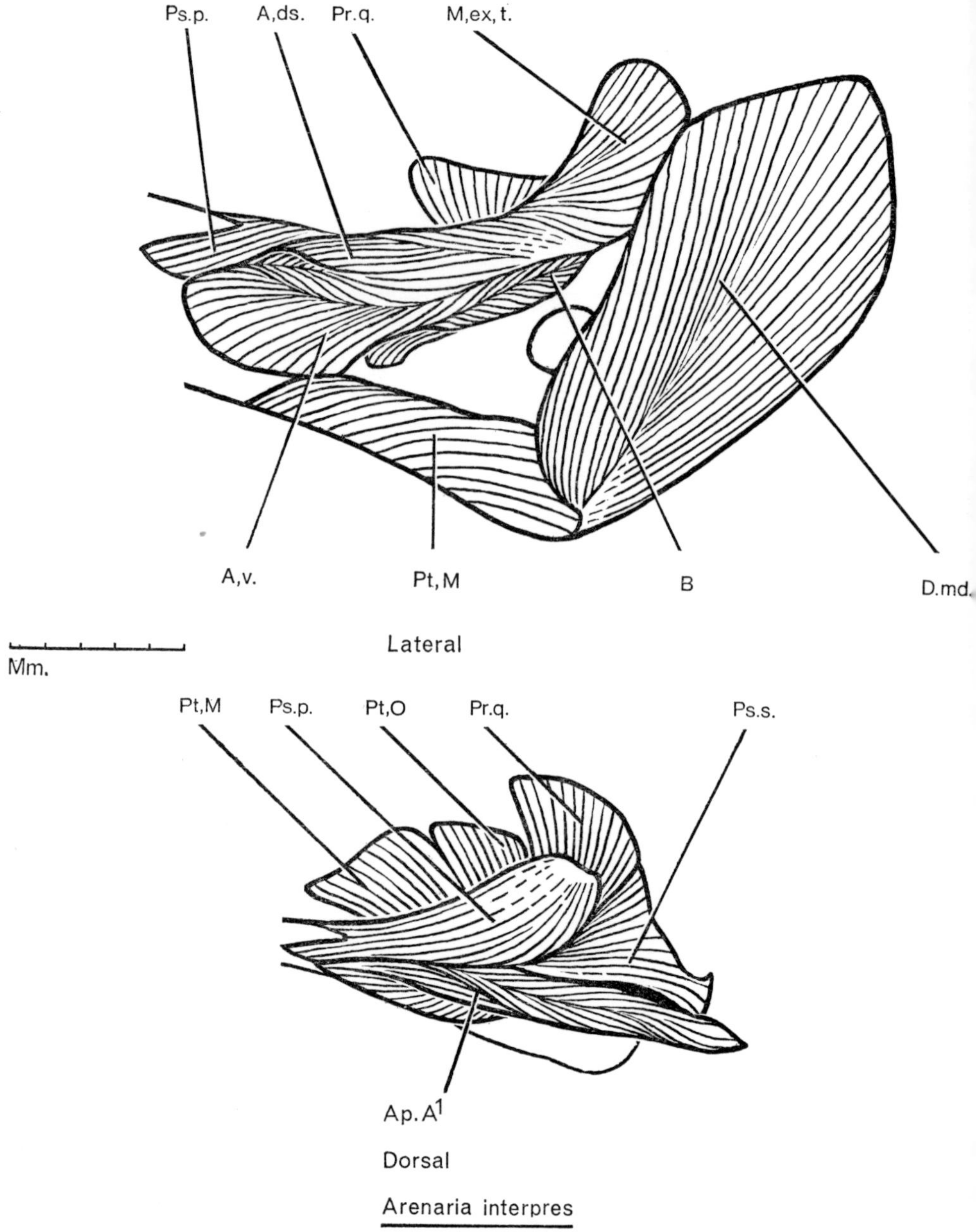

Plate 13.
Limosa lapponica: jaw musculature, lateral and dorsal aspects.

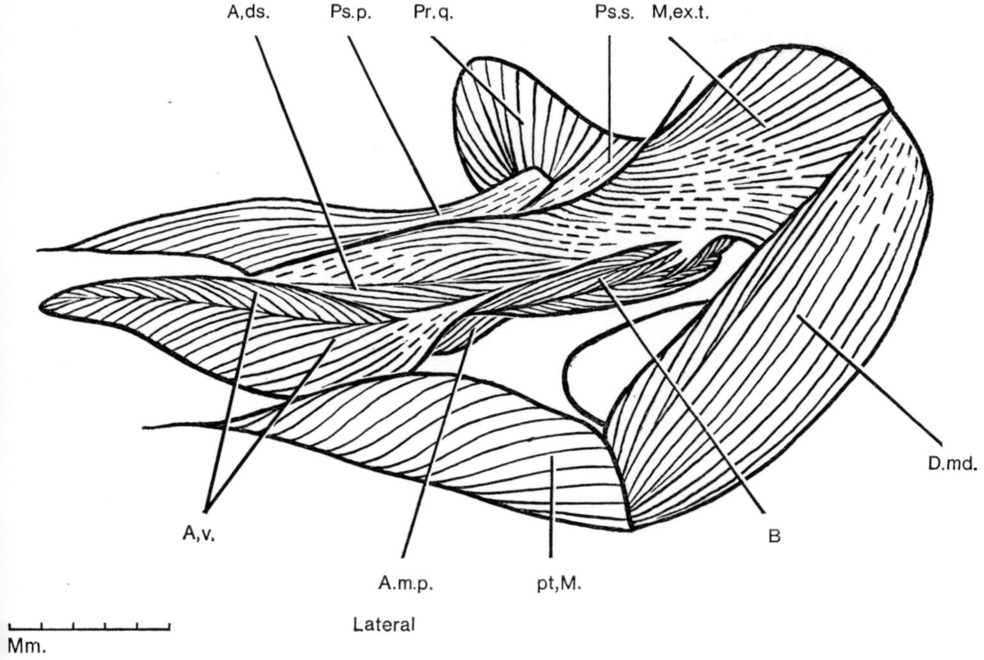

Lateral

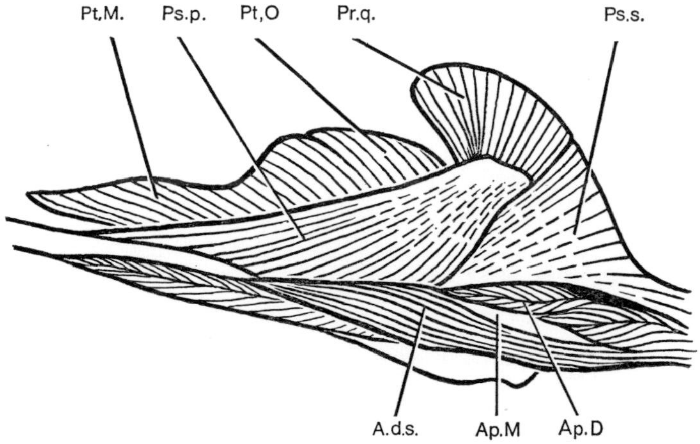

Dorsal

Limosa lapponica

Plate 14.
Limnodromus griseus: jaw musculature, lateral and dorsal aspects.

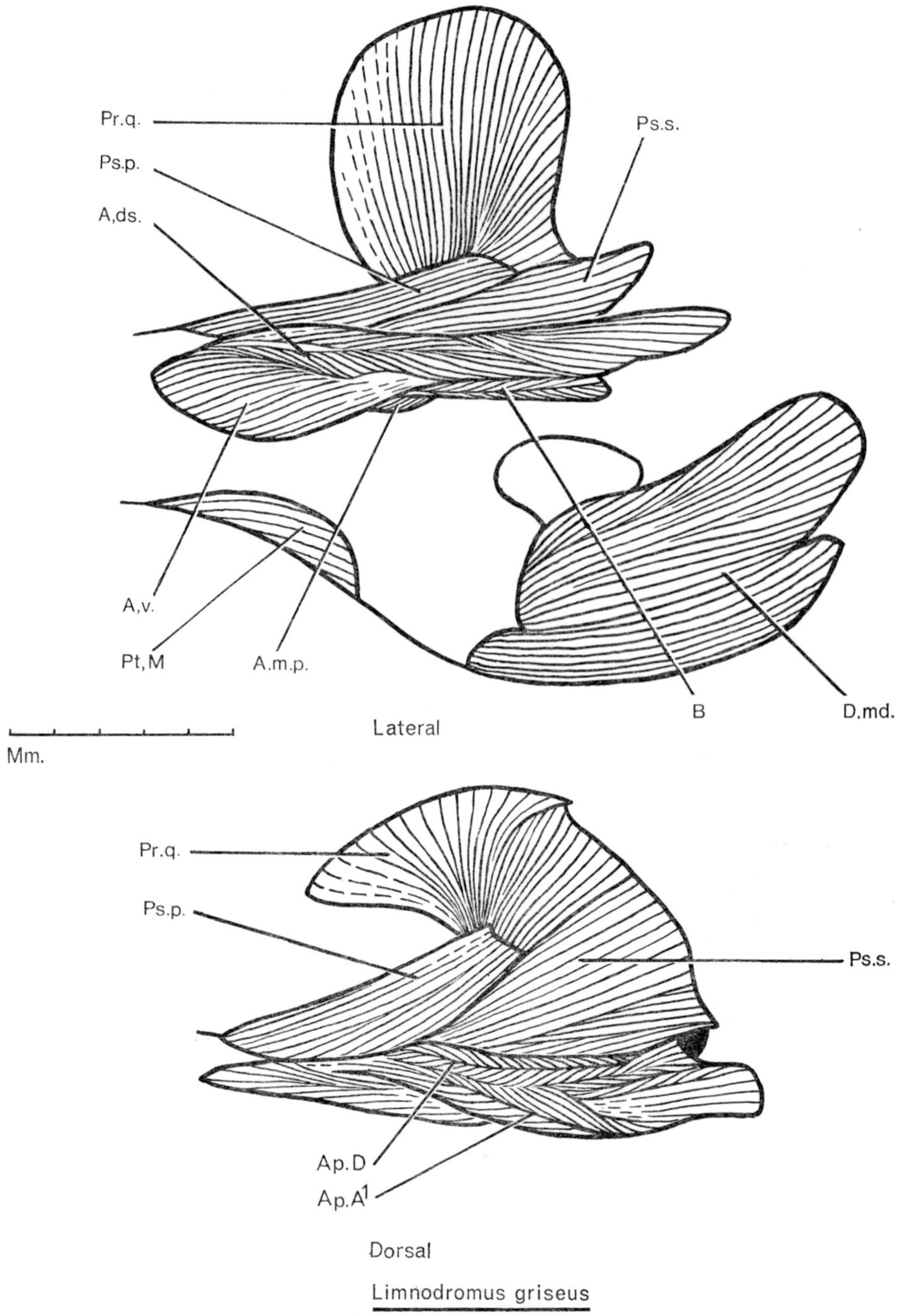

Plate 15.
Limicola falcinellus: jaw musculature, lateral and dorsal aspects.

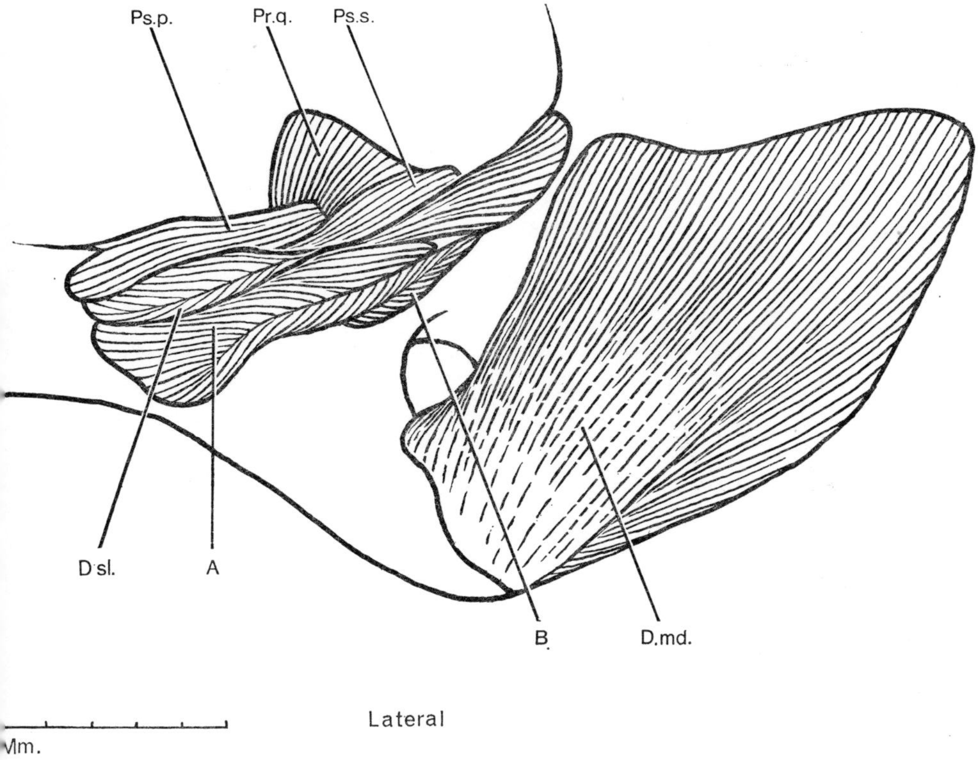

Lateral

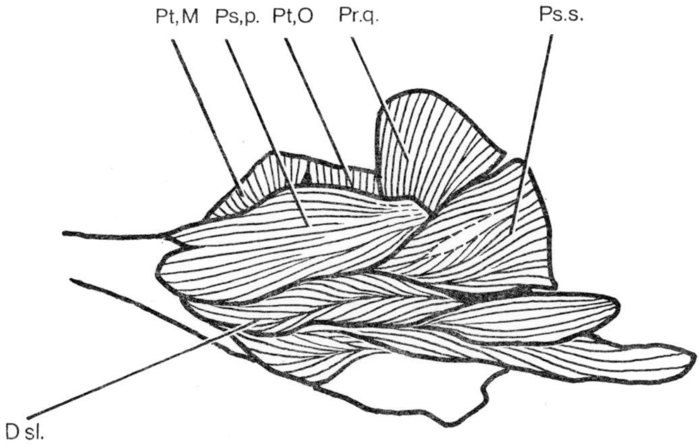

Dorsal

Limicola falcinellus

Plate 16.
Tryngites subruficollis: jaw musculature, lateral and dorsal aspects.

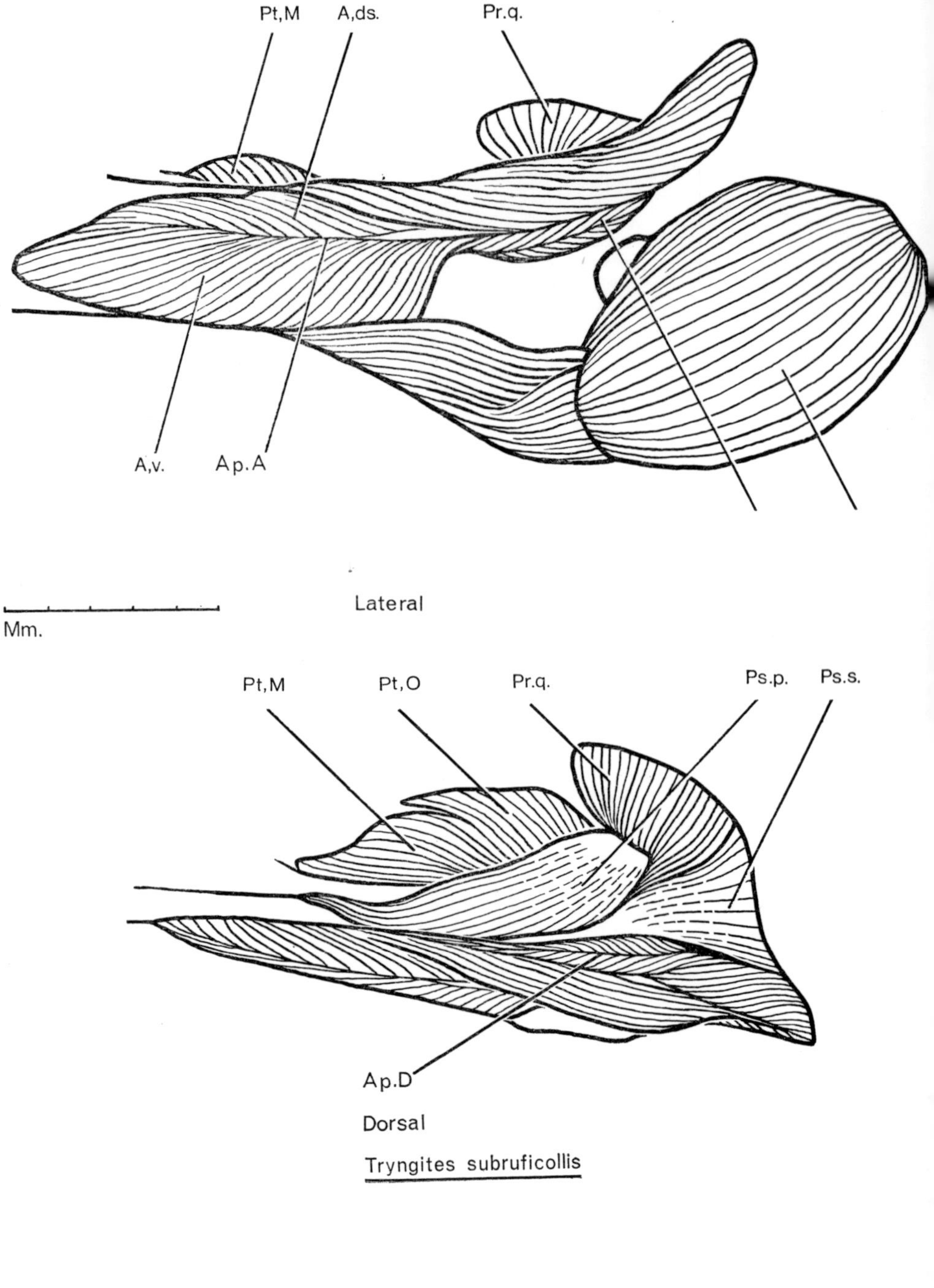

Plate 17.
Ibidorhyncha struthersii:
jaw musculature, lateral and dorsal aspects.

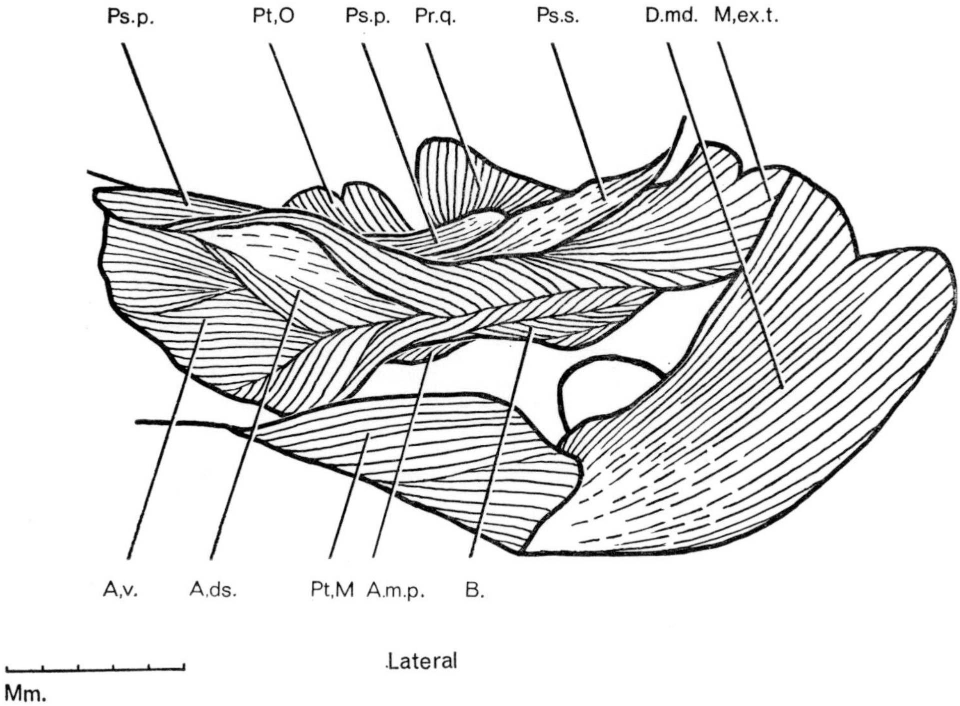

Lateral

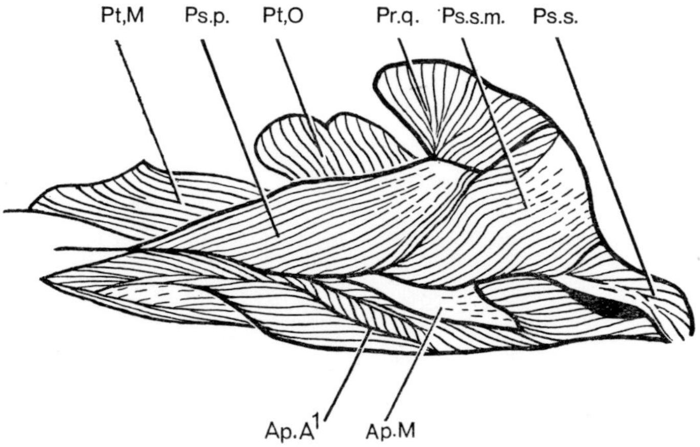

Dorsal

<u>Ibidorhyncha struthersii</u>

Plate 18.
Recurvirostra avosetta: jaw musculature, lateral and dorsal aspects.

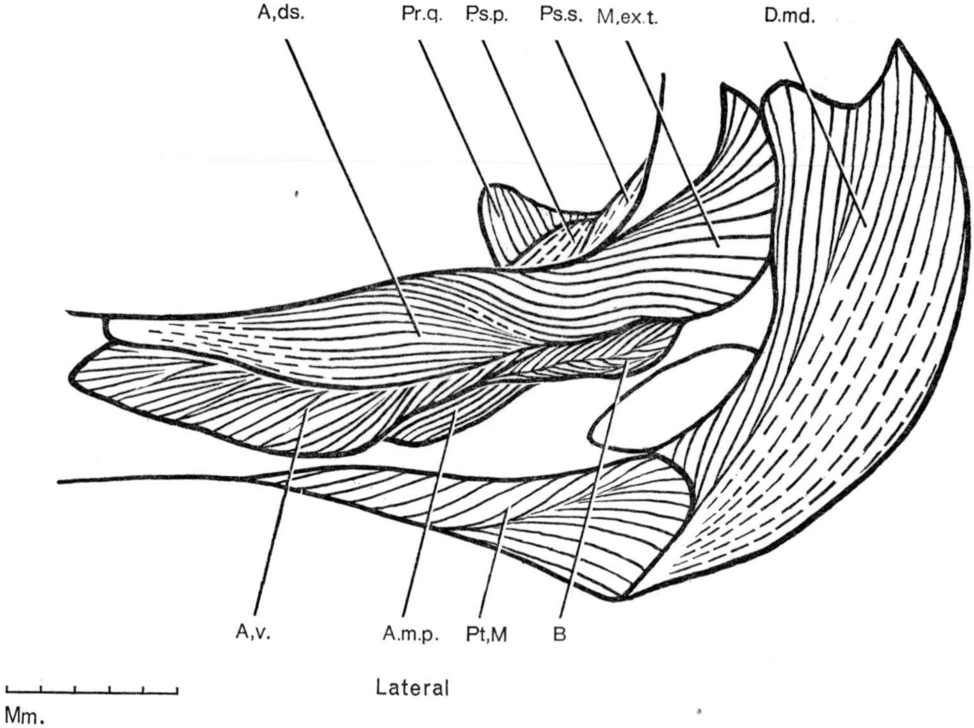

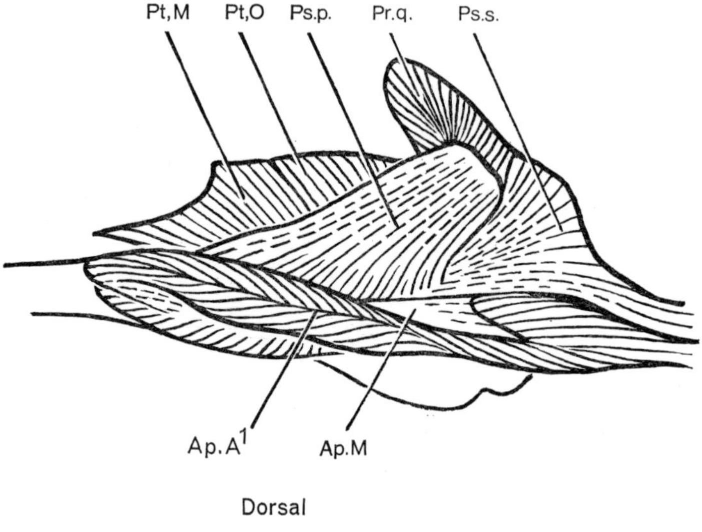

Plate 19.
Lobipes lobatus: jaw musculature, lateral and dorsal aspects.

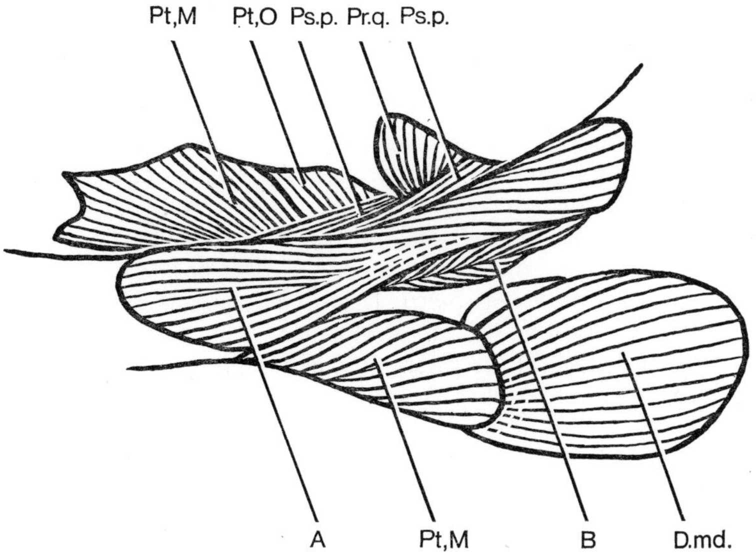

Mm.

Lateral

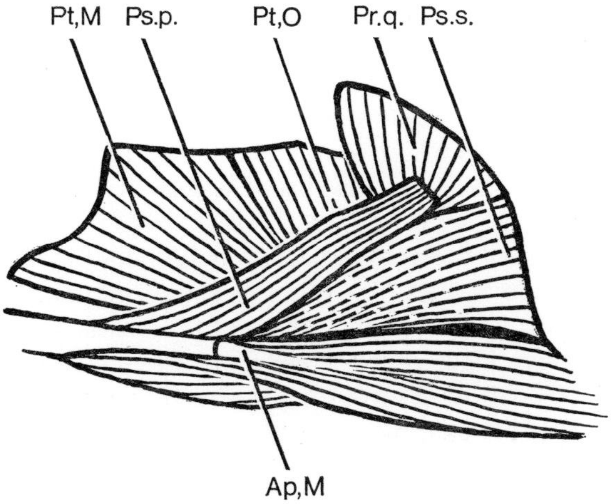

Dorsal

Lobipes lobatus

The fleshy mass medial to Ap. M in the rostral region is continuous ventrally with Part B. A raphe, Ap. D, arising on the otic process of the quadrate extends upwards into it, and may give rise to a well defined bipinnate slip (Ap. D slip), with fibres diverging rostrad. Some species show minor additional raphes arising in a similar way, and minor raphes arising from the medial edge of Ap. M may also transverse it.

Part A. Two sections are referred to. The dorsal section arises dorsal to Ap. A at its origin, where it is usually more or less continuous with Part M, and inserts narrowly on the dorsolateral surface of the surangular, rostral to Ap. M. Part A ventral section inserts broadly on the lateral surface of the surangular, immediately below the dorsal section.

Ap. A arises from the zygomatic process and fans out rostrally as a laterally concave sheet. This sheet commonly extends into Part A, dorsal section, where it is called A^1; ventrally it extends over the lateral surface of the ventral section, where it is referred to as A^2. The dorsal surface of the dorsal section often has some aponeurotic covering, usually continuous with Ap. M caudally. A lateral and ventral aponeurosis, Ap. P, is an important surface for insertion, and may cover more or less of the rostral lateral surface.

The ventral section consists of fibres arising from the lateral side of A^2, and inserting widely on the mandible. In some species there is a deep fossa on the lateral side of the surangular, and A^2 has a medial branch which attaches to the lateral edge of this fossa, while the lateral branch fans out across the muscle. In such cases, fibres arising between the two branches insert ventral and lateral to the fossa, while those medial to the medial branch insert within the fossa.

The insertion of the ventral section is bordered rostrally by M. pterygoideus, Part M. It is sometimes more or less overlapped by fibres arising from the ventral side of the dorsal section, and the two sections have fused in many species. The caudal half of Ap. A lies dorsal to Part B, and serves as an attachment for its dorsal fibres. N. mandibularis externus usually emerges through the ventral section, or at its edge.

Part B. The origin is fleshy and aponeurotic on the otic process of the quadrate, and the insertion is on the dorsal lateral surface of the surangular, behind and below the insertion of Ap. M. Part M lies ventral and medial to the rest of M. adductor externus, and dorsal to M. adductor posterior rostrally.

The main bulk of the muscle is contained between two aponeuroses, N and O. Ap. O is oriented obliquely, with the medial edge higher. Ap. N is less steeply oblique, and may be nearly horizontal; it lies lateral and dorsal to Ap. O. These aponeuroses arise only weakly on the otic process, but strengthen rostrally, and usually fuse at the insertion. Between them lies a raphe, Ap. B, arising on the otic process, but fading out short of the insertion. A further narrow strip of fibres arises on the ventral side of Ap. A and inserts on the dorsal surface of Ap. N. The most lateral and rostral of these usually insert with Part A ventral. Fibres run rostrad from Ap. A to Ap. N; caudad from Ap. N to Ap. B; rostrad from Ap. B to Ap. O; and caudad from Ap. O to the medial surface.

Comparison

Part M. The external temporal region is completely absent in *G. gallinago*, and vestigial in *C. alpina*. It is well developed in the remaining three representative species. In some specimens of *G. gallinago*, it arises on the surface of a group of fibres extending across the zygomatic process on to the wall of the orbit, but in most, the process is almost devoid of fibres, with Ap. M arising very weakly inside the muscle. Ap. M in this species frequently shows several small branches in transverse section, though always remaining thin. In *C. alpina*, Ap. M is commonly T-shaped in section, and in *T. totanus* and *N. arquata*, its medial edge is continued under the Ap. D slip to the medial surface of the muscle.

The Ap. D slip is present in all the representative species except *P. apricaria* and some specimens of *T. totanus*, and is particularly prominent in *C. alpina* by contrast with the simple structure of the rest of M. adductor externus.

Loss of the external temporal region has occurred in all Scolopacinae, and a vestigal condition is general in the Calidridinae (with least reduction in *Philomachus* and *Limosa*). Noteworthy reduction is also seen in *Rostratula*, *Haematopus*, small species of Charadriidae and Tringinae, *Arenaria* and the Phalaropodidae. Branching of Ap. M is usual in the Scolopacinae; in the Calidridinae, its form is remarkable in *Limicola*, being folded almost into a spiral. The median edge is extended to isolate the Ap. D slip in most larger Tringinae and in *Limosa* and *Limnodromus*. The varying development of the Ap. D slip is of great interest. Its prominence in *C. alpina* is typical of most Calidridinae. Greatest development is seen in *Limicola*, in which it forms the greater bulk of Part M, and crosses the dorsal edge of the mandible to insert widely on its lateral surface. Marked enlargement, with insertion rostral to Ap. M, is also seen in *C. canutus* and *C. maritima*. Exceptions in this subfamily are *Limosa*, in *C. acuminatus* and some specimens of *C. melanotos* and *Philomachus* in which it is absent. It is large in *Limnodromus*, but forms part of a generally much more complex muscle than in typical Calidridinae. Additional weak raphes traversing the fibres medial to Ap. M are prominent in *Limosa* and *Limnodromus*, though seen in many species. The Ap. D slip is also large in the Scolopacinae, where Ap. D originates from a strong crista on the zygomatic process. Origin from this site is also seen in *Haematopus*, but in all other species, origin is on the otic process. The slip is present in most moderate or large Tringinae, but usually weak. Greatest development is seen in *T. erythropus*, *T. nebularia*, *T. melanoleuca* and *Xenus*; in the latter, it covers two-thirds of the dorsal surface and inserts slightly rostral to Ap. M.

The Ap. D slip is absent in all other species, including all Charadriidae, Recurvirostridae and Phalaropodidae.

Part A. Ap. A^1 provides attachment for fibres of the dorsal section, separating them from the rostral region of Part M. In *N. arquata* and *T. totanus*, there is more complex structure, since fibres arising lateral to Ap. M enter into the structure of the dorsal section of Part A. In these species, A^1 diverges from Ap. A about where the postorbital ligament crosses it, and then runs rostromediad, dividing the dorsal portion obliquely into two. The fibres medial to it strictly speaking belong to Part M, and are often only weakly attached to Ap. A^1, though appearing to form part of the dorsal section of Part A. Variable minor pinnate arrangements are to be seen in this group of fibres. In *G. gallinago*, Ap. A^1 diverges from Ap. A at the origin, and acts as a strong raphe from which fibres diverge rostrad, the medial ones meeting the lateral fibres attached to Ap. M. In some specimens its laterodorsal edge is split, rostrally, so that its cross-section is Y-shaped.

A different type of structural complexity involving Ap. A^1 is seen in *P. apricaria*, though vestigially in some specimens. This is a bipinnate slip (A^1 slip) arising between Ap. A^1 and Ap. M, and extending across the dorsorostral surface of the muscle.

In *N. arquata* and *T. totanus*, fibres from the ventral edge of the dorsal section spread ventrad as a thin sheet overlapping the ventral section. They are attached to Ap. A^2, and are themselves covered by an extension of Ap. P. Ap. A^2 thus acts as a raphe, as also does its medial branch. In those two species and *G. gallinago*, regions of variable minor pinnate fibre arrangements are seen around the edges of the ventral section. At the other extreme, the ventral section in *C. alpina* is weakly aponeurotic, largely parallel fibred, and more or less merged anteriorly with the dorsal section.

The mandibular fossa in which the ventral section inserts is very deeply excavated in *N. arquata*, and is well developed also in *T. totanus* and *G. gallinago*.

A dorsal section of similar complex structure to *N. arquata* and *T. totanus* is seen in other large Tringinae, and in *Arenaria*. The arrangement described in *G. gallinago* also occurs in other Scolopacinae, while in *Limnodromus* there is a similar use of Ap. A^1, although in this case the medial fibres attached to it meet the lateral fibres attached to Ap. D, dorsal to Ap. M. *Xenus* also shows some approach to this condition, but Ap. A^1 diverges further forward.

The Ap. A^1 slip noted in *P. apricaria* occurs only in the Charadriidae and Recurvirostridae, and in all species of these groups, though vestigially in a few. At its most highly developed, the slip is strongly bipinnate and has a wide insertion on the dorso-lateral surface of the mandible. This condition is well seen in *Vanellus* and the Recurvirostridae.

Overlap of the ventral section by the dorsal is general in the larger Tringinae, though not always as extensive as in *N. arquata* and *T. totanus*. Extensive overlap also occurs in *Haematopus*, *Arenaria*, a few species of Charadriidae and *Ibidorhyncha*. Partial or complete fusion of the two sections is seen in most Calidridinae (not *Limosa* or *Limnodromus*), and in small *Charadrius* species, *Aechmorhynchus* and the Phalaropodidae. In most of these the ventral component is feebly developed. In *Tryngites*, however, fusion has produced a strongly bipinnate arrangement; the insertion of Part A extends far rostrad, and Ap. A is continued as a raphe between the sections. The extensive insertion overlaps the ventral edge of the mandible, and just reaches its lateral surface. In *Limosa* and *Limnodromus* there is a strongly bipinnate region at the dorsal edge of the ventral section, but the two sections remain separate. They are separate in *Rostratula*, but the ventral section is much the smaller.

The lateral mandibular fossa is well developed in many Scolopacidae, large *Tringa* species and *Limosa* making the closest approach to *Numenius*. It is weak in the typical Calidridinae, as also in the Phalaropodidae and Charadriidae. It is deep in *Haematopus*, and moderate in the Recurvirostridae; in *Recurvirostra* and *Himantopus* the insertion of Part A ventral is entirely confined within it.

Part B. The five representative species show moderate variation in structure. The insertion of Ap. N is broadest in *P. apricaria*, while in *N. arquata* and *G. gallinago*, minor superficial raphes may be detectable caudally. In addition, there is a further aponeurosis on the medial side of the muscle in *G. gallinago*, arising from a sharp spina on the otic process of the quadrate. Aps. B and A join by their medial edges in *N. arquata* and *P. apricaria*, but in *C. alpina*, the medial edge of Ap. B usually joins the ventral edge of Ap. D.

The insertion of Ap. N is generally relatively broad in the Charadriidae, and a marked expansion is seen in some species of *Vanellus*. Ap. B also broadens rostrally in a number of Charadriidae to cover the dorsal surface of fibres inserting lateral and ventral to Ap. N. This reaches an extreme in one specimen of *Vanellus tectus*, in which Ap. B extends along the whole caudal edge of Part A ventral section, with a narrow strip of fibres lying caudal to it, and plainly visible laterally. Such a lateral expansion recalls the structure seen in some other Charadrii (e.g., *Chionis*, *Pluvianus*) and the Lari.

Multiplication of raphes in the caudolateral region of Part B is particularly well seen in *Haematopus* and *Limosa*. In *Limosa* and *Limnodromus* the lateral edge of Ap. N is fused with Ap. A at its origin. Fusion of the medial edges of Aps. A and B is common, particularly in the Charadriidae and Tringinae, while fusion of Aps. B and D internally as in *C. alpina* is seen in many other typical Calidridinae. The medial edge of Ap. O commonly reaches the dorsal surface of the muscle, and in *Haematopus* it is bifid. The medial aponeurosis mentioned in *G. gallinago* is seen in all Scolopacinae, and should perhaps be considered a derivative of Ap. D.

The structure of Part B in *Rostratula* is distinctive, and unlike any other member of the Charadrii. There is only one aponeurosis, that of insertion, unless the weak superficial covering on the laterocaudal surface is counted. Fibres attaching to this aponeurosis do so at a very narrow angle, and the muscle is to all intents and purposes parallel fibred. Fibres ventral to the aponeurosis are limited to its caudal half, while those dorsal to it continue past its insertion to attach on the lateral surface of the mandible caudal to Part A ventral section.

Action. The primary actions of M. adductor externus are to elevate the depressed mandible or to maintain pressure in gripping prey by isometric contraction.

The torque produced by the muscle, as for any force acting on a lever, will be dependent upon the perpendicular distance of its line of action from the pivot, in this case the quadrate-mandibular joint. The trend towards downward and forward shift of the brain case in the Charadrii has resulted in reduction of this distance. Associated changes include early loss of the lateral mandibular expansion of Part N, closer siting of the insertions of aponeuroses M and N, and loss of the external temporal region. The resulting loss of effective force is partly compensated by utilizing multipinnate fibre arrangements, which are efficient also because of the smaller distance over which the muscle contracts. The culmination of these trends is well illustrated by *G. gallinago*, in which the mandible is sharply angled down close to the quadrate, with the adductors inserted together at the apex of this angle, and the highly pinnate M. adductor externus pulling along the line of the tomium.

Part A inserts furthest forward on the mandible, but is inserted at a more acute angle than parts M and B. The perpendicular distances of the aponeuroses to the pivot decrease in the order M, A, B. Zusi (1962) suggests that the proximal portions are important in initiating rapid closing of the jaws, while the distal portions serve chiefly to apply steady pressure in grasping. The contraction distance of Part B is the smallest, and as Bock (1964a) points out, its usually multipinnate structure is probably a consequence of this fact. Part B must play a major part in bringing about the rapid adduction over a short distance required for the capture of small active prey, the "mowing" movements performed by many waders, or the rapid mandible movements which accompany head jerking to pass prey up the bill.

The maintenance of pressure in grasping will be of particular importance to species which have to exert a steady pull in order to extract prey from the ground. Of particular relevance for this action are slips A^1 and D. Both have lines of action well above the pivot, and both are pinnate; their contribution to the torque of adduction must be considerable. Slip A^1 is oriented approximately along the line of the posterior dorsal edge of the mandible, while Slip D runs exactly parallel with the longitudinal axis of the skull. Slip D is efficiently sited for adduction and since it passes directly across the quadrate body, it will have little effect in swinging it outwards and thus a low retraction effect. It is particularly prominent in highly rhynchokinetic species which require forceful adduction over a short range of mandible movement, and a strong grasp during prey extraction. The low retraction component may be important to them when adduction occurs simultaneously with protraction. This combination of actions was seen in the captive Snipe when grasping a worm near the gape and simultaneously manipulating it with the upper jaw tip – or in one case, capturing a maggot while still gripping a worm higher up the bill.

The retractor effect is a secondary action of M. adductor externus. pointed out by Lakjer (1926), and to which renewed attention is drawn by Zusi (1962). This effect is the result of its force component acting backwards along the lower jaw on the quadrate, and tending to swing it outwards and downwards. The laterally situated parts of the muscle have lines of action more tangential to the arc of movement of the quadrate, and farther from its pivot, and will hence have a greater retraction effect. Part A, dorsal section, will be important in this respect, especially when augmented by Slip A^1. The backward force component is greater in species with a low angle of insertion of M. adductor externus, but this is largely offset by the associated shift of the long axis of the quadrate to a position more nearly in line with the tomium.

M. adductor externus normally acts synergically with M. pterygoideus, and will oppose its tendency to cause forward disarticulation of the quadrate-mandibular joint. It will do this most efficiently if attached at a low angle to the bill axis. Disruption forces with a lateral component arising during probing may be in part opposed by unilateral contraction of M. adductor externus. Some unilateral action may occur during manipulation of prey.

Von Kripp (1933a) suggested that M. adductor externus and M. depressor might contract synergically in aiding protraction of the upper jaw. Bock (1964a) justifiably doubts the usefulness of such an inefficient mechanism. Synergic action between the two muscles may, however, be expected at other times, as with other antagonistic muscle pairs.

The velocity ratio and mechanical advantage of muscles acting on the lower jaw will depend to a large extent on bill length relative to that of the skull, since the amount of adjustment that can be made in siting without gross morphological change is small. A rough indication of the velocity ratio of M. adductor externus, Part M, in the five representative species has been obtained by measuring the distance from the tip of the mandible to its pivot, and from the tip of Ap. M to the pivot. The position of the pivot was taken as the posterior edge of the lateral quadrate condyle, seen in lateral view; this is arbitrary, since the pivot is really a sliding one. Velocity ratios calculated from these measurements in the specimens dissected are as follows:

P. apricaria	0·17 to 0·19
T. totanus	0·08 to 0·09
N. arquata	0·05 to 0·06
C. alpina	0·11 to 0·12
G. gallinago	about 0·07

The figure for *T. totanus* is lower than its relative bill length (p. 39) suggests, but the importance of this factor is clear none the less. Compensation for reduced mechanical advantage resulting from increased bill length must be considered as one possible reason for increased complexity of muscle structure; however, the relationship between these factors is not simple, and must be interpreted with caution.

M. pseudotemporalis superficialis

M. pseudotemporalis superficialis is an adductor of the lower jaw. Its structure in the Charadrii is simpler than that of the Lari; nevertheless, Zusi's numbering can be used for two aponeuroses, although one (Ap. M) has undergone a significant change of insertion, as will be shown later in this account.

The origin is on the posterior wall of the orbit, and there is often a caudal lobe on the lateral side which may pass under the postorbital process to appear on the lateral surface of the skull in a vestigial pseudotemporal fossa. The dorsal edge of its orbital origin is bordered by a crista, and below this is a shorter crista which is the site of origin of an internal aponeurosis (Ap. B). The caudal lobe if present is bordered posteriorly by a crista representing the temporal crest.

Much of the surface of the muscle is aponeurotic, and this aponeurosis (M) is strongest laterally. The muscle narrows rostrally, and Ap. M becomes a strong tendon inserting on the medial side of the surangular, dorsal to the ramus mandibularis of Nerve V_3. In a few species, fibres arising medially run laterad across the dorsal surface of Ap. M; this modification is often incorporated into pinnate structure in the dorsal half of the muscle.

Transverse sections of the muscle are shown for fourteen species in Plate 26.

Comparison
The caudal lobe is absent in *C. alpina* and *G. gallinago*. The muscle is of complex structure only in *G. gallinago*, in which there is extensive overgrowth of the dorsal surface by fibres arising medially, and multiplication of raphes by variable branching of Aps. M and B. In *Calidris alpina*, the two aponeuroses are joined. In *N. arquata* there is a narrow band of fibres arranged in unipinnate fashion along the medial edge. More or less fusion with M. adductor externus, Part M, is seen at the insertion in *G. gallinago*.

Relatively simple structure is the rule in most species. The complexity seen in *G. gallinago* is found also in other Scolopacinae except *Lymnocryptes*, in which the muscle is exceptionally thin. Overgrowth of the dorsal surface by medial fibres is also marked in *Haematopus*, and shown in a lesser degree by one specimen each of *Vanellus tectus* and *V. coronatus* and by *Ibidorhyncha*. In one specimen of *V. chilensis* and in *Pluvianellus*, the overlapping fibres form a well marked bipinnate slip with fibres diverging rostrad. Less highly developed pinnate structure at the dorsal surface, is seen in one specimen of *Pluvialis squatarola* (right side only), *Limnodromus*, *Calidris canutus* and *Limicola*.

A unipinnate band of fibres along the medial edge has also been seen in *Charadrius asiaticus*, *Eudromias*, *Aechmorhynchus*, *Numenius phaeopus*, *Xenus*, *Himantopus* and *Recurvirostra*. The medial edge is sharply emarginated in *Aechmorhynchus*, *Bartramia*, *Catoptrophorus* and *Heteroscelus*.

Action. The principal function is adduction of the lower jaw. M. pseudotemporalis superficialis is inserted near M. adductor externus, Part M, and will have a similar mechanical advantage; it is usually inserted more steeply than Part M, and will thus be more efficient. Seen dorsally, the midline of the muscle runs rostrolaterad from origin to insertion, but its line of action probably lies nearer to the lateral side where Ap. M is situated. It may thus pull parallel with the long axis of the skull, or more usually somewhat medially. A medial component in adduction may be of some value in overcoming lateral external forces, or in returning the mandibular rami to rest after bowing.

The variation in site of insertion in the Charadrii deserves comment. Loss of the double insertion seen in some other Charadrii (q.v.) is related to reduction in development of the muscle, but it is interesting that only the Charadrioidea have retained the insertion dorsal to N. ramus mandibularis. This site is further from the quadrate-mandibular pivot, and thus has a slightly greater mechanical advantage. More important may have been the need to accommodate a bulky M. pseudotemporalis profundus despite changes in skull morphology.

Other variations in development of the muscle show a similar picture to that for M. adductor externus. With increasing specialization for rhynchokinesis, the lateral lobe is reduced and lost, and the angle of insertion decreases. Starck & Barnikol remark on the hypertrophy of M. pseudotemporalis superficialis to compensate for reduction of M. adductor externus in species which they investigated. It is less easy to demonstrate such a simple relation among the Charadrii; more usually, reduction or development of the two muscles seem to progress on similar lines. The bipinnate medial slip is a feature shown by many other Charadriiformes, but retained by few Charadrioidea. The complex structure shown by some Scolopacidae has probably arisen secondarily to compensate for general reduction in bulk of both adductors.

M. pseudotemporalis profundus and M. adductor posterior

Lakjer regarded N. pterygoideus as separating these two muscles. Starck & Barnikol treat them as constituting a single "medial muscle complex", but suggest a division based on Barnikol's (1953a) study of innervation. According to this division, Lakjer's M. adductor posterior would include an element of M. pseudotemporalis profundus. Zusi, however, retains Lakjer's criterion, and the same course is followed here.

These muscles act to lower the upper jaw at the same time as they raise the mandible. Since both their attachments move, the treatment of the quadrate as the site of origin is arbitrary.

M. pseudotemporalis profundus originates fleshily from the lateral surface and the anterior ventral edge of the orbital process of the quadrate, and by an aponeurosis attached to the distal edge of the process. This aponeurosis covers much of the dorsal surface, and may be folded into the muscle medially. The bulk of the fibres are parallel, and run rostroventrad; fibres posterior to the aponeurosis tend to diverge and run ventrad. The insertion is wide and fleshy on the medial surface of the surangular and prearticular, and the muscle frequently overlaps its dorsal edge to make further insertion on its lateral surface. The main insertion is bordered rostrally by the medial origin of M. geniohyoideus.

M. adductor posterior arises on the proximal region of the orbital process and the quadrate body. The origin includes the lateral surface and the rostral edge of the medial surface of the orbital process, and the anterior lateral surface of the body. Insertion is on the dorsal surface of the mandible, just posterior to the insertion of Ap. C, and to the medial surface, immediately dorsal to that of M. pterygoideus. Part O, with which there may be some fusion.

Comparison

Great variation in the bulk of M. pseudotemporalis profundus is revealed by inspection, but a quantitative approach would be needed for an adequate survey. Among the representative species, the muscle appears best developed in *P. apricaria* and *N. arquata*. In *G. gallinago* it is small and narrow, and oriented exactly in line with M. protractor 2. In *T. totanus*, the dorsal aponeurosis is turned down, and a band of fibres medial to it diverge rostrad in unipinnate fashion. Rostrally, the aponeurosis fades out, and these medial fibres run parallel with the rest. M. adductor posterior is most clearly visible laterally in *C. alpina*.

Extremes of development of M. pseudotemporalis profundus appear to be the very broad muscle seen in *Haematopus*, some *Vanellus* spp., *Arenaria* and *Recurvirostra*, and the very small and narrow one of *Rostratula*, *Gallinago* and *Lymnocryptes*. A unipinnate arrangement along the medial edge, similar to *T. totanus*, is also seen in other large *Tringa* species, *Catoptrophorus*, *Heteroscelus* and *Phalaropus*. A more highly developed structure is found in *Haematopus*, *Arenaria*, *Aphriza* and *Scolopax*, all of which possess an internal aponeurosis arising on the rostral edge of the orbital process, from which fibres diverge rostrad. This aponeurosis is particularly strong in *Haematopus*, in which it arises from a broad flat flange on the orbital process, and extends across most of the width of the muscle.

M. pseudotemporalis profundus usually overlaps the mandible at its insertion. This feature is particularly well marked in the Calidridinae, and in *Limicola Micropalama* and several species of *Calidris*, the lateral insertion takes the form of a distinct fork. In *Limicola*, two-thirds of the dorsal surface of the muscle is made up of fibres running to this fork. A mandible overlap is absent in many Charadriidae and Recurvirostridae because it is displaced by a large Apl. A^1 slip. It may also be lacking, however, when Part A, dorsal section, is weak, so that the entire dorsal edge of the mandible rostral to Cr. 1 is exposed. This is seen in *Aechmorhynchus, Bartramia, Tringa flavipes, T. stagnatilis, T. solitaria, T. ochropus, T. glareola* and the Phalaropodidae.

Variations in the amount of the insertion of M. adductor posterior which can be seen laterally depend to a large extent upon the degree of overlap by M. adductor externus. The muscle appears most markedly well developed in *Rostratula*.

Action. M. pseudotemporalis profundus is both an adductor of the lower jaw and a retractor of the upper. Zusi suggests that it may thus be important in co-ordinating the closing of the jaws. Its attachment far along the mandible, and to the tip of the orbital process, give it a high mechanical advantage compared with other adductors and retractors. Like the more distal parts of M. adductor externus, it is probably important in maintaining a grip on prey. Its action must require modification by synergists when "uncoupled" movements of the two jaws are taking place for manipulating prey – e.g., if the upper jaw is depressed past the "closed" position, particularly when unaccompanied by adduction.

The force exerted on the mandible by M. pseudotemporalis profundus, particularly its posterior fibres, has a considerable medial component. This may be of importance in returning the mandible to the resting position in species employing bowing of the rami during prey swallowing, and also in counteracting lateral forces. Zusi points out that support of the mandible on the quadrate will be a major function of M. adductor posterior since its low mechanical advantage must render it of little use in jaw closure.

The basically parallel fibred structure of M. pseudotemporalis profundus in all the species studied is understandable in view of the long distance over which it acts. Its prominent overlap on to the dorsal lateral surface of the mandible in many Calidridinae appears to be occupying space made available by the reduction of M. adductor externus, Part A; this development may thus be in part compensatory. The complete absence in a few species of any attachment of M. adductor externus, Part A, to the dorsal edge of the mandible, is not accompanied by any clear hypertrophy or reduction of other muscles. This feature occurs particularly in species feeding on small aquatic prey.

M. pterygoideus

Lakjer treated this large muscle complex as consisting of dorsal and ventral portions which could be subdivided into lateral and medial parts.

Plate 20.
Jaw musculature in four species of Charadrii showing relationship of parts M and O of M. pterygoideus to the path followed by N. pterygoideus.
M. pseudotemporalis superficialis and M. pseudotemporalis profundus removed.

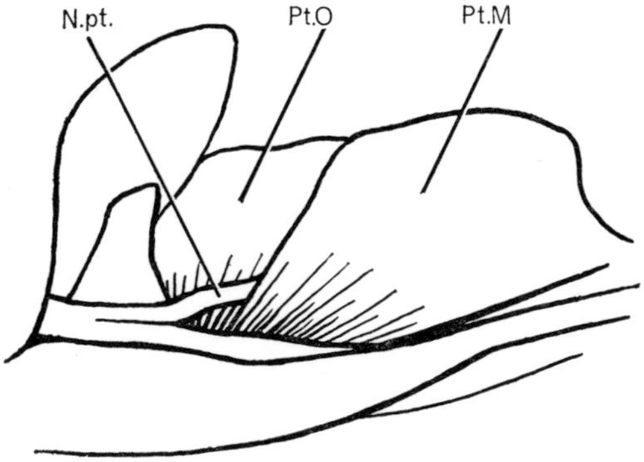

Tringa totanus

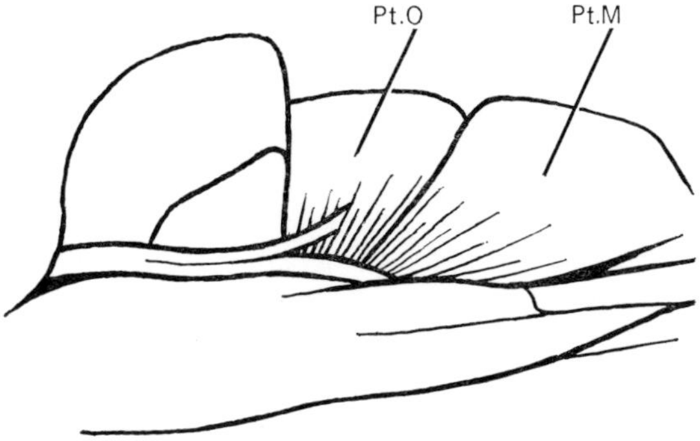

Pluvialis apricaria

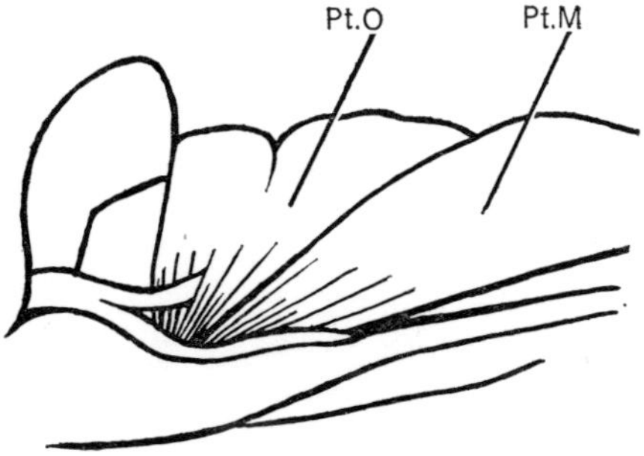

Pluvianus aegyptius

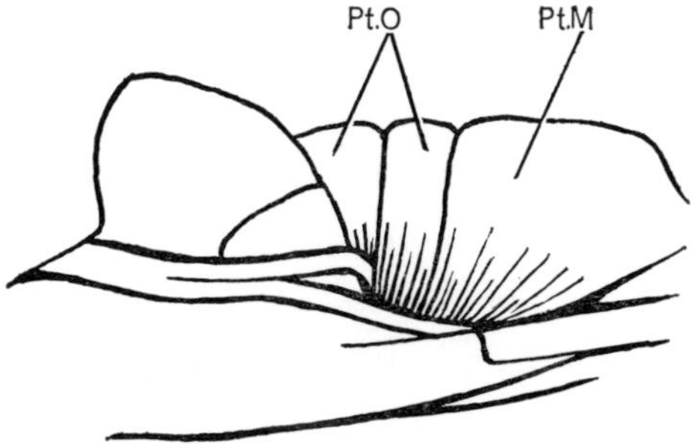

Peltohyas australis

Pathways of N.pterygoideus

Zusi has pointed out inconsistencies in the application of this terminology by later workers, and suggests a three part division based on aponeuroses. This division is used here; the parts are named after their aponeuroses of insertion. Its attachment to the mandible is arbitrarily considered as the insertion, in conformity with previous accounts.

M. pterygoideus, Part M, has an extensive fleshy origin on the dorsolateral surface of the caudal half of the palatine, excluding its caudomedial tip. It is also attached by a strong aponeurosis, A^1 to the lateral and posterolateral edge of the palatine. The lateral edge of Ap. A^1 is folded slightly into the muscle to act as a weak superficial raphe from which fibres diverge caudad. Its medial edge is also folded in, but much more deeply, marking the boundary with Part N. It acts as a strong raphe, fibres of Parts M and N diverging from it caudad, and fades out caudally. Ap. M covers much of the dorsal surface of this portion, and narrows laterally to a strong insertion on the dorsomedial surface of the mandible, immediately rostral to that of Ap. O. There is fleshy insertion just below this, and also on the ventrolateral surface of the caudal end of the mandible.

Part N originates on the concave ventral surface of the palatine, fleshily, and by a superficial ventral aponeurosis, A^2, attached to the palatine at the rostral end of the insertion, and along its medial flange. There is also origin on the medial and sometimes the ventral surface of the pterygoid. Ap. A^2 is fused laterally with Ap. A^1. Part N inserts on the medial surface of the internal process of the mandible, and by a strong aponeurosis, N, attached to the rostrodorsal tip of the process. Ap. N runs rostroventrad through the muscle, and fibres diverge rostrad from it. Since Ap. N does not span the whole width of the part, this is a circumpinnate arrangement.

Part O originates fleshily on the dorsolateral and sometimes the ventral surface of the pterygoid, and on the medial caudal edge of the palatine. There is also attachment to the pterygoid by a ventral aponeurosis (Ap. C) and one or more internal aponeuroses are found in many species. Ap. O covers the dorsolateral surface, and provides a strong, narrow insertion on the dorsal medial surface of the mandible, just rostral to the articulation with the quadrate. There is also fleshy insertion below this.

Comparison

The lateral insertion of Part M reaches the caudal edge of the retroarticular process in all the representative species except *C. alpina*.

In Part N, a distinctive feature shown by *N. arquata* is a second, shorter raphe, ventral to Ap. N, and also with fibres diverging rostrad around it. Parts M and O are separated by a groove, and in all but one of the five, *N. pterygoideus* passes through this groove. The exception is *P. apricaria*, in which the nerve penetrates Part O, posterior to the groove (Plate 20).

The pterygoid is typically approximately crescentic in section rostral to the basipterygoid process; the concave surface faces dorsolaterally. In *N. arquata*, however, an extra flange is developed to produce a section which is nearer triangular, with dorsolateral, ventral and medial surfaces. Part O has extensive origin on the ventral surface, and has additional internal aponeuroses arising from a very strong curved crista on the rostral end of the ventral surface.

Failure of the insertion of Part M to reach the caudal edge of the mandible is a feature shown by all members of the Calidridinae except *Limosa* and *Tryngites*, and also by the Phalaropodidae and some small species of *Charadrius*. The space left is filled by the origin of a bulky *M. stylohyoideus*. The lateral insertion is entirely lacking in *Limicola*. The most extensive lateral insertion is seen in *Aphriza*, in which some fibres are attached to the ventral end of the postorbital ligament. In *Haematopus*, the pinnate region at the lateral edge of Ap. A^1 is highly developed, and the infolding is double, forming a deep groove.

Part N shows little diversity. No other species besides *N. arquata* has been found to possess a second raphe, although Ap. N itself is extremely stout in *Haematopus* and *N. phaeopus*. Ap. N is distinctly weak in some small species, and scarcely detectable in a few Calidridinae.

The course followed by *N. pterygoideus* is of much interest. The condition in which it passes between Parts M and C was found without exception in all Scolopacidae and Phalaropodidae examined, while it penetrates Part O in all Charadriidae, Haematopodidae and Recurvirostridae. In *Rostratula* it displays a condition unique in the order; instead of entering the muscle in a lateral position, it runs mediad in the groove between Parts M and O, finally entering the muscle near the pterygoid-palatine articulation. A wide gap between the origins of Parts M and O is seen in *Ibidorhyncha* and a few *Vanellus* species.

A flange at the rostral end of the pterygoid similar to that of *N. arquata* is seen in *N. phaeopus* and in *Haematopus, Xenus, Catoptrophorus, Scolopax, Philohela, Limosa* and *Limnodromus*. The extra (ventral) surface is usually occupied by Part N, but in *Scolopax* and *Limnodromus* Part O takes origin from both dorsolateral and ventral faces, restricting Part N to the medial surface. Extensive ventral insertion of Part O is also seen in *Limosa*. Other genera lack the prominent curved crista seen in *Numenius*, but there are a number of small cristae in the same region in *Limnodromus*.

Action. M. pterygoideus is primarily a retractor of the upper jaw and an adductor of the lower. Its actions, however, are complex and subtle, and have attracted considerable interest. Valuable discussions are those of Bock (1960b), Yudin (1961) and Zusi (1962). Zusi shows that its pull on the mandible acts not only to cause adduction, but also to hold the palatal mechanism in place on the parasphenoid rostrum. As well as this, it moves the mandible forward and inward on the sliding hinge of the quadrate condyles as adduction proceeds.

Bock discusses the functions of the various parts of M. pterygoideus in passerines, and points out that the lateral parts of the muscle will be of greatest importance in adduction. This is equally true for Part M in the Charadrioidea. As a consequence of its insertion some way forward of the mandible-quadrate articulation it travels through a greater distance than other parts of the muscle, a fact reflected in its largely parallel fibred structure. Since its pull is rostromediad in direction it will also aid sliding forward of the mandible during adduction. The unipinnate region at the anterior lateral edge of Part M is sometimes well developed, and may contribute to maintenance of a sustained grip on prey. Yudin points out that the lateral part of the muscle will act to straighten the bowed mandible, and suggests that the insertion on the lateral surface of the mandible is of importance for this function. An important feature of M. pterygoideus as an adductor is that its angle of attachment to the mandible increases as the mandible is depressed – the exact opposite of the other adductors. It may therefore be particularly useful to species with a wide range of mandible movement, particularly if they grasp food with a widely open bill (e.g., *P. apricaria*) or take large prey (e.g., *N. arquata*).

The retractor function of M. pterygoideus is of great importance for the refined kinetics of the Charadrioidea. Bock has pointed out that the low mechanical advantage of M. pterygoideus dorsalis medialis (=Part O) renders it of little use for adduction, and he considers retraction to be its main function. Some features of its retractor action merit discussion. It is attached mainly to the pterygoid (the connection with the palatine* retained by Part O in all species may be necessary to reduce the risk of disruption of the pterygo-palatine articulation) and its pull has a considerable lateral component. This is an efficient arrangement since the pterygoid is increasingly pulled into a laterally directed path as retraction proceeds by the quadrate. The basipterygoid processes and posterior broadening of the parasphenoid rostrum serve to maintain this path accurately and reduce the risk of disarticulation. The caudal pull of Part N aids in holding it against these bony guides,

* In fact limited mainly to the hemipterygoid, which is fused with the palatine in adult birds.

and the resultant force of the two parts must act along a line close to its direction of movement. The lateral component of pterygoid movement is greatest in extreme rhynchokinetic forms in which the pterygoids are most steeply angled to the parasphenoid rostrum to begin with, and in these species, the bony guides are supplemented by the antero-dorsal edge of the auditory meatus. Part O is proportionately largest, and has most extensive attachment to the palatine in highly rhynchokinetic species; the abbreviation of Part M is presumably also a consequence of orbit shortening.

Variations in the course followed by N. pterygoideus through the muscle are of great interest. The existence of two well defined alternative pathways clearly associated with taxonomic groupings suggest reorganization of the muscle mass during the history of the Charadrii. The changes in functional emphasis which must have accompanied such a history are difficult to surmise.

Part N contracts over a short distance only, and supplies a major part of the force for retraction. Its bulk and circumpinnate structure reflect these facts, although there is no basitemporal attachment as in some passerines. (See e.g., Fiedler 1951, Bock 1960b.) Like Part O, it can have only a small adduction effect, and these two parts may be almost alone responsible for retraction in situations where the upper jaw tip is deflected below the resting position unaccompanied by adduction. Part N also acts to cause bowing of the mandibular rami in at least some species. The mechanism of this process as envisaged by Yudin, is that the pull of Part N (M. pterygoideus ventralis medialis in his account of *Larus*) on the medial process of the mandible rotates the posterior end of the mandible about its articulation on the quadrate, thus swinging the rami outwards. Yudin adds that in consumption of very large objects requiring maximum depression, the lateral part of M. depressor may assist bowing, but he considers that in other positions the depression component would be disadvantageous. It may be remarked that in waders, the orientation of the occipito-mandibular ligament places it in more direct opposition to the pull of Part N than in *Larus*. This is partly offset by the backward and outward movement of the quadrate-mandibular articulation which results from retraction, but M. depressor would further increase the range of movement possible in this direction by sliding the mandible back on the quadrate condyles. Retraction simultaneous with depression has been observed in *N. arquata* and *G. gallinago*, suggesting that synergistic action between these muscles is a normal feature, and may be more often employed in bowing than Yudin suggests.

Two possible further parts played by M. pterygoideus in swallowing may be briefly considered. By its action in retracting the palate, the passage of food from the buccal cavity to the oesophagus may be assisted. As the palatine only moves a very small distance repeated retractions would be necessary, but this may be useful in some circumstances, e.g., in swallowing a large worm. This could be a reason for the repeated retraction of the upper jaw tip, unaccompanied by mandible movement, seen while the captive Snipe was consuming specimens of *Lumbricus*. Closing of the choenae and infundibular slit accompanying swallowing has been observed in *Gallus domesticus* (Farner, 1960). Only M. pterygoideus, Part N appears capable of doing this, presumably by its increase in thickness on contraction, but in the Charadrioidea, its effect must be limited to the infundibular slit since the choanae are flanked by the widely separated medial crests of the palatines; moreover, its pinnate structure would greatly reduce any increase in thickness as it contracts.

M. pterygoideus must play a vital part in preventing disarticulation by environmental forces. Zusi considered support of the mandible on the quadrate to be the principal function of Part O in the Lari. Parts M and O will be effective in counteracting forces acting laterally or ventrally on the articular region of the mandible; Part N, by its bowing action, in opposing inward pressure on the rami during probing; and the entire muscle in reducing the risk of backward disarticulation.

M. protractor quadrati et pterygoidei

(Short form: M. protractor)

Origin is from the posterior wall of the orbit and more or less of the interorbital septum. Insertion is on the quadrate and pterygoid. Two main groups of fibres may be distinguished. The first arise medially and rostrally, mainly from the interorbital septum, and insert on the medial surface of the pterygoid, caudal to the basipterygoid process, and on the adjacent region of the quadrate; this insertion is usually aponeurotic on its lateral face. The second group arise caudally and laterally, and insert on the medial surface of the orbital process and part of the quadrate body. They frequently extend a short way on to the caudolateral surface of the orbital process. In the majority there is little distinction between the two groups at their origins, but in some species they may be sharply marked off by a difference in fibre direction. Where this is the case, the fibres of the first, rostral, group are called M. protractor 1, and those of the second group M. protractor 2.

Comparison
In the five representative species, the quadrate and M. protractor are proportionately smallest in *T. totanus*. The muscle is enormously enlarged in *G. gallinago*, and occupies the whole interorbital septum anterior to the optic nerve. M. protractor 1 and 2 are sharply separated in this species; the general fibre direction of M. protractor 1 is ventrad, and that of M. protractor 2 rostrad, in line with M. pseudotemporalis profundus.

The great size of the muscle in *G. gallinago* is shown also by all other Scolopacinae and by *Limnodromus*, and M. protractor 1 and 2 are similarly well differentiated. In other species, this differentiation is much less, and the muscle is generally much smaller, though its enlargement merits comment in *Rostratula*, *Haematopus* and the Calidridinae.

Action. This muscle elevates the upper jaw by imparting forward movement to the palatal mechanism. The fibres attached to the orbital process (M. protractor 2) swing the quadrate about its otic articulation, pushing the pterygoid dorso-rostro-mediad; the anterior fibres of the muscle (M. protractor 1) aid in swinging the quadrate and also act directly on the pterygoid.

The anterior part of the interorbital septum is potentially an extensive site for the origin of this muscle. It has been used in this way, however, only by the Scolopacinae and *Limnodromus*; this may be a consequence not only of hypertrophy for probing, but also of the relatively very anterior position of the quadrate in these groups. The anterior part of the interorbital septum does, however, provide origin for this muscle in several other groups (e.g., Anseriformes, Picidae) in which the quadrate is not exceptionally far forward, and mechanical analysis and comparison of these groups would be desirable to elucidate this feature.

M. depressor mandibulae
(Short form: M. depressor)

This muscle arises on the cranium and inserts on the posterior surface of the articular.

In its simplest form, the muscle has no internal aponeuroses, but its surface is aponeurotic in three principal areas. Aponeurosis A is attached to the ridge which marks the ventral edge of the temporal fossa and the lateral edge of the exoccipital. It is usually rather weak and short. Aponeurosis B is attached to the ventral edge of the exocippital. It is a strong aponeurosis, covering much of the dorsal surface of the muscle, and is frequently deeply folded. At its medial edge the occipitomandibular ligament runs from the exoccipital to the internal process of the mandible. Aponeurosis M is attached to the ventral and ventrolateral edges of the articular which is frequently prolonged into a retroarticular process.

The attachment to the skull is also fleshy, to the exoccipital, and often also to the squamosal, lateral and dorsal to Ap. A. There is a wide area of fleshy insertion on the posterior end of the articular, and on Ap. M.

Internal aponeuroses if present arise principally in three situations: from infolded regions of Ap. B; by the infolding of the dorsal edge of Ap. M; and from the retroarticular process.

Comparison

Among the representative species, most pronounced development is seen in *N. arquata*, in which the origin of M. depressor overlaps much of the external temporal region of M. adductor, Part M. The retroarticular process is well developed in *C. alpina* and *G. gallinago*. In *C. alpina* a strong vertical raphe arises from the process. In *G. gallinago* there are several raphes in the muscle, appearing U-shaped in transverse section; some of these apparently arise by branching of a raphe attached to the retroarticular process, others by infolding of Ap. B. The dorsal edge of Ap. M is infolded in *T. totanus* and *N. arquata*, with a narrow unipinnate band of fibres diverging caudad above it. It is particularly strong in *N. arquata*.

Marked enlargement of M. depressor is seen in a number of species; those which deserve particular mention in this respect are *Haematopus*, *Scolopax*, *Arenaria*, *Aphriza*, *Limicola* and *Recurvirostra*. Its great bulk in *Limicola* is particularly striking in view of its generally small or moderate size in all other Calidridinae. The retroarticular process is generally well developed in the Calidridinae (except *Tryngites*), and is also long in *Haematopus*, *Arenaria*, *Aphriza* and *Recurvirostra*.

A single vertical raphe arising from the process is general in the Calidridinae and Arenariinae, while multiplication of raphes as in *G. gallinago* is seen in other Scolopacinae and in *Limnodromus*. An infolded dorsal edge to Ap. M is found in most Tringinae and a few species of *Vanellus*. In other species examined, raphes are either absent or very weak.

Action. The principal action is to lower the mandible. The lateral part of the muscle has a greater mechanical advantage, frequently increased by elongation of the retroarticular process. These lateral fibres must play a major part when maximum depression occurs, particularly against resistance; the medial region of the muscle will be of importance in effecting rapid opening. Other things being equal, reduction in the extent of depression may be expected to be reflected in shortening of the muscle.

M. depressor also aids protraction of the upper jaw by its action on the quadrate. The mechanism of this action has been the subject of some controversy, discussed under skull, jaws and kinetics. Zusi (1967) gives evidence that the presence of a well developed post-orbital ligament need not imply strict coupling of the actions of the two jaws as proposed by Bock (1964a). The findings of the present investigation support this view. By manipulation of fresh specimens I have found independent jaw movement to be possible in waders, and this is clearly a necessity for the variety of manipulative actions they can perform. A capacity to increase the force of protraction by the action of M. depressor is probably also important to most species, especially some highly rhynchokinetic forms in which the muscle and retroarticular process are hypertrophied – e.g., *Scolopax, Philohela, Coenocorypha, Gallinago undulata,** *Limicola*. The medial fibres attached to the retroarticular process insert at a steeper angle than the lateral part, and their forward component may be important in maintaining tension on the ligament when coupling is required.

As noted earlier, Yudin (1961) suggests that the lateral fibres of M. depressor may aid in bowing of the mandible during the swallowing of extremely large objects by *Larus*. He doubts if it plays a part in this mechanism normally since he considers the depression component would be disadvantageous. Observations of retraction accompanying depression in *N. arquata* and *G. gallinago* suggest that synergistic action of M. depressor and M. pterygoideus, Part N, may regularly occur. Since several of these observations have been made while swallowing was taking place, it seems likely that mandible bowing is often performed during depression rather than adduction; hence, M. depressor may participate to a greater extent than Yudin suggests.

The capacity of M. depressor to bring about rotation of the posterior end of the mandible on the quadrate condyles would enable it to play some part in opposing transverse environmental forces. It is also suitably sited to oppose forward dislocation.

* Skeleton only examined.

Tongue and Hyoid Apparatus

Tongue

The length of the tongue relative to that of the bill is of basic importance to an understanding of its role in feeding. The ratio of tongue to bill has been investigated by a series of measurements covering all the Charadrioidea examined, and where possible from a series of specimens for each species. Tongue length has been measured from the level of the tips of the postero-lateral papillae, and bill length from the point of junction of the nasal and jugal bars. Other measurements of bill length give very similar results when plotted against tongue length, but with a wider scatter due to greater measurement error. As tongue/bill ratio may be affected by differences in the form of the junction of nasal and jugal bars, however, small differences in ratio are best disregarded.

Fig. 1 records the measurements taken as a scatter diagram. This shows a clear linear relationship between tongue and bill length for the majority of species. Not all species conform to this, however, and scatter appears to increase with size; calculation of a regression equation has not, therefore, been carried out. It is clear, however, that the equation to which the measurements approximate is one in which the constant 'a' has a negative value, where the form of the equation is represented by $y=a+bx$. Therefore, a slight increase in proportionate tongue length may be expected with increase in bill length, but the evidence points against any allometric relationship. An abridged summary of measurements (only 30 species included) is given in Table IX.

Most interspecific differences in proportionate tongue length are small and probably involve little, if any, change in the slope of the line; longer series of measurements would be required to investigate them further. In several groups, however, reduction in tongue length is very marked and deserves further comment. This occurs principally in larger species, including *Haematopus*, all the Recurvirostridae and several genera of Scolopacidae. Among the latter, the larger Tringinae are especially noteworthy. The relative length of the tongue reaches its lowest values in *Numenius* spp., and is low also in *Bartramia*, and in *Tringa nebularia*, *T. melanoleuca* and *T. erythropus*. In the latter three species the short series of measurements available suggest an inverse relationship with bill length; more data are needed to confirm this and some apparent reduction in large specimens of *T. totanus*. *Catoptrophorus*, similar to them in many ways, has a longer tongue, which in absolute values is the longest in the Tringinae (closely

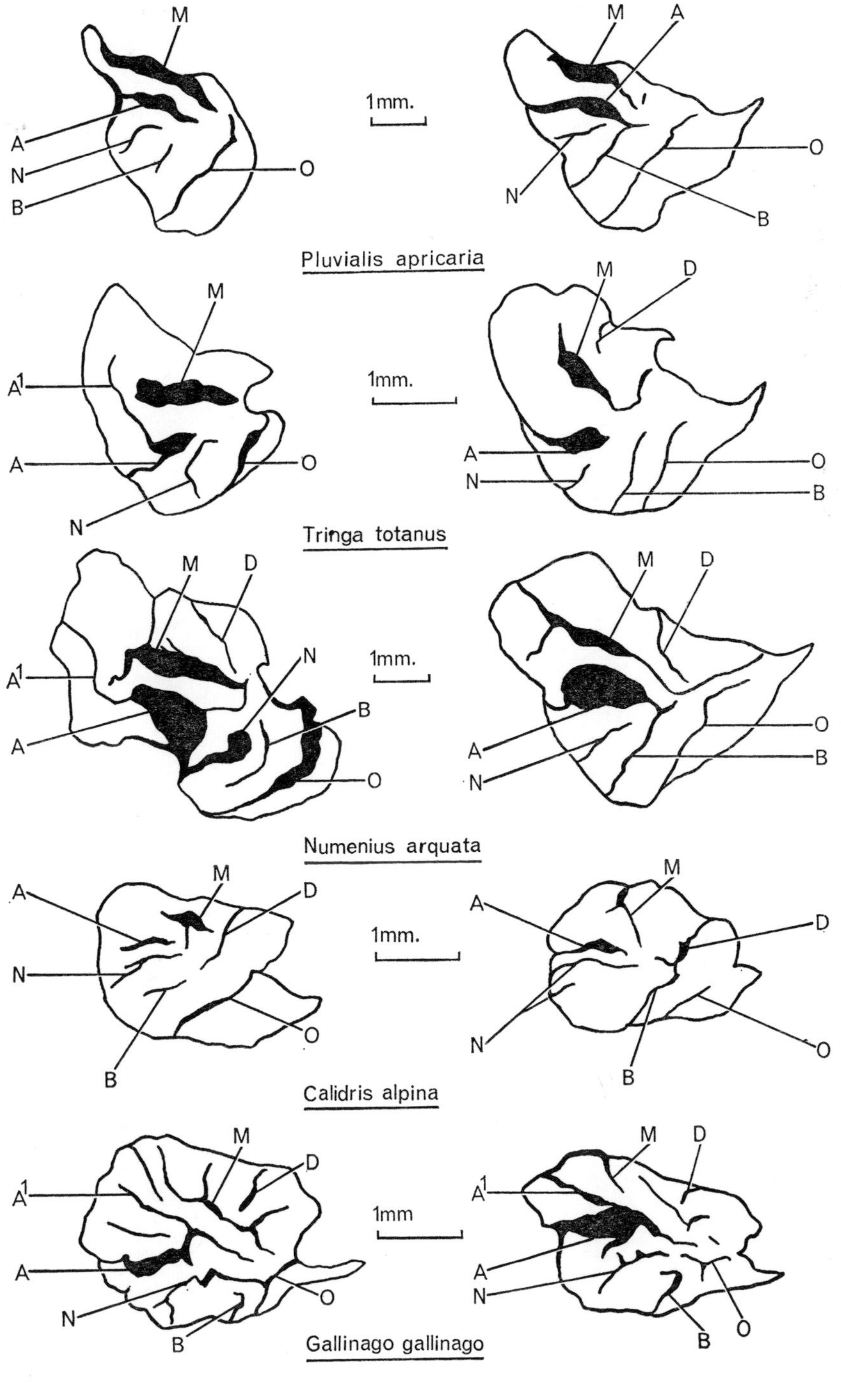

Plate 21.
Transverse sections of M. adductor mandibulae externus in the five representative species. Both sections from the region of the muscle traversing the body of the quadrate, the left-hand diagram showing the more anterior of the two. Letters refer to aponeuroses.

Plate 22.
Transverse sections of M. adductor mandibulae externus in five species of Scolopacidae. For explanation see Plate 21.

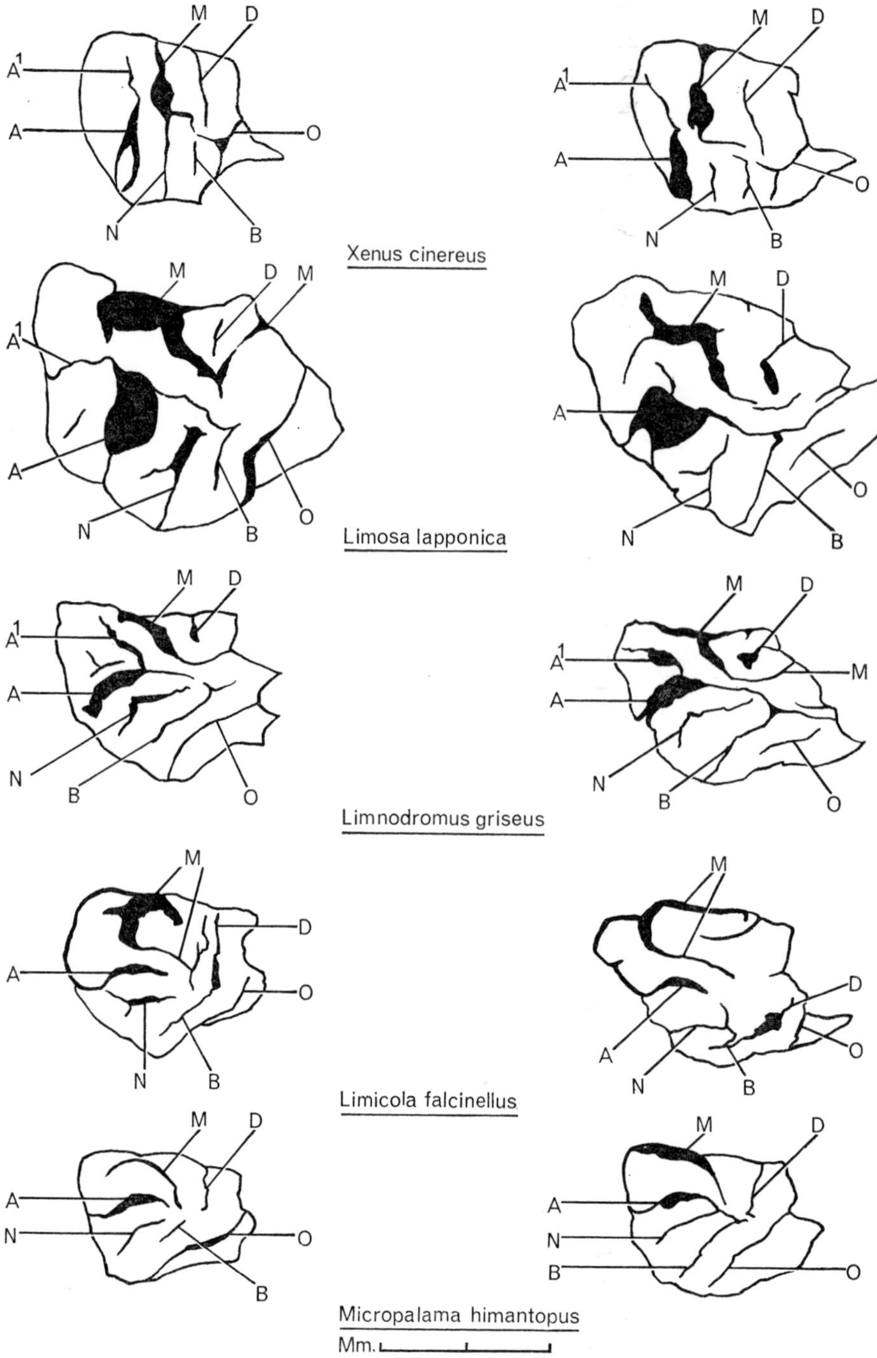

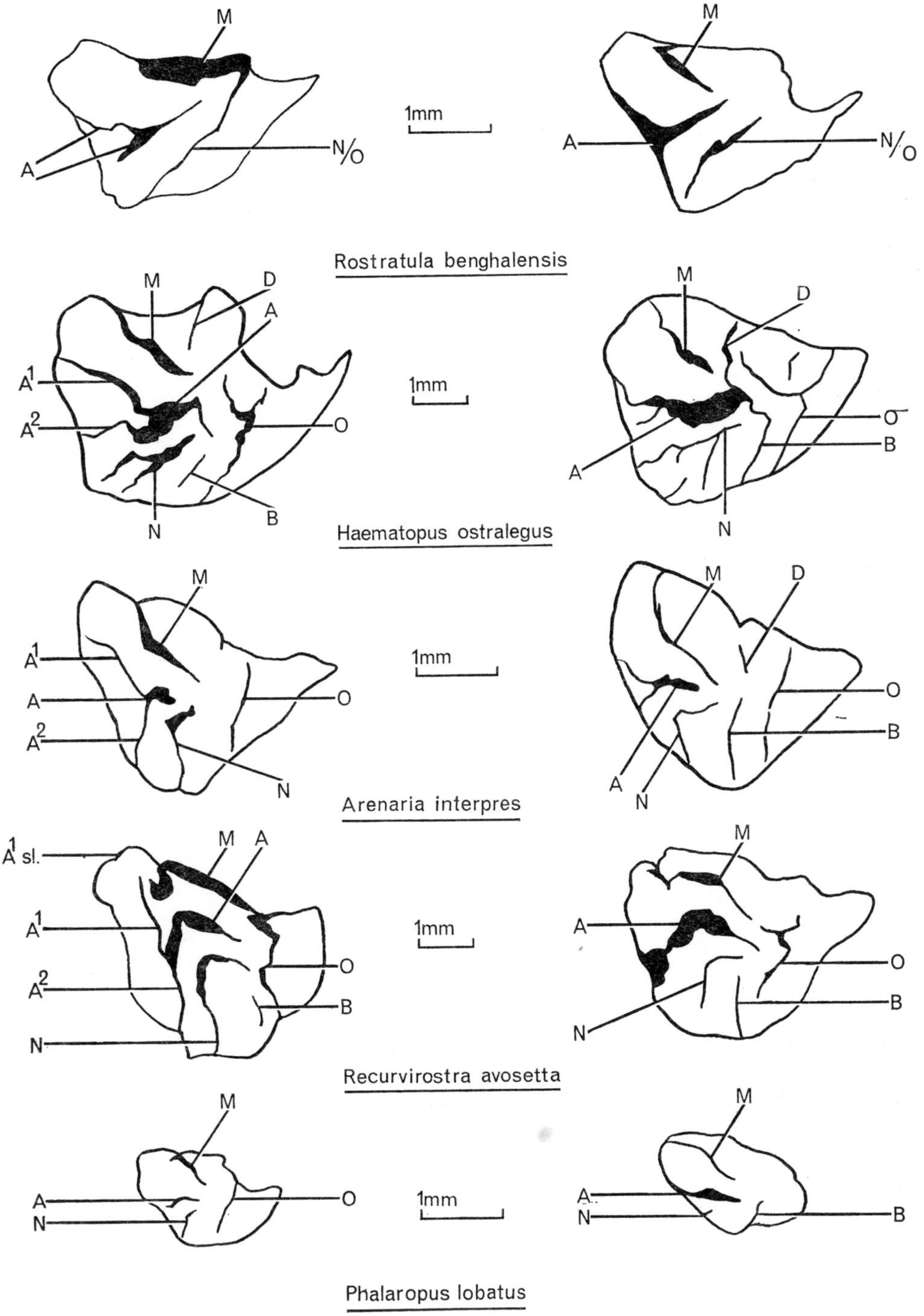

Plate 23.
Transverse section of M. adductor mandibulae externus in five species of Charadrioidea of different families. For explanation see Plate 21.

Plate 24.
Transverse sections of M. adductor mandibulae externus in four species of Charadrii of different superfamilies. For explanation see Plate 21.

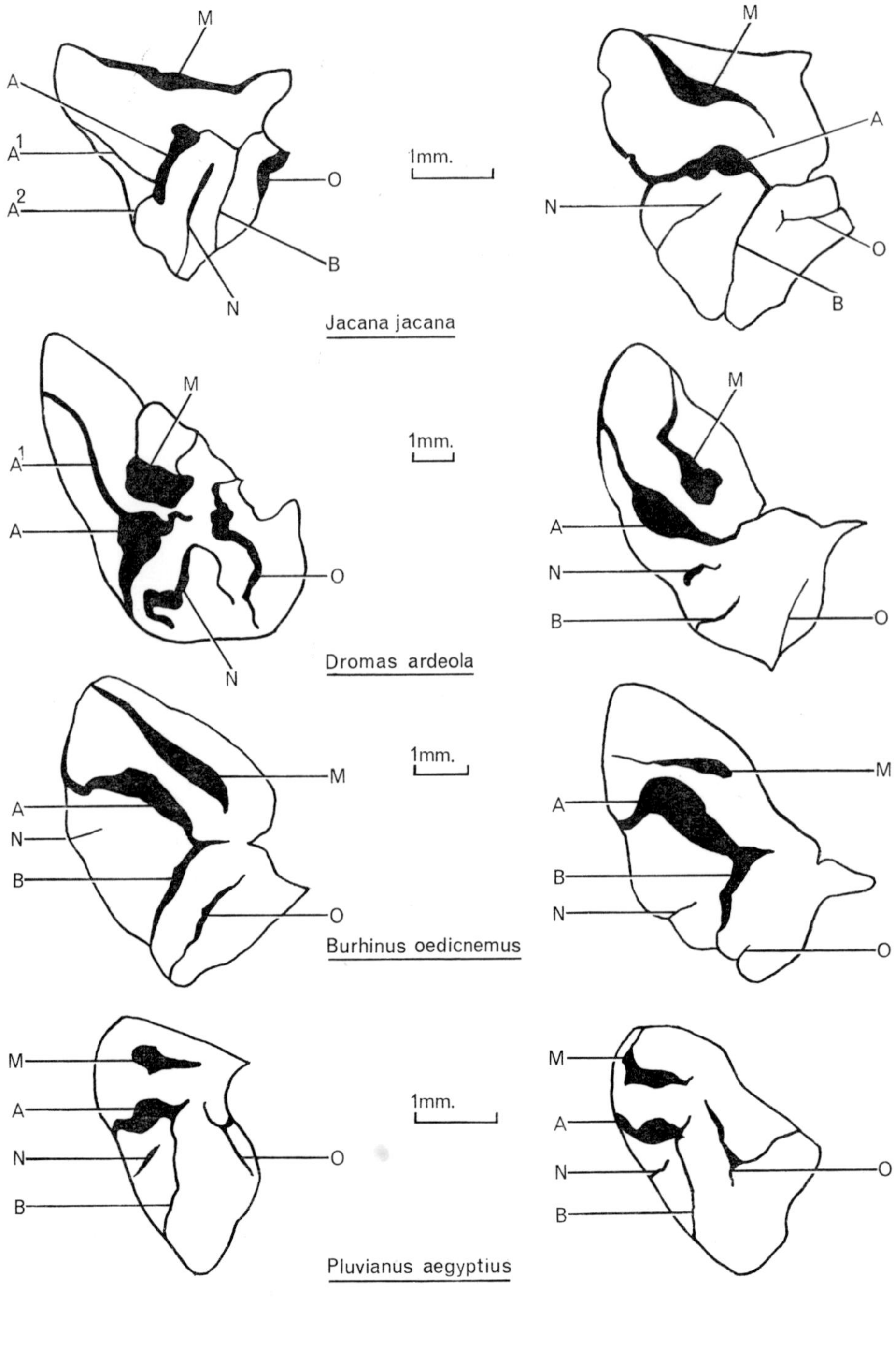

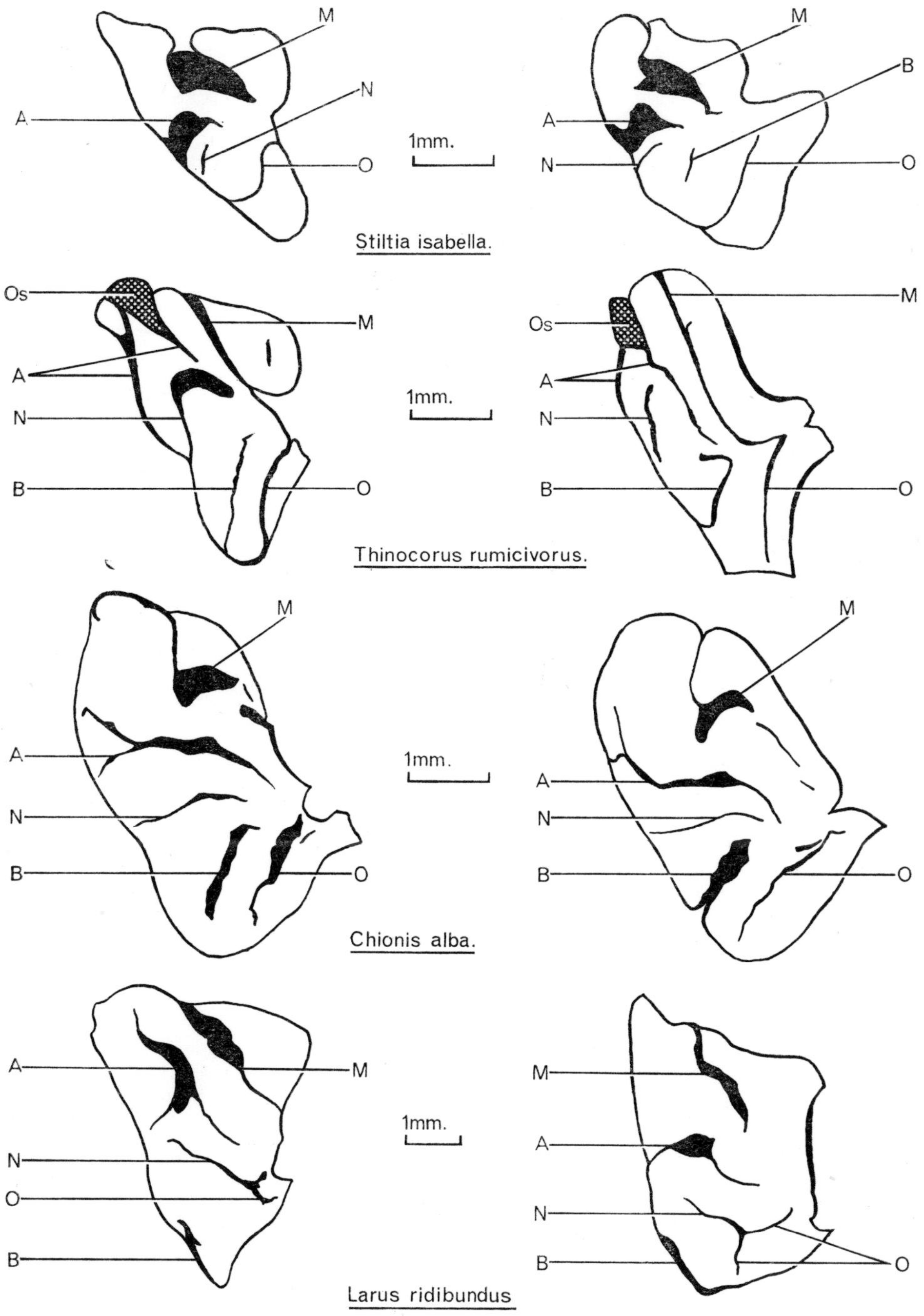

Plate 25.
Transverse sections of M. adductor mandibulae externus in three species of Charadrii of different superfamilies and in *Larus ridibundus* (S.O. Lari). For explanation see Plate 21. The ossified region of origin of Ap. A, continuous with the fused zygomatic and postorbital processes in *Thinocorus* is labelled 'Os'.

Plate 26.
Transverse sections of M. pseudotemporalis superficialis in fourteen species of Charadrioidea. Sections made at about the midpoint of the fleshy portion of the muscle. All to the scale given at the bottom of the plate except *Calidris alpina* and *Limicola falcinellus.*

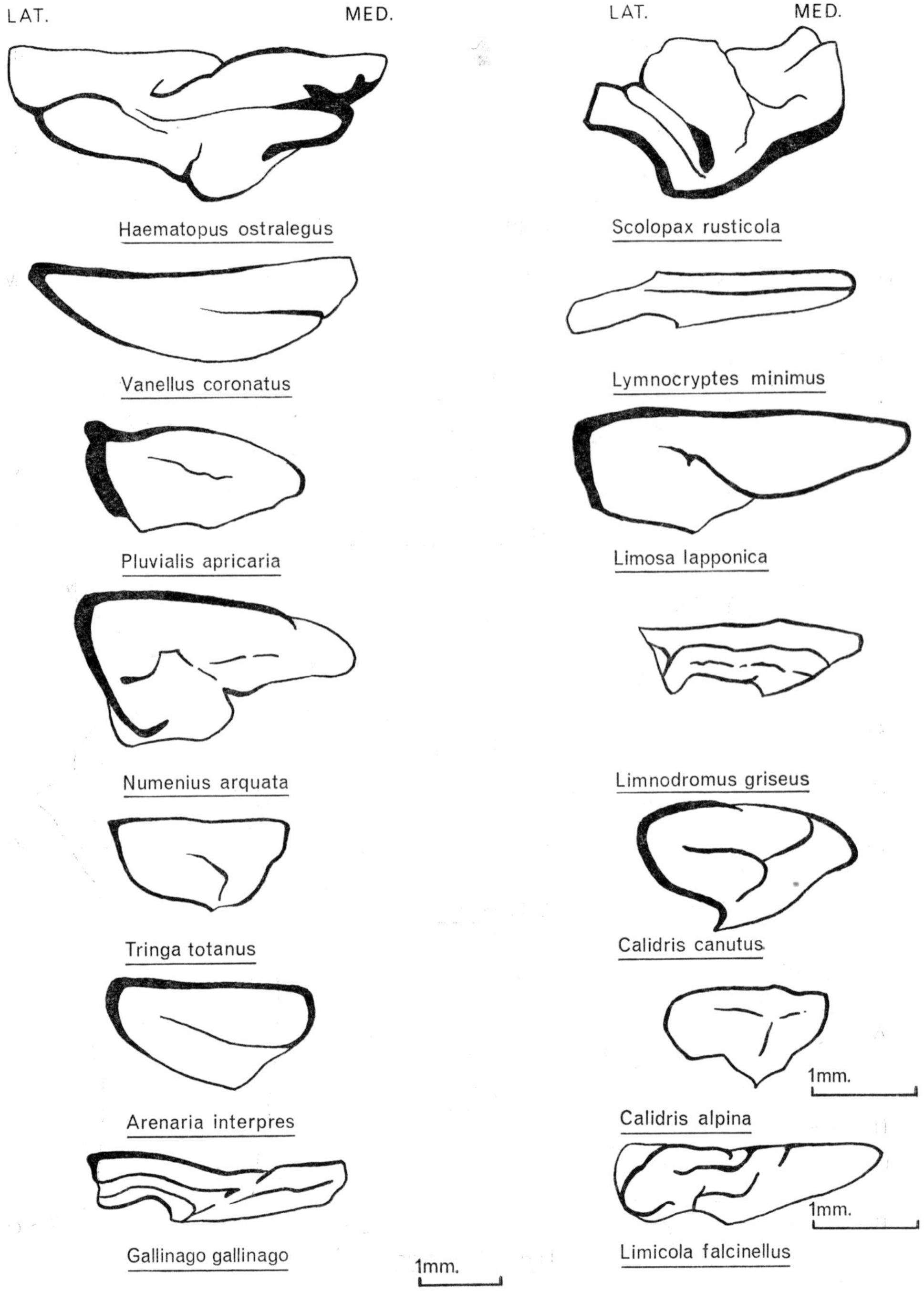

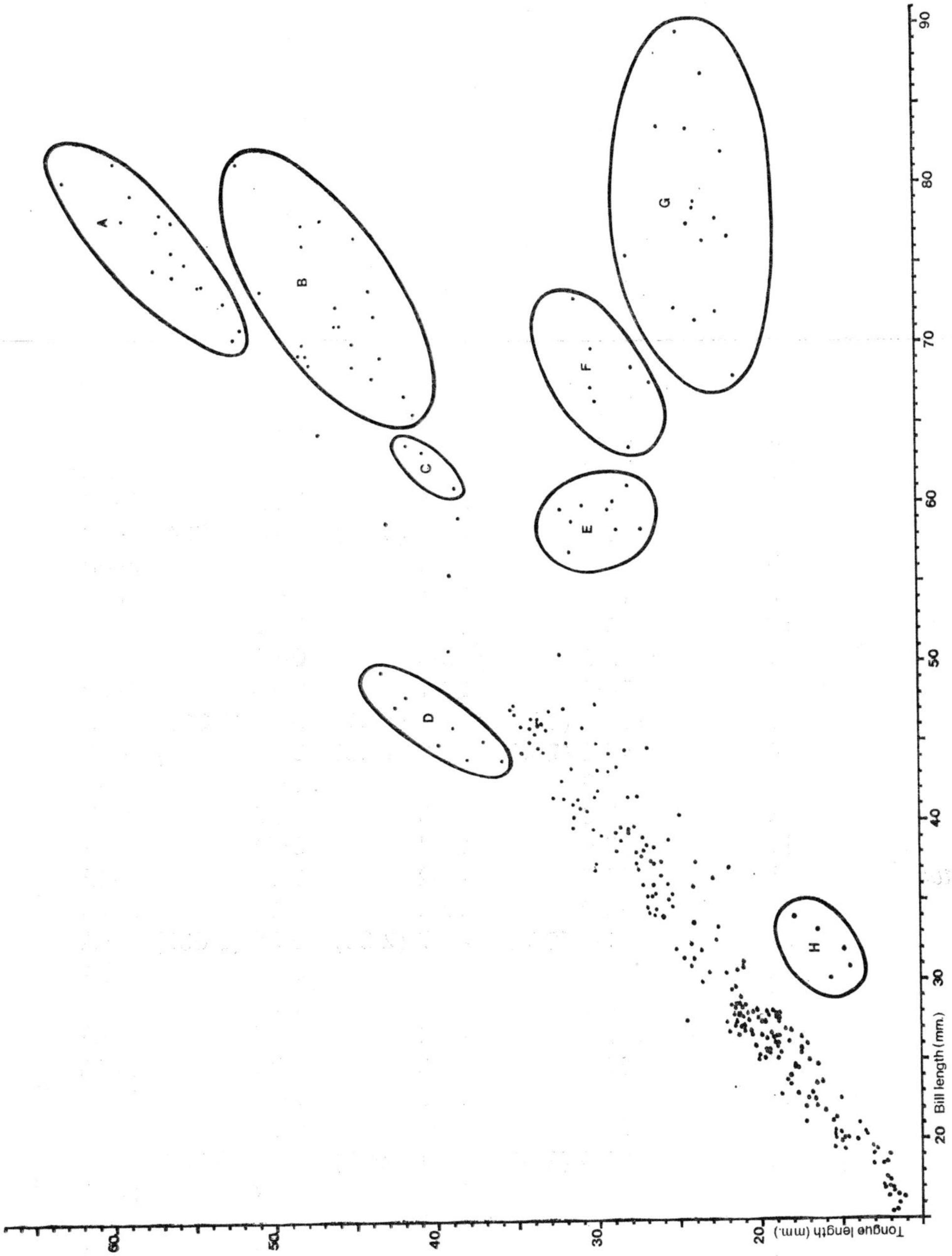

Fig. 1.
Relationship of tongue length to bill length in 75 species of Charadrioidea. *Numenius arquata* and *Limosa* spp. omitted for space reasons. Most species (including *P. apricaria, T. totanus* and *C. alpina*) are clustered in the lower part of the graph. The position of a few others can be indicated as follows:
A *Scolopax & Philohela*
B *Gallinago gallinago*
C *Catoptrophorus*
D *Rostratula*
E *Tringa erythropus, T. nebularia, T. melanoleuca*
F *Himantopus*
G *Haematopus & Numenius phaeopus*
H *Bartramia*

Table IX.
Tongue/bill ratios in 30 species of Charadrioidea. The approximate position of the angle of the gape is also shown, expressed as millimetres anterior or posterior to the junction of nasal and jugal bars. Standard deviations in brackets for representative species.

Species	Number measured	Mean bill	Mean tongue	Mean ratio	Angle of gape *
Rostratula benghalensis	8	46·1	39·6	0·86	1–3P
Haematopus ostralegus	10	79·2	23·2	0·30	4–A2P
Vanellus vanellus	6	28·0	20·4	0·72	0–2P
Pluvialis apricaria	18	28·1	20·6 (0·89)	0·78 (0·024)	1–2P
P. squatarola	10	31·8	22·2	0·70	2–3P
Charadrius hiaticula	7	17·4	12·1	0·70	1P
C. melanops	10	16·6	11·8	0·71	0–1A
Bartramia longicauda	5	32·0	15·8	0·49	6–7P
Numenius phaeopus	6	74·3	24·1	0·33	4–5P
N. arquata	20	129·8 (13·01)	31·1 (2·01)	0·24 (0·018)	0–4P
Tringa totanus	14	45·0 (2·40)	31·0 (1·88)	0·68 (0·045)	0–3P
T. nebularia	4	58·9	30·9	0·52	3–4P
T. ochropus	3	37·0	22·8	0·62	0–2P
Actitis hypolencos	10	27·6	20·4	0·74	0–2P
Catoptrophorus semipalmatus	3	62·7	40·2	0·64	0–3P
Arenaria interpres	10	26·0	17·6	0·68	0–1A
Gallinago gallinago	21	71·4 (3·70)	45·7 (2·80)	0·64 (0·030)	5–6A
Scolopax rusticola	14	75·3	55·4	0·73	6–7A
Lymnocryptes minima	12	45·8	33·9	0·74	5A
Limosa lapponica	9	100·4	48·4	0·48	3–4A
Limnodromus griseus	5	65·6	47·6	0·72	5–7A
Calidris canutus	15	38·0	27·2	0·72	3–5A
C. pusilla	11	21·7	16·1	0·74	3–4A
C. alpina	18	35·5 (3·05)	26·1 (2·59)	0·73 (0·009)	4–5A
Micropalama himantopus	4	42·2	32·6	0·77	5–6A
Tryngites subruficollis	3	22·3	17·2	0·77	1P
Philomachus pugnax (♂)	4	39·1	29·3	0·74	2–3A
Himantopus himantopus	7	68·0	28·9	0·42	3–5P
Recurvirostra avosetta	4	86·3	26·1	0·30	1–2P
Phalaropus fulicarius	2	25·8	19·2	0·75	1–2A

* i.e., its posterior limit in the rictus.

Plate 27.
Tringa totanus, hyoid.
Abbreviations:
Bas. basihyal.
Cer. ceratohyal.
Ent. entoglossum.
Ep. epibranchials.
Uro. urohyal.

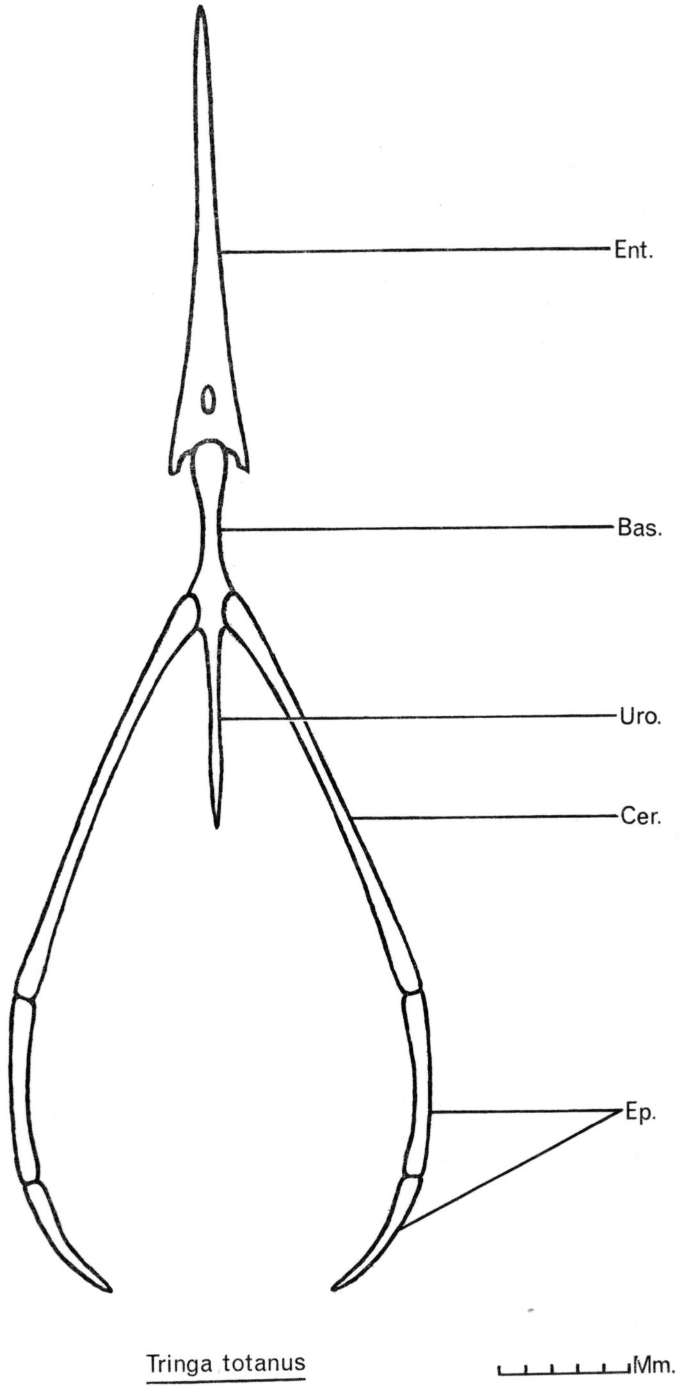

Plate 28.
Hyoids of various Charadrioidea. Cartilage distribution, as revealed by bulk staining with New Methylene Blue, is indicated by stippling. Entirely cartilaginous regions are indicated by dense uniform stippling. Lighter stippling is used to indicate intensity of blue staining in ossified regions.

Key:
1. *Tringa totanus.*
2. *Rostratula benghalensis.*
3. *Gallinago gallinago.*
4. *Limosa lapponica.*
5. *Scolopax rusticola.*
6. *Limnodromus griseus.*
7. *Numenius arquata.*
8. *Recurvirostra avosetta.*
9. *Haematopus ostralegus.*
10. *Calidris alpina.*
11. *Arenaria interpres.*
12. *Aechmorhynchus cancellatus.*
13. *Peltohyas australis.*
14. *Lobipes lobatus.*
15. *Bartramia longicauda.*
16. *Tryngites subruficollis.*
17. *Pluvialis apricaria.*
18. *Vanellus tectus.*

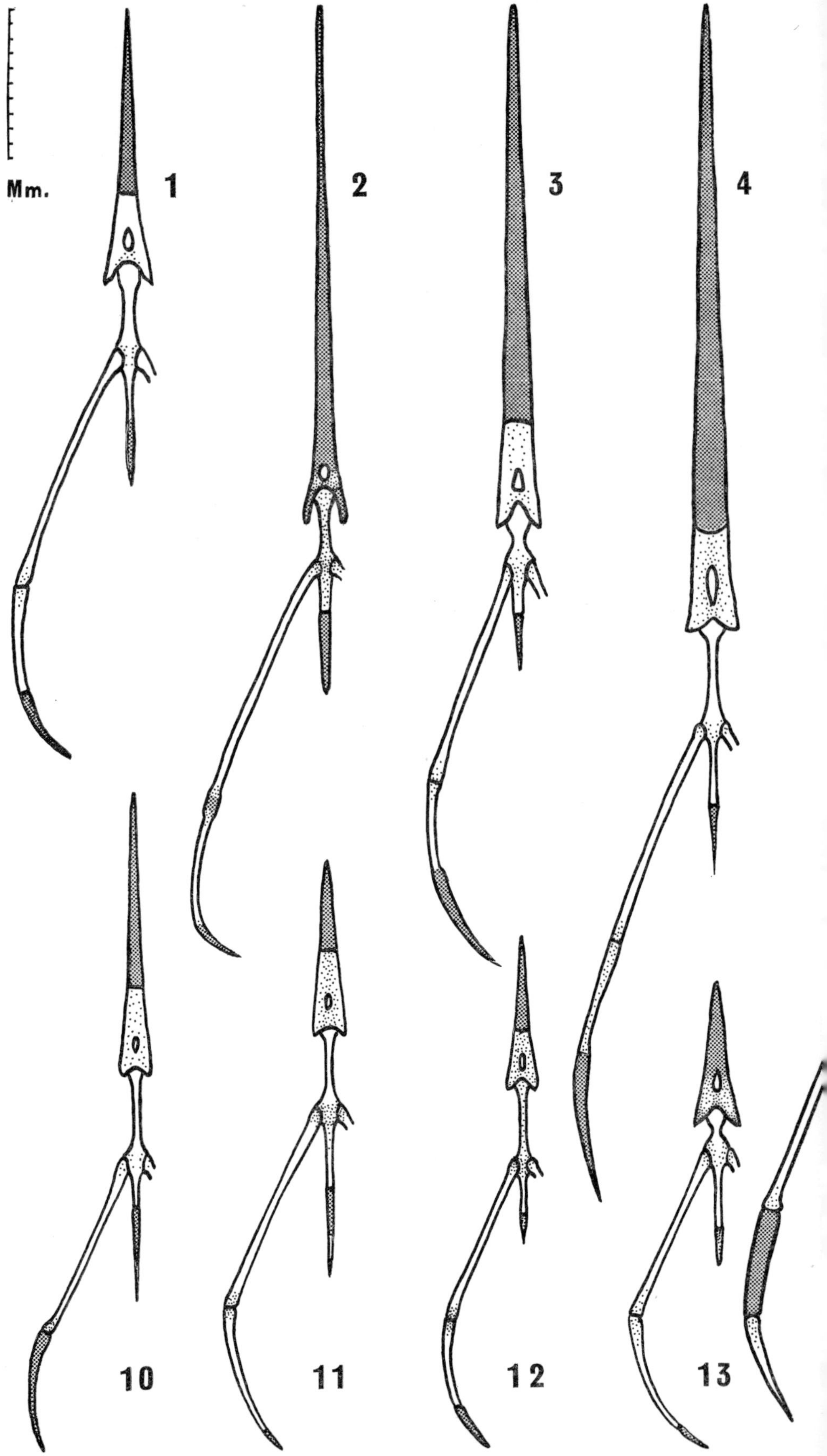

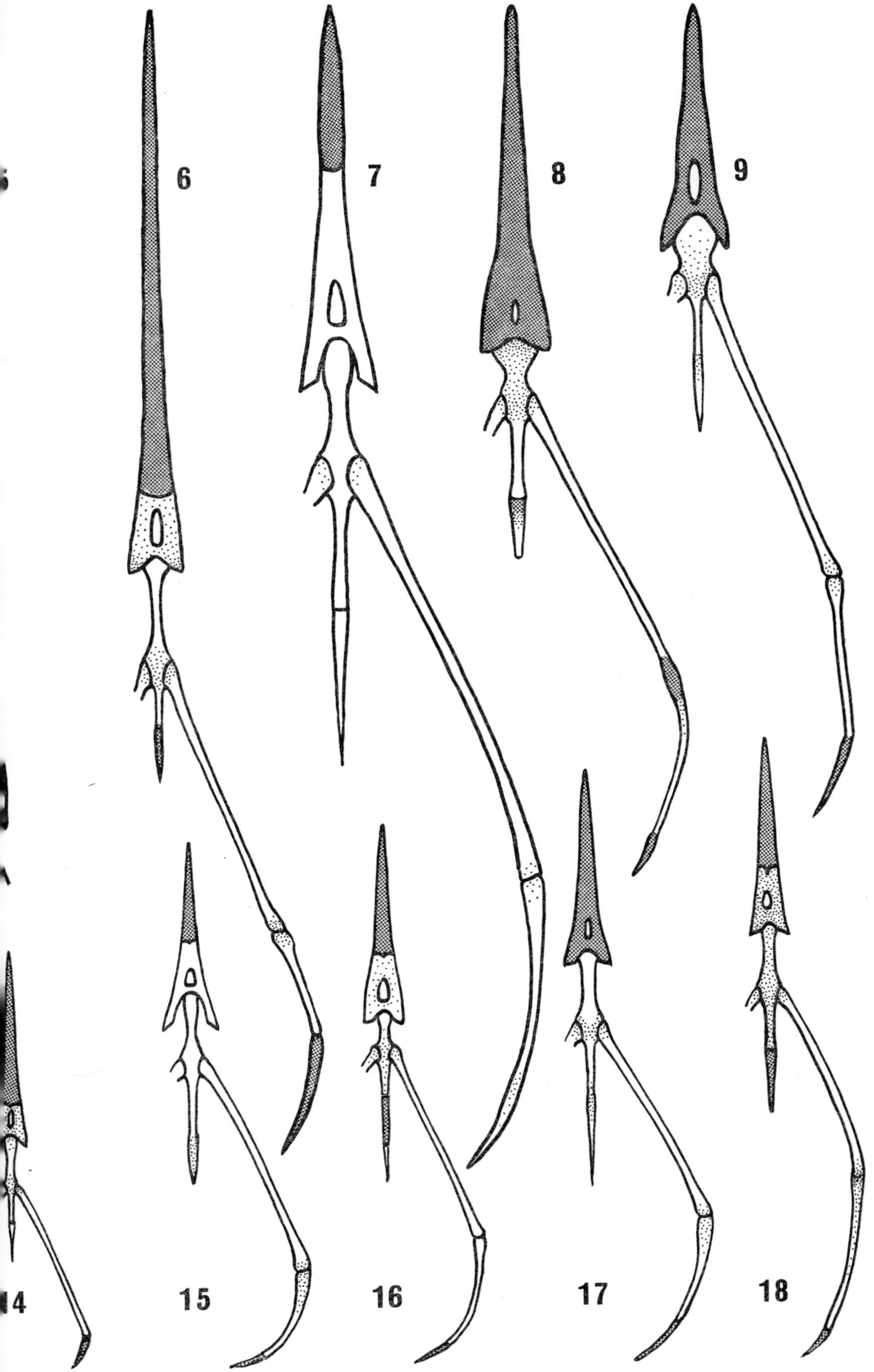
6
7
8
9
14
15
16
17
18

approached by *Xenus*). *Bartramia* has the shortest bill of species showing marked tongue shortening.

Among the Scolopacinae, the disparity between *Scolopax* and *Gallinago* is noteworthy, and is greatest between long-billed specimens of each genus. *Scolopax* spp. are the longest-billed waders maintaining the same linear relationship between tongue and bill, and have the longest tongues in absolute measurements. Measurements for the Calidridinae generally, including *Limnodromus*, lie close to the approximate regression line, but relative tongue length is considerably less in *Limosa*. Nevertheless, the tongue in *Limosa* is considerably longer than in *Numenius* specimens of similar bill length, and in a few specimens is exceeded in absolute length only by some *Scolopax* individuals. The longest tongue relative to the bill, among the Charadrioidea is seen in *Rostratula*.

Action. A full understanding of the action of the tongue is hindered by the difficulty of observation. The following types of action are likely to occur:

1. Assisting in the movement of prey up the bill and towards the mouth. This is probably effected by very rapid backward and forward movements. This action has been observed in *Gallus domesticus* under experimental conditions (S. White, University of Liverpool, personal communication), and may be used by most birds, but would seem particularly useful to long-billed species, especially highly rhynchokinetic probers in which consumption is sometimes commenced or even completed before the bill is withdrawn.

2. Manœuvring prey into a convenient position for swallowing. This would depend on lateral tongue movements, which are likely to be restricted, especially in long-billed species.

3. Pushing food into the buccal cavity. This will normally be carried out by the papillate posterior border of the tongue; the tongue tip could perhaps be directly employed in short-billed waders if the bill were held widely open, but this action has not been observed.

Tongue reduction relative to bill length has occurred particularly in species exhibiting pronounced bony reinforcement of the lower jaw, since this occludes much of the bill lumen and reduces the space available for accommodation and movement of the tongue. It may also be related to swallowing large prey whole, a feature associated with tongue atrophy in some other groups, e.g., Pelecaniformes,

Alcedinidae. In *Numenius*, the extreme reduction of the tongue prevents its use during probing, and thus total removal of nearly all prey is needed before consumption can even begin. Moderate shortening in *Limosa* presumably shows a compromise between bill reinforcement and use of the tongue during probing.

Hyoid Skeleton

The names for skeletal components of the hyoid apparatus adopted here are those used by Fisher & Goodman (1955b). An alternative nomenclature, based on reptile affinities is that of Fürbringer (1922). The distribution of cartilage has been investigated by bulk staining with New Methylene Blue. Examination of juveniles of various ages indicates that ossification proceeds rapidly, and is probably completed by the first winter. Details given below are based on dissections of birds in adult plumage wherever possible.

a. The hyoid "horns" each consist of a ceratohyal anteriorly, and an epibranchial posteriorly. The ceratohyal is entirely bony; the epibranchial is bony, but usually retains cartilage at one or both ends. The cartilaginous regions are in some cases long and expanded, e.g., *Scolopax*

b. The median basihyal is rodlike in the majority of species. If M. stylohyoideus inserts widely on the basihyal, its dorsal surface bears a pronounced median ridge, and its anterior end may be expanded, as in *Recurvirostra*. In *Haematopus*, the basihyal is short, and completely expanded into a flat plate.

The basihyal is generally proportionately longer relative to the tongue in species with M. hyoglossus obliquus of type 2, though it is short in the Scolopacinae. Its greatest proportionate length is seen in *Aechmorhynchus*.

c. The urohyal forms a posterior continuation of the basihyal, behind its articulation with the ceratohyals, and ventral to the larynx and anterior end of the trachea. It is fused with the basihyal in most species but there is a well defined articulation in *Numenius* and less obviously in *Catoptrophorus*. The posterior end of the urohyal is usually cartilaginous.

d. The entoglossum is the skeletal element supporting the tongue. It articulates with the anterior end of the basihyal by means of a swivel joint which permits extensive downward flexion, but no upward flexion and little lateral movement. The posterior end is broad, and produced into two backwardly projecting processes. Anteriorly, it tapers to a point. The entoglossum is entirely cartilaginous in *Haematopus, Recurvirostra, Ibidorhyncha, Vanellus vanellus, V. chilensis* and all Charadriidae of other genera. In *Himantopus* there is a small bony area on either side of the articulation with the basihyal, and in *Rostratula* the posterior processes are largely bony, with a partly ossified region extending well anterior to this. In *Vanellus* (apart from the two noted above), and in all Phalaropodidae and Scolopacidae, the entire base is bony. In very small species, e.g., *Charadrius melanops, Calidris temminckii*, the cartilage appears to be replaced by tough connective tissue.

The ventral side of the entoglossum is deeply grooved in its posterior half. In species with a bony base to the entoglossum, the groove is deep, and bordered by two sharp flanges. A fenestra pierces the groove just anterior to the basihyal. In species with an entirely cartilaginous tongue, the groove is shallow and the fenestra reduced. The entoglossum is usually more or less dorso-ventrally flattened, but is cylindrical in *Rostratula*.

A strong ligament connects the anteroventral tip of the basihyal to the ventral surface of the entoglossum at their articulation. Anterior to the ventral groove, the underside of the entoglossum is clad in a tough sheet of connective tissue, arising posteriorly as a median aponeurosis on which insert fibres of M. hyoglossus anterior and M. ceratoglossus *anterior*.

Musculature

The nomenclature of avian tongue muscles presents just as confusing a picture as that of jaw muscles. The account given by Gadow and Selenka (1891) has been followed by most subsequent studies, but usually with variations and innovations. George and Berger (1966) refer to most studies of importance and clarify synonymy in a number of cases. References to the Charadrii are few. The general study by Kautz (1931) which has apparently been little used includes some details of the tongue myology of *Limosa*, and Feninger (1937) gives short descriptions for several species.

The terminology and order followed here are those used by George and Berger, except for the name "*M. cleidohyoideus*" which has been adopted from Gadow and Selenka.

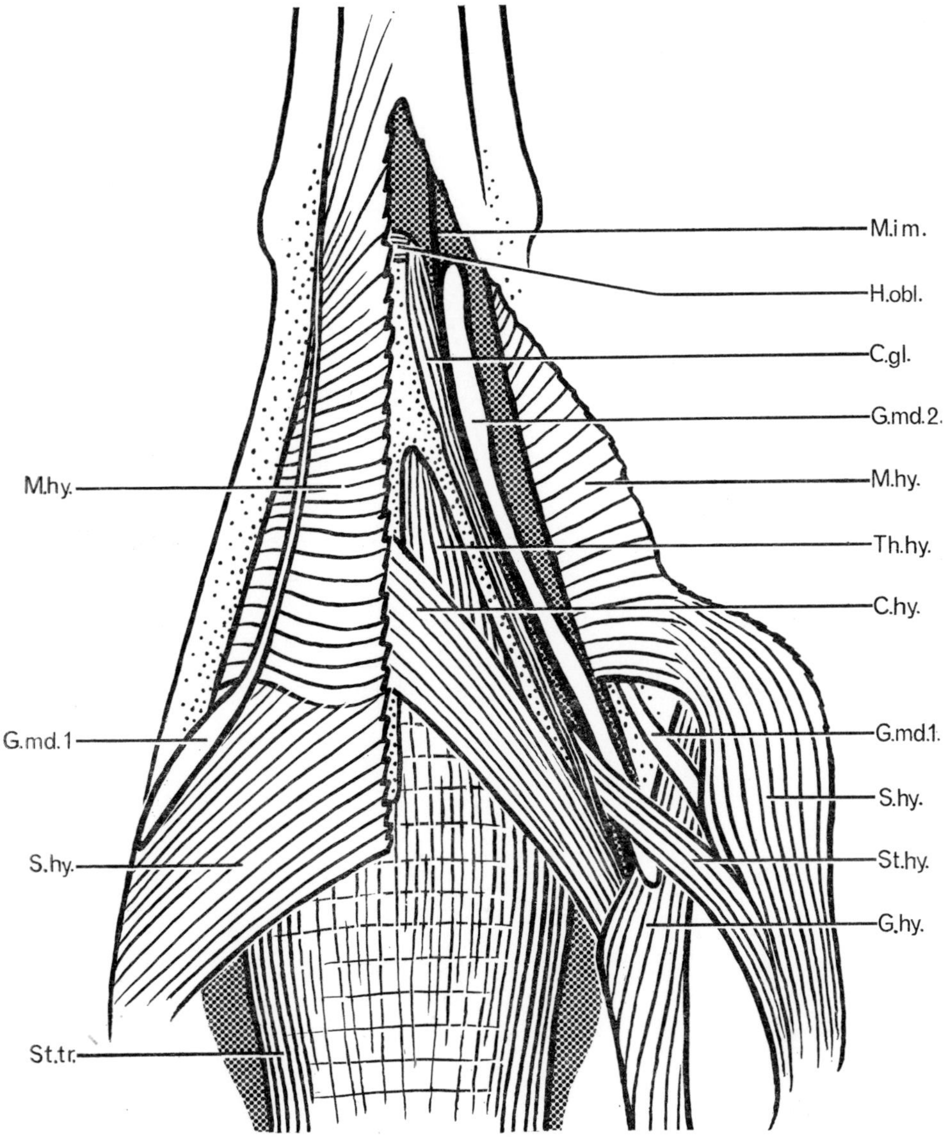

Tringa totanus.

Plate 29.
Tringa totanus: superficial hyoid muscles. M. mylohyoideus, M. serpihyoideus, M. stylohyoideus and M. geniohyoideus freed by cuts along ventral midline and sites of origin, and turned aside on the left. Abbreviations for this and succeeding plates (32–37) showing hyoid anatomy:

Bas. basihyal.
C.gl. M. ceratoglossus.
C.gl.ant. M. ceratoglossus anterior.
C.gl.ap. superficial cponeurosis of M. aeratoglossus anterior.
C.gl.t. tendon of M. ceratoglossus.
Cl.hy. M. cleidohyoideus.
Con.gt. M. constrictor glottidis.
Ent. Entoglossum.
G.cr.ar. Gl. crico-arytenoideus.
G.gl. M. genioglossus.
G.hy. M. geniohyoideus.
G.hy.i. M. geniohyoideus, insertion.
G.hy.o.(det.) M. geniohyoideus, detached origin.
G.md.1. Gl. mandibularis 1.
G.md.2. Gl. mandibularis 2.
H.ant. M. hyoglossus anterior.
H.med. M. hyoglossus medialis.
H.obl. M. hyoglossus obliquus.
Lig. Ligament connecting basihyal and entoglossum.
M.ap. Median aponeurosis.
M.hy. M. mylohyoideus.
M.i.m. Middle internal maxillary artery.
S.hy. M. serpihyoideus.
St.hy. M. stylohyoideus.
St.tr. M. sternotrachealis.
Th.ar. M. thyroarytenoideus.
Th.hy. M. thyrohyoideus.

Plate 30.
Tringa totanus: hyoid musculature, ventral aspect, after removal of tongue from head. For abbreviations see Plate 29.

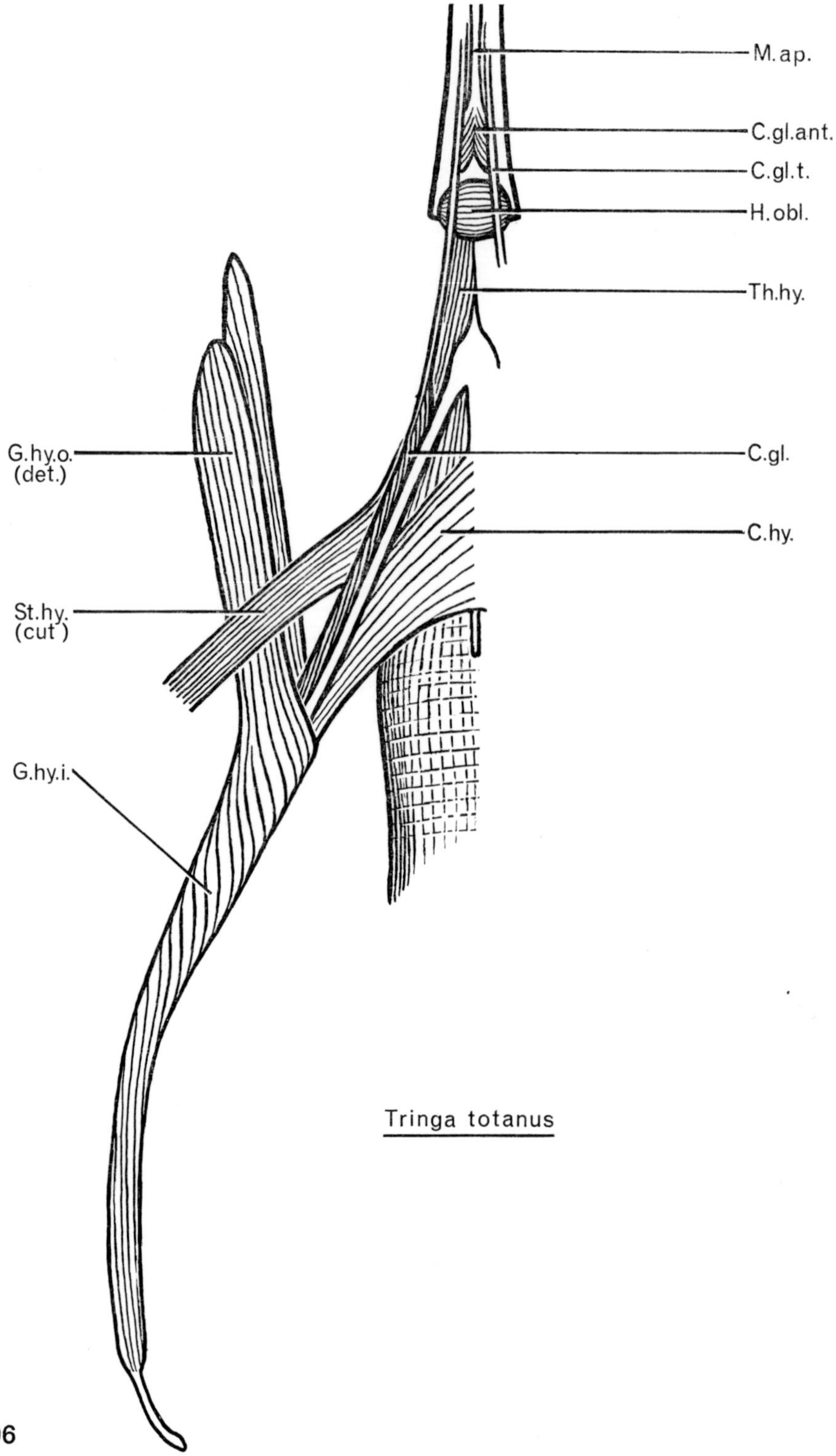

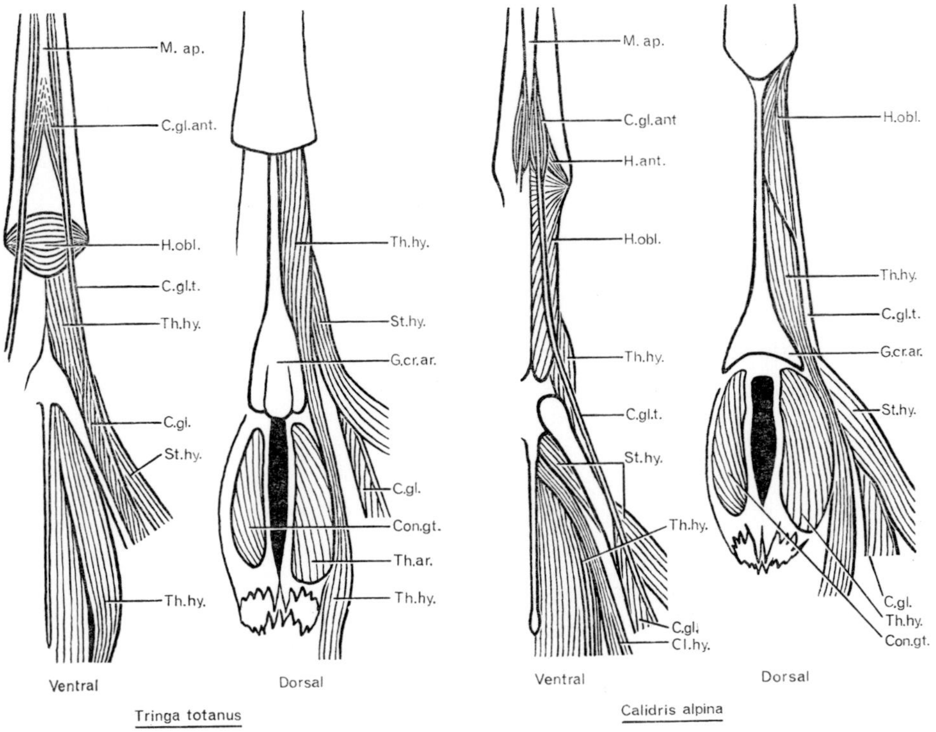

Plate 31.
Tringa totanus and *Calidris alpina:* dorsal and ventral aspects of hyoid musculature showing detail in the region from the larynx to the base of the tongue. The epidermal papillae at the posterior edge of the larynx have been left in position. M. thyroarytenoideus removed on right-hand side. For abbreviations see Plate 29.

M. mylohyoideus

The origin is fleshy, from the medial surface of the mandible, and from the lateral ventral edge of the floor of the oral cavity. The muscle runs ventrad, medial to M. geniohyoideus and is continuous at the ventral midline with M. mylohyoideus from the other side. The posterior edge of the muscle lies ventral to the anterior edge of M. serpihyoideus.

The muscle is moderately or well developed in the species examined, except *Numenius phaeopus*, in which it is vestigial.

Action. M. mylohyoideus raises the anterior part of the floor of the buccal cavity, and thus plays an important part in support of the tongue and in completion of the action of swallowing. It must also tend to draw the mandibular rami together, but this action must be weak at best, and is probably unimportant.

M. serpihyoideus

The muscle originates on the caudolateral surface of the mandible, ventral to M. stylohyoideus. It runs rostroventrad, and inserts mainly on the ventral midline; its most anterior fibres, however, run forward to insert on the floor of the oral cavity, lateral to the base of the tongue. Its posterior edge is composed of fibres arising ventral to the internal process of the mandible which should perhaps be referred to M. constrictor colli, with which it is closely associated. M. serpihyoideus is well developed in all the species examined.

Action. M. serpihyoideus raises the larynx and posterior part of the floor of the buccal cavity; its contribution to the mechanism of swallowing is similar to that of M. mylohyoideus.

M. stylohyoideus

The origin of M. stylohyoideus lies medial and dorsal to M. serpihyoideus on the caudolateral surface of the mandible. The muscle runs towards the ceratohyal, and follows it for some way before inserting on some part of the tongue skeleton. The exact site of insertion shows marked variations which may be conveniently grouped as follows:

1. Insertion to the anterior end of the basihyal, immediately posterior to its articulation with the entoglossum.

This arrangement is found in several Charadriidae (*Vanellus albiceps, V. tectus, V. tricolor* and *Charadrius asiaticus*), and Tringinae (*Aechmorhynchus, Bartramia, Numenius, Actitis* and *Xenus*) and also in *Scolopax, Limosa* and *Tryngites*. The insertion is ventral to M. thyrohyoideus in *Vanellus tectus* and lateral to it in the others.

2. M. stylohyoideus fuses with M. thyorhyoideus near the posterior end of the basihyal, and the two insert as one at the anterior end of the basihyal.

Exhibited by some Tringinae (*Tringa erythropus, T. totanus, T. nebularia, T. melanoleuca* and *Heteroscelus*) and Charadriidae (*Vanellus indicus, V. miles, Eudromias ruficollis*).

3. Insertion near the ceratohyal/basihyal articulation.

The remaining Charadriidae and Tringinae fall into this group, and in most of them the insertion lies partly on the basihyal, and partly on the dorsal anterior tip of the ceratohyal. In this category may also be included *Haematopus, Gallinago, Philohela, Limnodromus* and *Calidris acuminatus*, in which the main insertion lies on the basihyal, and the Recurvirostridae in which it is restricted to the ceratohyal.

4. Insertion on the anterior ends of the ceratohyal and urohyal.

This most posterior site of insertion is exhibited by the great majority of Calidridinae, including *C. alpina* ,by the Phalaropodidae and by *Arenaria*. The attachment usually covers the dorsal and medial surfaces of the ceratohyal, and the lateral surface of the urohyal. The insertion is most extensive in *Limicola*, in which the lateral surface of the ceratohyal and the ventral surface of the urohyal are also included, and is particularly well developed also in *Calidris canutus* and *C. maritima*. A few fibres extend on to the basihyal in *Philomachus*, *Calidris tenuirostris* and *C. minutus*.

Action. M. stylohyoideus is the principal retractor of the tongue, and thus plays a vital part in prey manipulation and consumption.

Goodman & Fisher (1962) point out that when the mandible is depressed, the origin of M. stylohyoideus will be raised, and they consider that synergistic action of M. stylohyoideus and M. depressor is likely in the Anseriformes.

M. geniohyoideus
The muscle arises on the mandible and inserts on the epibranchial. As in several other groups of birds, medial and lateral portions can be distinguished. The medial origin is sited dorsally on the medial surface of the mandible, anterior to M. pterygoideus. Part M. The lateral origin, which is the weaker, is on the angular and surangular, anterior to M. adductor externus, Part A, ventral. The part of the muscle arising medially surrounds the posterior ends of M. ceratohyoideus and M. ceratoglossus for a short distance before making its attachment to the epibranchial. The lateral part joins the hyoid "horn" superficially and slightly caudal to the medial part.

The two origins may show more or less continuity along the ventral edge of the mandible; their separation is generally most emphasized in the Calidridinae, and least in the Charadriidae. The lateral origin of M. geniohyoideus usually extends to about the horizontal midline of the mandible. In *Tryngites* it extensively overlaps Ap. 2 portion, 1st mand. part, but in the other species examined the boundaries of the two are adjacent. In *Numenius phaeopus*, *Haematopus* and the Recurvirostridae, the lateral origin is scarcely developed.

Action. The action of this muscle is to pull the tongue forward. Moller (1931) pointed out that the lateral portion (reduced or absent in a few Charadrioidea and most other Charadrii) is more efficient as a protractor, since its line of action is closer to the direction of movement of the tongue. The presence of a lateral origin must also increase the power of tongue protraction.

Manipulation of fresh specimens suggests that contraction of M. geniohyoideus alone would be likely to buckle the ceratohyals, and that synergistic action of other muscles may be essential to its efficient working. M. ceratohyoideus and possibly M. ceratoglossus seem likely to be of importance in this respect, since they are inserted on the ceratohyal.

M. genioglossus

This is a narrow muscle which arises on the ventral medial surface of the mandible just posterior to the symphysis, and runs caudad along the ventral side of the tissue forming the floor of the oral cavity medial to the duct of the Gl. mandibularis 2. It passes dorsal to M. mylohyoideus and inserts feebly on connective tissue in the region of the tongue base.

A weak M. genioglossus is present in *Vanellus albiceps;* apart from this it is found only in a few Tringinae. In *Bartramia*, *Catoptrophorus* and *Numenius* it is well developed, and comparatively wide; in *Aechmorhynchus* it is narrow, and in *Heteroscelus* it is very faint and weak. In *Bartramia* and *Numenius*, it passes upwards at the insertion, which lies lateral to the basihyal, but in the others the muscle does not extend so far posterior and fades out ventral to the tongue base.

Action. This muscle is a protractor of the tongue, a function which can presumably be adequately performed by M. geniohyoideus alone in most species.

M. ceratohyoideus

The origin is on the ventral surface of the anterior end of the ceratohyal. The muscle runs antero-mediad and broadens to insert on the midline, immediately ventral to the anterior half of the urohyal. Very little variation in this muscle has been encountered.

Action. This muscle contributes to the raising and support of the larynx, together with M. thyrohyoideus (q.v.). By contracting simultaneously with MM. mylohyoideus and serpihyoideus, it will participate in raising the floor of the buccal cavity. A further function, perhaps important, may be as a synergist in tongue protraction, since its pull on the ceratohyal has a medial component which will oppose the lateral force component of M. geniohyoideus.

M. ceratoglossus

The origin is fleshy, on the dorsal surface of the anterior end of the ceratohyal. An aponeurosis arises on the lateral surface, and narrows to become a tendon, from which fibres diverge caudad. About level with the posterior end of the basihyal, the fibres fade out, the tendon continuing to its insertion on the posterior ventral surface of the entoglossum. In most species, more fibres arise on the rostral part of the tendon, this time diverging rostrad. These are referred to here as "M. ceratoglossus anterior". In *Charadrius* and *Eudromias*, they are separated only by a short gap from the rest, but in most species they are restricted to the region of insertion. In *Tryngites* there is no gap between M. ceratoglossus anterior and the rest of the muscle; both are distinctly hypertrophied.

The site of insertion on the entoglossum is the flange on its posterior ventral surface, and the fossa medial to this. Typically, the tendon is attached to the flange, and the fibres of M. ceratoglossus anterior insert in the fossa, and on the posterior end of a broad and strong median aponeurosis which runs forward to the tip of the tongue. The posterior tip of this aponeurosis may bifurcate, each branch running for a short distance along the medial edge of M. ceratoglossus anterior.
The fibres of M. ceratoglossus anterior may mingle to a greater or less extent with those from the other side, or with M. hyoglossus anterior or medialis.

No rostral fibres were found in *Philomachus*, *Aechmorhynchus*, *Himantopus*, *Recurvirostra* and *Phalaropus*.

Action. M. ceratoglossus rotates the entoglossum downwards about its articulation with the basihyal. Since the downward movement of the tongue is stopped by the floor of the bill, contraction past this point will cause the posterior end of the tongue to be raised. This action would be required to bring the postero-lateral processes of the tongue into a suitable position to push food back into the mouth when M. stylohyoideus contracts. In doing this it may contract synergically with M. hyoglossus obliquus to maintain the position of the entoglossum relative to the basihyal as it presses against the food.

M. ceratoglossus anterior apparently acts on the cartilaginous anterior part of the entoglossum in the same way as M. hyoglossus anterior. Gadow and Selenka point out that unilateral contraction of M. ceratoglossus can turn the entoglossum laterally on the basihyal. The narrow bills of most waders reduce the capacity for this action, but it may be utilised in steering food into the mouth.

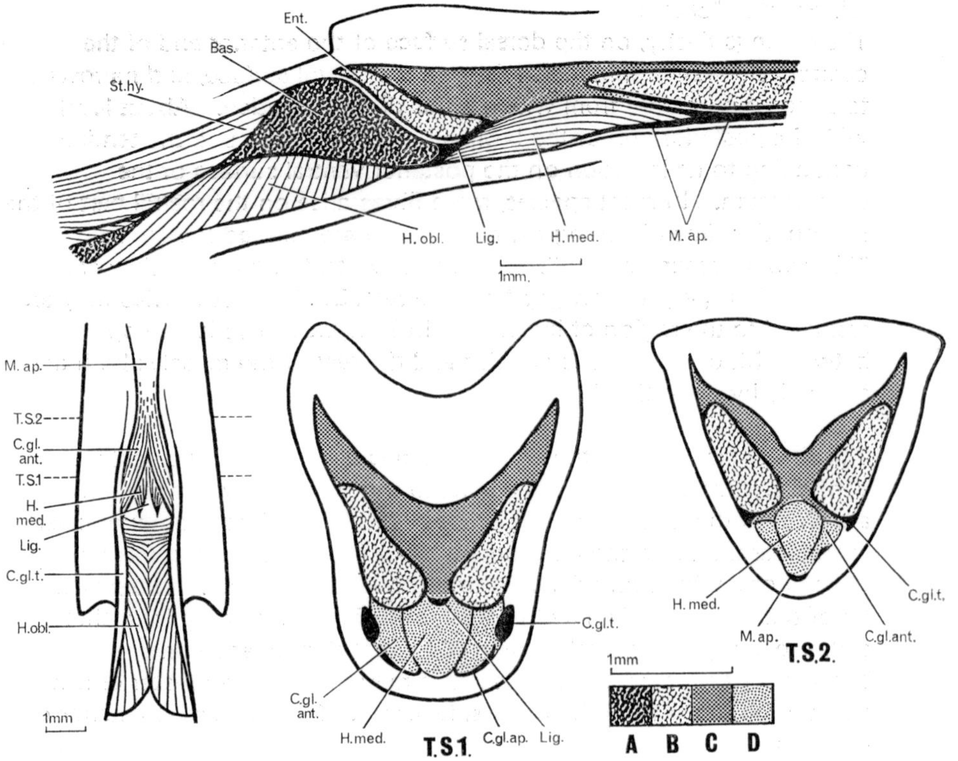

Plate 32.
Vanellus vanellus: detail of musculature in region of tongue base.
Top:
longitudinal section of anterior region of basihyal and base of tongue, slightly lateral to sagittal plane.
Bottom, left:
Ventral aspect of same region.
Bottom, middle:
Transverse section at level indicated by T.S.1. on ventral aspect drawing.
Bottom, right:
Tranverse section at level indicated by T.S.2. on ventral aspect drawing.
Key to shading:
A Bone.
B Cartilage.
C Loose connective tissue.
D Muscle cut transversely to fibre direction.
(Fibre direction is shown where muscles are cut approximately longitudinally; skin is left unshaded.)
For abbreviations see Plate 29.

M. hyoglossus obliquus

M. hyoglossus obliquus has origin on the ventral and lateral surfaces of the basihyal, and inserts on the posterior lateral process of the entoglossum. Two principal structural types may be distinguished:

1. The right and left muscles are continuous ventrally, forming a band of fibres which passes under the basihyal. The muscle extends little further posterior than the posterior lateral process of the entoglossum, and unless the basihyal is very short, is confined to its anterior end.

2. The right and left muscles meet ventrally, but remain separate for most of their length, any fusion being confined to the anterior end. The muscle extends far back along the basihyal, often to its posterior end, and seen from the ventral surface, fibres diverge rostrad from the midline.

The muscle is of type 1 in the majority of species. This is seen in *Haematopus*, all Recurvirostridae and Phalaropodidae, and in nearly all

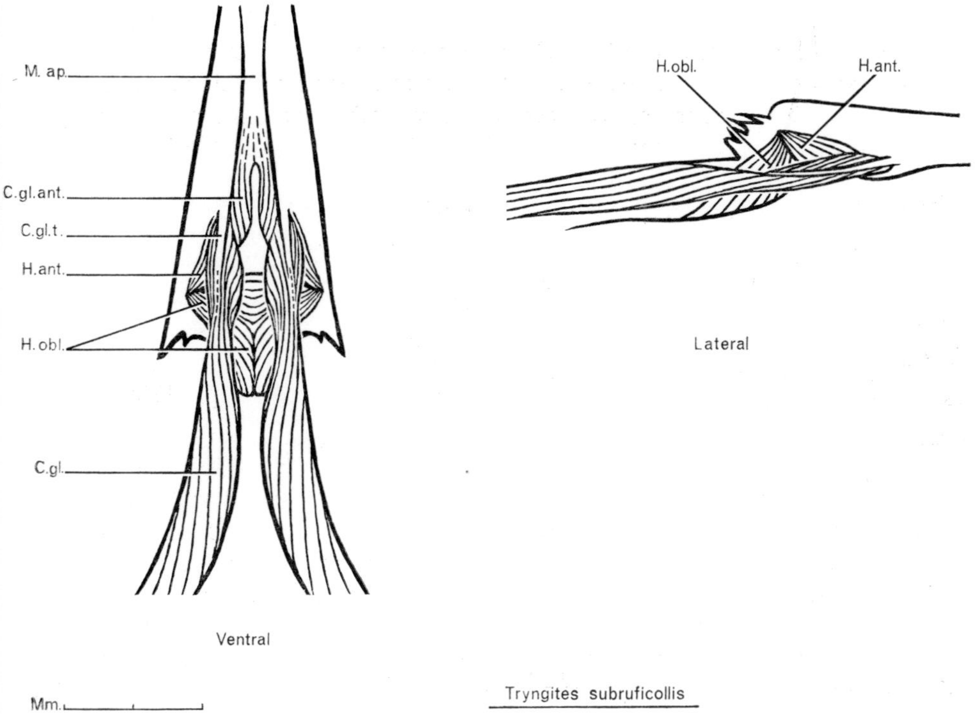

Plate 33.
Tryngites subruficollis: musculature in region of basihyal and tongue base. For abbreviations see Plate 29.

Charadriidae and Tringinae. Among the latter two groups, exceptions exhibiting type 2 are *Pluvianellus, V. vanellus, V. malabaricus, V. coronatus, V. indicus, Aechmorhynchus* and some specimens of *Heteroscelus*. In the two latter genera, asymmetrical development is shown by some individuals.

Type 2 is found in all Arenariinae, Scolopacinae and Calidridinae, although in most Scolopacinae, the fused anterior portion of the muscle is the bulkier. A well-marked feature in many of these species is an aponeurosis arising at the origin on the entoglossum. This frequently extends caudoventrad as a weak raphe, from which fibres diverge caudad. In *Scolopax rusticola*, this aponeurosis, together with a few fibres, passes lateral to the tendon of M. ceratoglossus and attaches to the anterior tip of the ceratohyal. Attachment to the ceratohyal is also seen in *Philohela* and *Limicola*.

Action. M. hyoglossus obliquus rotates the entoglossum upwards about its articulation with the basihyal. Since this articulation does not allow upward flexure, M. hyoglossus obliquus serves either to return the depressed tongue to this position, or to resist depression by pressure against a food item.

Plate 34.
Thinocorus rumicivorus: musculature in region of basihyal and tongue base. For abbreviations see Plate 29.

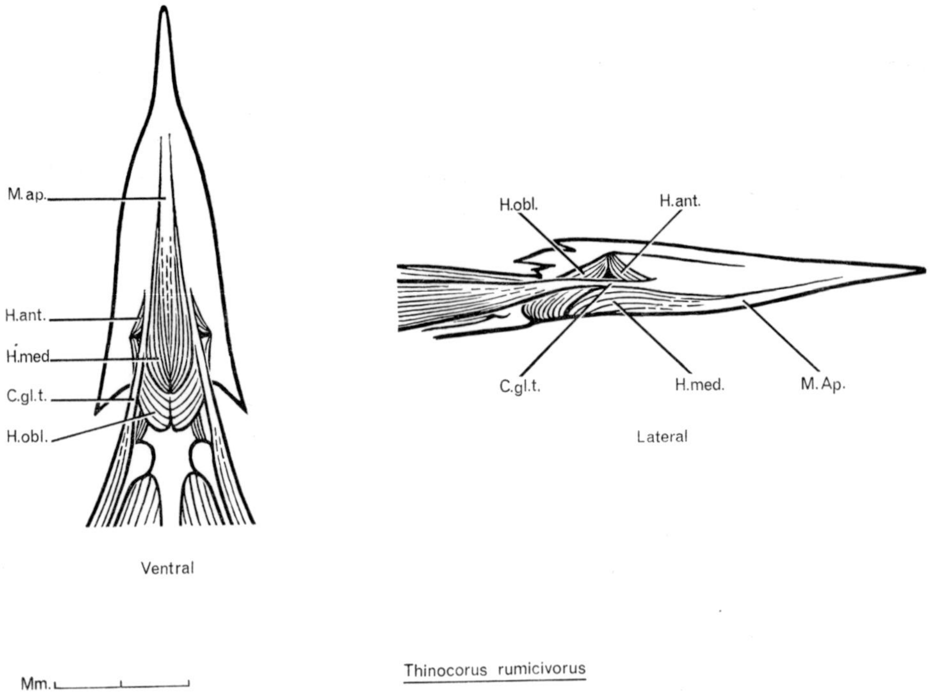

Posterior extension of the origin increases the force of the muscle, not only by hypertrophy, but also because the more posterior fibres will pull at a steeper angle to the radius joining the point of insertion and the pivot. The action of M. hyoglossus obliquus on the entoglossum can be regarded as that of a simple first-class lever. The distance between the insertion and the pivot cannot be greatly increased without substantial changes in the morphology of the skull and buccal cavity, and lengthening of the tongue may therefore be expected to result in a reduced mechanical advantage at its tip. Posterior extension of the origin may thus be an important adaptation to maintain sufficient power to utilize a long tongue.

M. hyoglossus obliquus of type 2 is seen in the majority of highly rhynchokinetic species; *Xenus, Limosa* and *Numenius* are exceptions. This probably reflects the importance of the tongue for supplementing the manipulative action of the upper jaw in such species; a powerful M. hyoglossus obliquus is probably needed to maintain rigidity as the tongue is moved rapidly backwards and forwards under the prey.

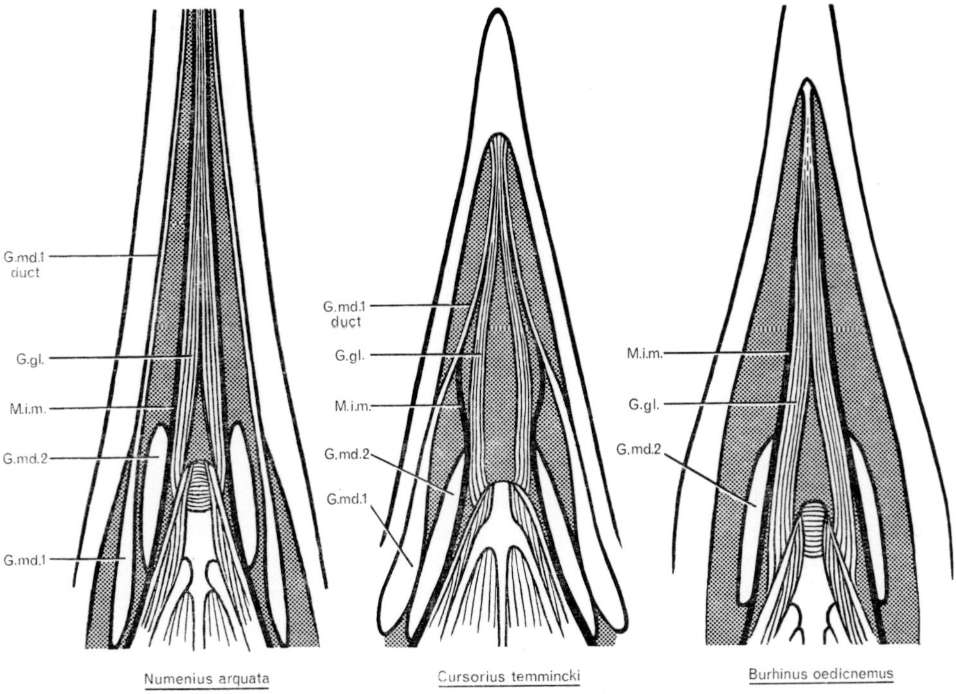

Plate 35.
M. genioglossus in three Charadrii, *Numenius arquata, Cursorius temmincki* and *Burhinus oedicnemus.*

M. hyoglossus anterior

This muscle is missing in some groups of birds, and in its absence the name M. hyoglossus anterior has been applied by some workers to the group of fibres here termed "M. ceratoglossus anterior".

As understood here, M. hyoglossus anterior arises on the lateral posterior edge of the entoglossum immediately anterior to M. hyoglossus obliquus and runs antero-ventrad to insert on the median ventral aponeurosis of the tongue. This insertion is usually anterior to that of M. ceratoglossus, though the fibres of the two generally merge to some extent at the insertion. Fusion between right and left muscles dorsal to the median aponeurosis is frequent; alternatively, a separate median group of fibres may be found, arising on the antero-ventral tip of the basihyal, and the ventral surface of the entoglossum, and inserting on the median aponeurosis. This median muscle is here termed M. hyoglossus medialis. A similar muscle in the Psittaciformes has been termed M. Mesoglossus (Mudge 1903), but use of this term is avoided in the present account in the absence of more certain knowledge of their homologies.

M. hyoglossus medialis is prominent in *Vanellus*, and can be clearly seen ventrally (Plate 32). It is present also in all other Charadriidae but concealed from ventral view by the overlap of Hyoglossus anterior. It was not found in any other families of the Charadrioidea. M. hyoglossus anterior is very weak in *Micropalama*, *C. alba* and *Numenius phaeopus*, and absent in *Phalaropus* and *Lobipes*.

Action. This muscle, and the rostral fibres of M. ceratoglossus, pull the median aponeurosis of the tongue backwards, and by so doing, the cartilaginous anterior portion of the tongue is bent down. There are no antagonistic muscles to oppose this action; upon relaxation, the tongue will straighten owing to the elasticity of the cartilage. This mechanism is probably used to facilitate sliding the tongue forward under a food item held in the bill, and perhaps in aiding manipulation with the tip of the tongue.

M. thyrohyoideus

The posterior end of the cricoid cartilage is the site of origin. The medial part of the origin may show some separation from the rest, and evidently corresponds to a M. thyroglossus fused rostrally with M. thyrohyoideus. The muscle is frequently augmented by fibres arising from the floor of the oral cavity; these are closely associated with M. cleidohyoideus, and are described under that heading.

The insertion is at the anterior end of the dorsal surface of the basihyal, just posterior to the entoglossum; if M. stylohyoideus makes a separate insertion, this lies lateral to that of M. thyrohyoideus.

Action. The action of M. thyrohyoideus is to draw the dorsal surface of the larynx upwards and forwards towards the tongue, and thus to bring them into line, aided by M. ceratohyoideus. It is thus an antagonist of MM. cleidohyoideus and sternotrachealis, whose actions pull the larynx downwards and backwards, out of line with the tongue. It is likely, however, that it often works synergically with them, enhancing their retractor effect. This would be an important mechanism for raising the tongue tip with the bill open, in conjunction with M. stylohyoideus.

M. sternotrachealis

This muscle, and M. cleidohyoideus belong to the group which Gadow and Selenka treat as composing the "sterno-hyoideus system", considering them to be derived from a single primitive sternohyoid layer. George and Berger point out that his interpretation is still unproven.

M. sternotrachealis originates in waders, as in most birds, on the sterno-coracoidal process of the sternum. It inserts on the trachea a short distance anterior to its bifurcation, and continues cephalad as a thin sheet adhering closely to its ventral lateral surface. It strengthens anteriorly and usually broadens to cover most of the ventral surface of the trachea. The insertion is on the ventral and lateral surfaces of the cricoid, superficial fibres usually continuing across it to merge with M. thyrohyoideus. The small amount of variation observed in the species examined does not appear to merit comment.

Action. M. sternotrachealis moves the trachea and larynx posteriorly and ventrally, and thus contributes to lowering of the buccal floor in swallowing.

M. cleidohyoideus

This name is used by Gadow & Selenka; the muscle appears to fall into the group discussed by George and Berger under the heading of M. ypsilotrachealis. It originates from the ventro-medial surface of the clavicle, and runs cephalad in contact with the skin of the neck. For much of the length of the neck it is usually diffuse, and closely associated with dermal muscles; in this respect it resembles M. sternohyoideus of Parrots (Mudge 1903).

Its manner of insertion shows great variation, both within and between species. A common site of attachment is the medial anterior surface of the ceratohyal, where there may be fusion with M. stylohyoideus. In the Calidridinae, *Arenaria*, Phalaropodidae and *Lymnocryptes*, the muscle follows the caudal edge of M. stylohyoideus, to insert on the anterior end of the urohyal. Posterior to the insertion, the muscle is commonly augmented by fibres arising on the ventral surface of the horny covering of the larynx, or on the floor of the oral cavity just lateral to this. These fibres may also contribute to M. thyrohyoideus medially. In some cases, they may form a separate slip which alone makes the insertion, while M. cleidohyoideus merges with M. thyrohyoideus. More usually they are fused with M. cleidohyoideus or connected to it by variable small slips. All these variants have been recorded in *Calidris alpina* alone, and probably occur in most other species examined. In cases where the fibres arising on the floor of the oral cavity form an isolated slip, they correspond, according to insertion, to either M. dermoglossus or M. thyrohyoideus accessory of Fisher & Goodman (1955b). Owing to the variation encountered, these terms cannot be employed here.

In *Vanellus vanellus*, *V. chilensis* and *V. cayanus*, M. cleidohyoideus inserts on the posteroventral edge of the cricoid, and no fibres insert on the ceratohyal. Insertion on the ceratohyal is also lacking in *Scolopax*. In *Tringa nebularia*, *T. erythropus* and *T. melanoleucos*, M. cleidohyoideus appears to fade out in the anterior cervical region.

Action. By their action on the larynx, this muscle and M. tracheohyoideus lower the floor of the mouth to accommodate food as it is being swallowed. They may also enable the posterior papillae of the larynx to play an active role in pushing food into the oesophagus. Synergic action with M. thyrohyoideus has been discussed above. The reduction noted in large *Tringa* spp. may perhaps be connected with the swallowing of slippery aquatic prey.

M. thyroarytenoideus and M. constrictor glottidis
These two muscles of the larynx appear to correspond very closely to the description given for *Grus americana* by Fisher & Goodman. No significant variation has been observed.

Epidermis and Salivary Glands

Epidermal Papillae

The epidermis lining the bill and buccal cavity in birds has received less attention than many other features of the jaw apparatus. Seed eating birds have attracted particular interest (e.g., Sushkin (1927), Beecher (1953), Sims (1955)) and epidermal features in waterfowl are included in the review of Goodman & Fisher (1962). The only reference to the Charadrioidea appears to be that of Feare (1966) for *Calidris maritima* (which closely resembles other *Calidris* spp. in this respect).

On the roof of the buccal cavity and bill, backwardly directed papillae are found:

a. In longitudinal rows on the lining of the bill.

b. In a transverse row near the anterior end of the choana.

c. In weak longitudinal rows on the lateral edges of the palate.

d. Fringing the choana.

e. In a transverse row posterior to the choana and infundibular slit.

On the floor of the buccal cavity and bill, papillae are found:

f. At the posterior margin of the tongue; the most lateral of these are often very large.

g. At the posterior margin of the larynx – a double transverse row of large, crowded papillae.

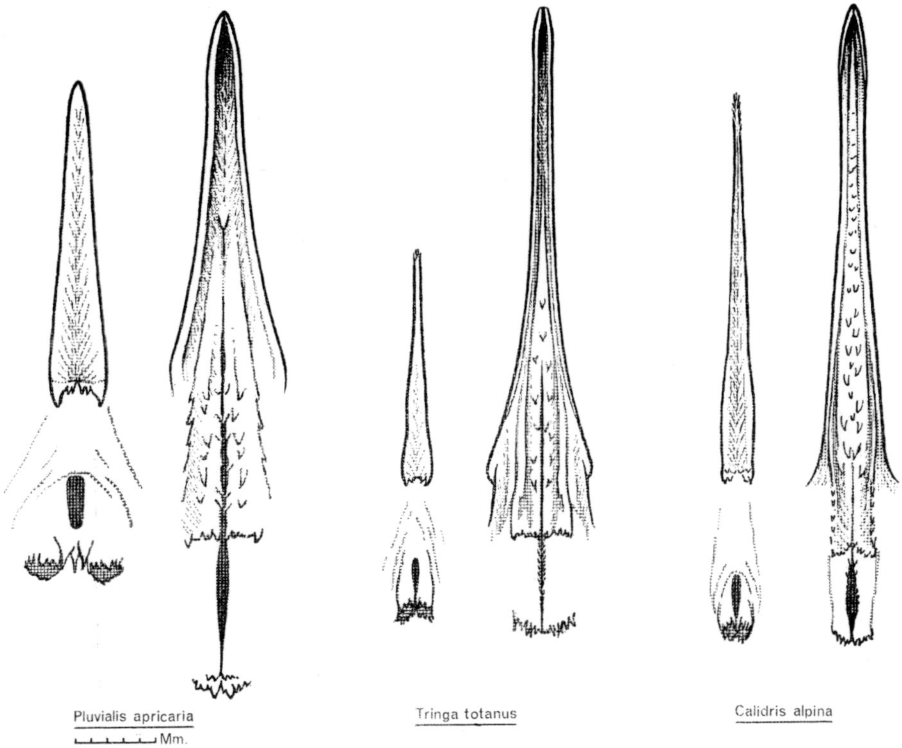

Plate 36.
Epidermal features of pharynx, tongue, palate and lining of upper jaw in *Pluvialis apricaria, Tringa totanus* and *Calidris alpina.*

The extent of papillae in group a. corresponds closely with the situation of the tongue in what appears to be its resting position, with the posterior margin about level with the posterior extremity of the gape. They extend noticeably beyond the tip of the tongue in *Lymnocryptes.* In all Scolopacinae these papillae are small and very numerous; the most anterior bill papillae of *Lymnocryptes* show this condition in an extreme form. The Scolopacinae, *Limosa* and *Limnodromus* lack papillae of group b. In *Rostratula*, the papillae of group a. are rounded, not backwardly directed, and separated into two rows by a median ridge.

The posterior extremity of the gape is situated well forward in highly rhynchokinetic species, normally anterior to the junction of the nasal and jugal bars; the most anterior position is seen in the Scolopacinae. In most moderately rhynchokinetic species, it lies behind this point, reaching an extreme in *Bartramia.* Its relative position is indicated in Table IX.

Action. The close correspondence between the length of the tongue and the extent of the papillae lining the upper bill indicates their

Plate 37.
Epidermal features of pharynx, tongue, palate and lining of upper jaw in *Numenius arquata* and *Gallinago gallinago.*

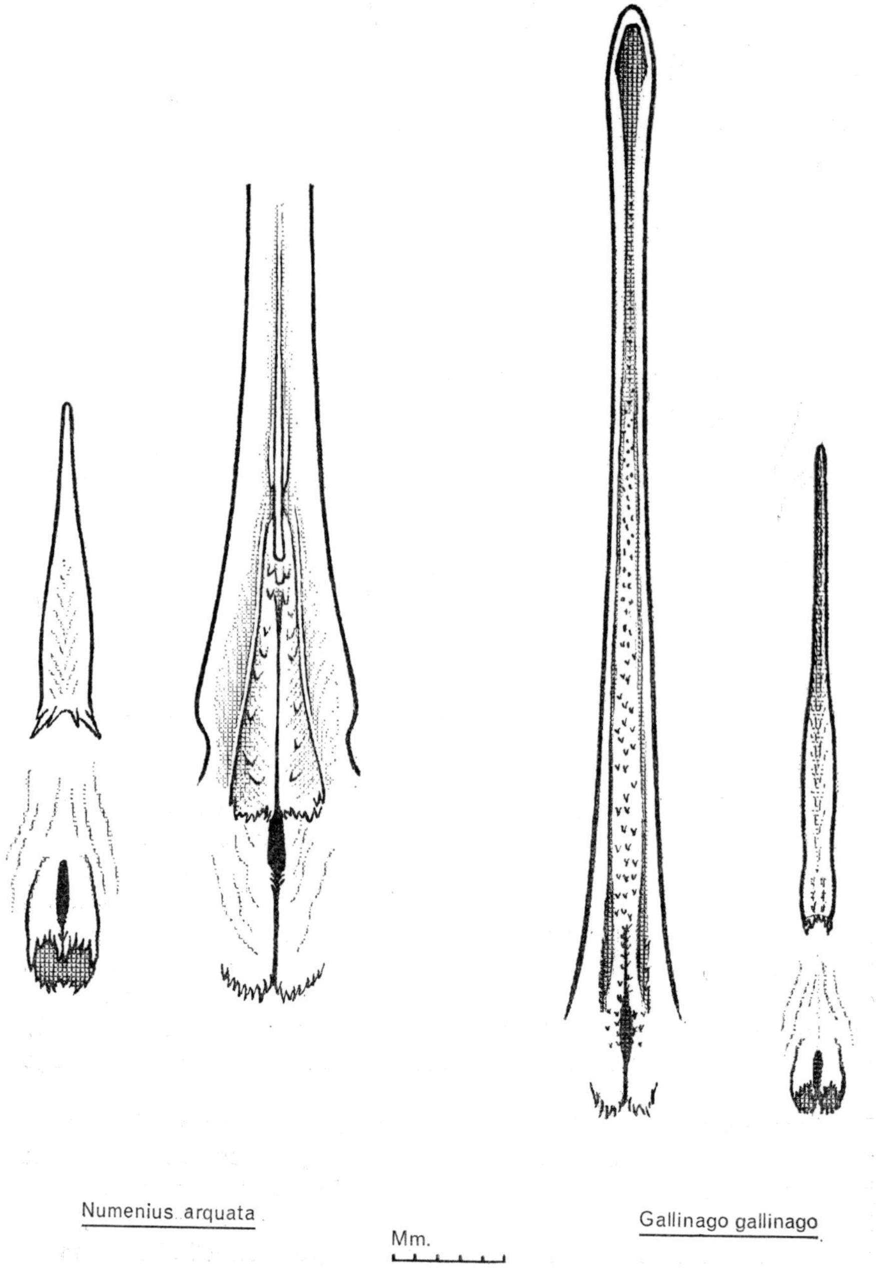

importance for efficient tongue action. Their orientation allows only backward movement of the food item although the tongue moves in both directions. Their extension beyond the tongue in *Lymnocryptes* suggests a function in aiding the initial grasp of food items by the bill tip.

The absence of papillae from the surface of the tongue itself is interesting. Such a feature would seem extremely useful, particularly to probing species with long tongues. However, a papillate tongue might be exposed to dangerous forward pulling forces during probing, when prey slipped from the grasp of the jaws. Papillae may also hinder manipulation and rapid action by adding to the overall bulk of the tongue. Papillate tongues are found in relatively few avian groups (e.g., Sphenisciformes, Anatidae, Picidae), suggesting that there may be yet other disadvantages.

The large papillae at the posterior margin of the tongue are important for thrusting food into the buccal cavity, while those of the larynx and palate aid swallowing.

Salivary Glands

General accounts of histology and morphology of the avian salivary glands have been given by Cholodkowsky, 1892; Holting, 1912; Greschik, 1913; and Antony, 1920. The study by Antony covers a wide range of species, and the terminology she proposes is adopted here, with a slight modification for Gl. mandibularis. An alternative nomenclature is advanced by Farner, 1960.

Gl. mandibularis

Antony uses this term to cover a complex of glands situated in the floor of the buccal cavity. She distinguishes anterior, posterior, internal, external and medial glands. Unfortunately, there seem to be no clear criteria for the identification of these glands. Two pairs are present in most waders, and will be referred to simply as glands 1 and 2.

Gland 1 lies lateral and dorsal to M. stylohyoideus, and lateral to the origin of M. geniohyoideus.

Gland 2 lies medial to gland 1, and medial also to the origin of M. geniohyoideus.

Plate 38.
Tryngites subruficollis showing highly developed salivary glands. In the drawing from ventral aspect, the two mandibular rami have been split apart and deflected laterally.
Abbreviations:
G.a.or. Gl. angularis oris.
G.md.1. Gl. mandibularis 1.
G.p.a. Gl. palatinae anterior.
G.p.d. Common median duct of right and left Gll. palatinae.
G.p.p. Gl. palatinae posterior.
Md.(def.) Deflected mandibular ramus.
M.pt. M. pterygoideus.
V.i.p. Infrapalatine vein.

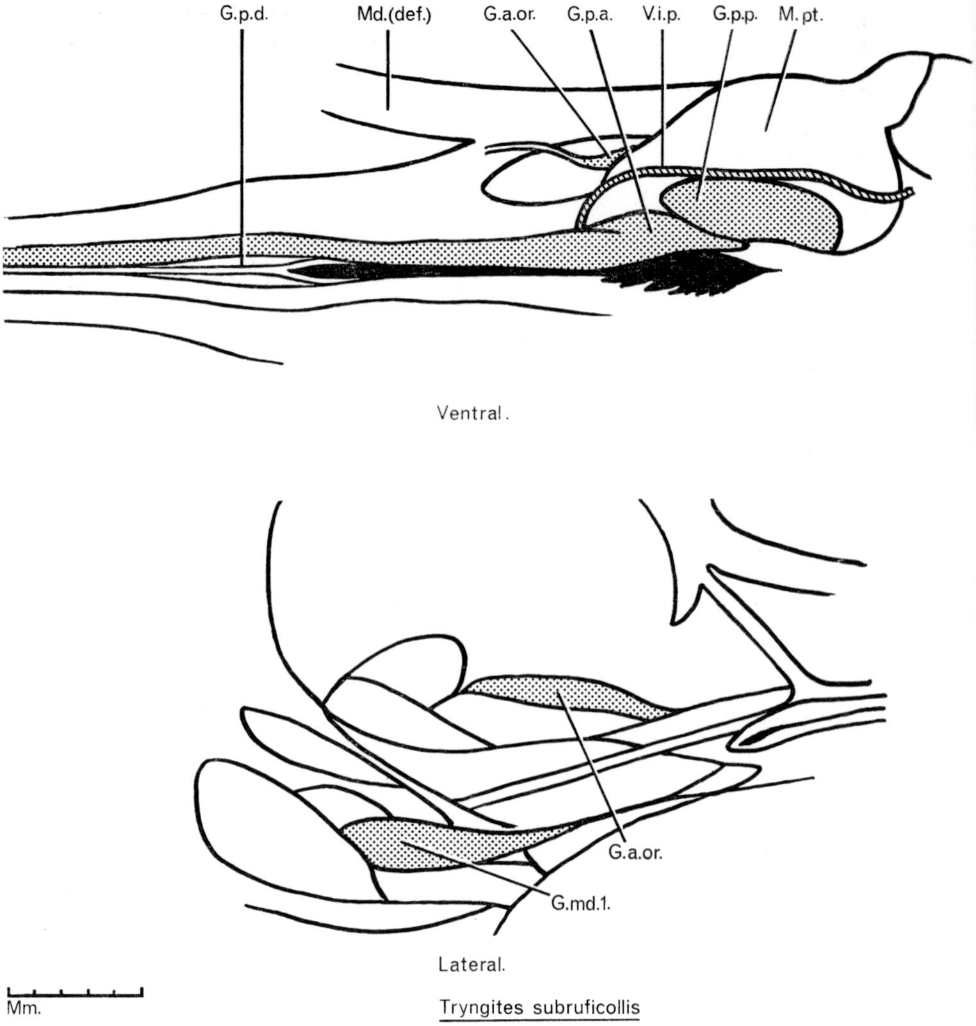

The duct of gland 1 runs dorsal to M. mylohyoideus to open in the region of the symphysis between right and left dentaries, or just beyond. Gland 2 opens near the base of the tongue.

The mandibular glands are well developed in the majority of species. Gland 2 shows least variation, and is present throughout. Gland 1 is absent from the Recurvirostridae and *Limnodromus*, and is vestigial or small in most Charadriidae and Tringinae and in *Gallinago* and *Lymnocryptes*. It is, however, large and prominent in all Calidridinae except *Limosa* and *Limnodromus*, in the Arenariinae and Phalaropodidae, and in *Aechmorhynchus* and *Scolopax*. In this hypertrophied condition, it runs along the dorsal border of M. stylohyoideus to the retroarticular process. Normally the posterior end of the gland is swollen, but in the Phalaropodidae, it is evenly enlarged and parallel sided.

Gl. angularis oris

This gland opens at the angle of the gape as its name implies. In waders it normally lies anteromedial to M. pseudotemporalis profundus, but may somewhat overlap it.

It is present in all species examined, but is much reduced in *Haematopus*, *Gallinago* and *Recurvirostra*. Its small size merits comment also in *Rostratula*, *Numenius*, *Xenus*, *Scolopax*, *Philomachus* and *Himantopus*. It appears best developed in *Charadrius asiaticus*, *Eudromias*, *Pluvialis*, several species of *Vanellus* and in *Tryngites*.

Gl. palatinae

The medial edge of the palatine, just anterior to the medial crest and origin of M. pterygoideus, Part N, is the site of this gland. It appears to be absent in most species, and in many, could not be identified with certainty. It is clear in most species of *Vanellus*, in *Bartramia*, *Numenius*, *Catoptrophorus*, *Actitis*, *Scolopax*, *Calidris melanotos*, *C. acuminatus*, *Tryngites* and *Phalaropus*. It is greatly enlarged in *Tryngites* and continued far forward along the upper jaw. Another, similar gland (– Gl. pal. posterior, Antony) is present in *Tryngites* behind the medial, crest of the palatine, both glands sharing the same duct.

The ducts of the right and left glands join to form a single median duct lying between them, and this duct continues forward to open near the bill tip in most species; in *Numenius* it apparently opens about level with the anterior end of the nostril. In several species of *Vanellus* and in *N. arquata*, a separate narrow gland lies alongside the duct anteriorly, probably corresponding to Antony's Gl. maxillaris.

Gl. cricoarytenoideae
Unlike the preceding glands which are paired, this is a single median structure lying immediately anterior to the larynx. Its duct runs dorsal to the basihyal to open to the buccal cavity at the base of the tongue. It is present throughout, and shows little variation; hypertrophy by forward extension in some specimens of *N. arquata* deserves mention.

Functions. Antony has shown that in general, the secretion of the salivary glands in birds fulfills a lubricatory function. Glands are absent or poorly developed in species feeding on slippery aquatic prey. In waders, lubrication in the bill is probably important to facilitate rapid and easy motion of the tongue. Hence, the mandibular glands, opening below the tongue are generally much more highly developed than the palatine glands opening above it. Gland 1, which provides lubrication in the anterior part of the bill, is largest in highly rhynchokinetic species with a proportionately long tongue. Exceptions to this (*Gallinago, Lymnocryptes, Limnodromus*) are species which probe in very wet substrates and often feed on slimy prey.
Gl. angularis oris and Gl. cricoarytenoideae which provide lubrication to assist swallowing also show reduction in these species.

Cervical Muscles acting on the Head

This account deals only with the six neck muscles inserting on the cranium. Nevertheless, consideration of the entire cervical musculature would repay future investigation in this group.

A detailed survey of the skeleton and musculature of the neck region in birds has been made by Boas (1929). He distinguishes three sections* on functional and morphological grounds, and Zusi (1962) adopts a similar approach in his study of four Lari, though his allocation of vertebrae to sections differs from that of Boas for *Larus marinus.* The muscles considered here originate predominantly on the anterior section (Section I). Zusi allocates the first five vertebrae to this section (except in *Rynchops*), and this appears valid also for the waders examined. (Boas, using different criteria, encountered some variation in the constitution of the neck sections in a few species of waders.)
Section I and the skull can be flexed only downwards, though upward movement of Section I with respect to Section II is possible.
Section II can only be flexed upwards, while Section III can be flexed downward, and also upwards at its anterior end.

* Following Zusi and Storer (1969) the term "sections" is used here in preference to "segments" as employed by Boas and Zusi (1962).

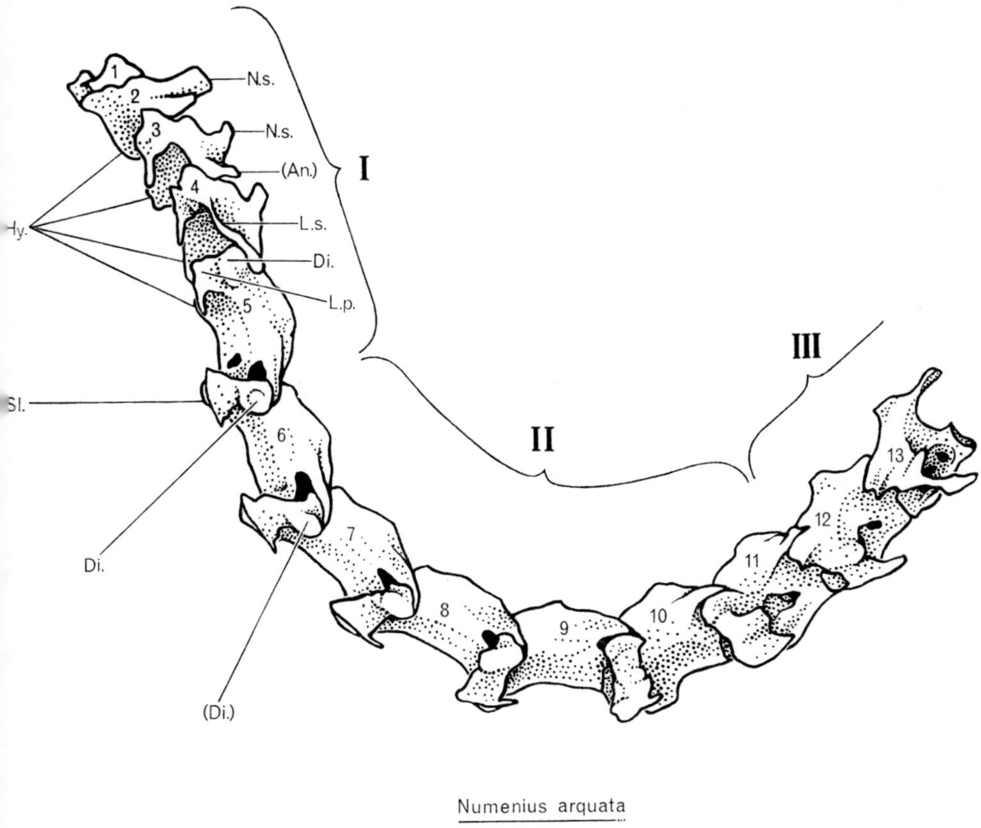

Plate 39.
Numenius arquata, cervical vertebrae. Segments indicated by large Roman numerals, numbering of vertebrae by small Arabic numerals. Division into segments follows Zusi (1962), but the cervico-dorsal vertebrae are not depicted.
The vertebrae are oriented with pre- and post-zygapophyses completely opposed; compare curvature with species shown in Plate 42.
Surface features labelled are those serving as points of origin in some or all Charadrii for muscles inserting on the skull. Those not utilised in *Numenius arquata* are bracketed.
Abbreviations:
An. anapophysis.
Di. diapophysis.
Hy. hypapophysis.
L.p. lateral process.
N.s. neutral spine.
Sl. sublateral process.

If the vertebrae are arranged with the pre- and post-zygapophyses completely opposed, it can be seen that the five vertebrae of Section I form a unit which is distinctly kinked upwards with respect to Section II. This kink is more pronounced in probing species, and most of all in the Scolopacinae. Plates 39 and 40 illustrate this for the five representative species. Numbering of vertebrae from front to back, and terminology for parts of vertebrae, are the same as those used by Zusi.

The dermal muscles, M. dermotemporalis and M. constrictor colli show little noteworthy variation, except for the hypertrophy of the former in the male of *Philomachus*, and are not included in this account.

M. complexus

This muscle originates by slips arising on several anterior cervical vertebrae. Possible sites of origin are the anapophysis of 3; the transverse process of 4; the lateral strut of 4; and the diapophyses of 5, 6 and 7. None of the species investigated utilized all these sites.

Plate 40.
Cervical vertebrae of *Pluvialis apricaria, Tringa totanus, Calidris alpina* and *Gallinago gallinago,* oriented with pre- and post-zygopophyses completely opposed for comparison of curvature. See also *Numenius arquata,* Plate 39.

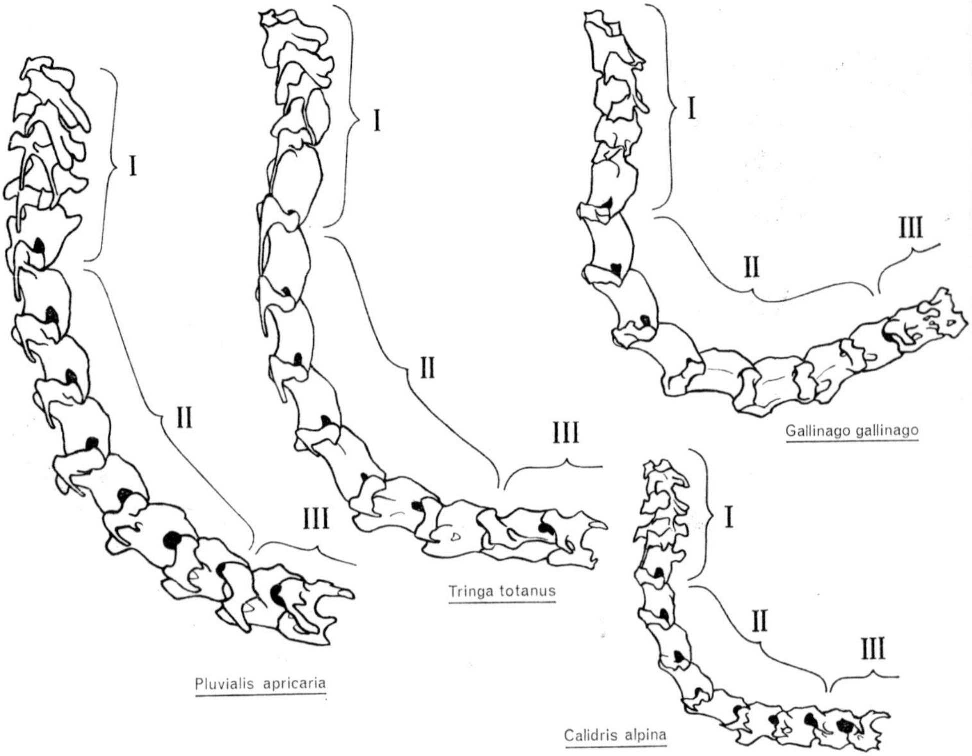

The commonest combination is the lateral strut of 4, and the diapophyses of 5 and 6. The attachment to 6 is frequently made by a superficial aponeurosis. Of the five representative species the combination 4, 5 and 6 is shown by *P. apricaria, N. arquata* and *C. alpina.* The slip to 4 is absent in one specimen of *C. alpina,* and in all specimens of *G. gallinago.* In some individuals of *N. arquata,* the attachment to 4 is very extensive, including the lateral process, as well as the lateral strut, and is subdivided into minor slips. A similar feature is seen in the specimens of *Vanellus malabaricus* and *V. miles.* The sites of origin for other species examined are shown in Table X.

Insertion is made on the raised dorsal rim of the occipital. Hypertrophy of the muscle may involve fusion for some distance in the dorsal midline between the right and left MM. complexi, and increase of insertion area by means of a superficial aponeurosis at the anterior edge of the muscle – features well shown by *N. arquata* and *Haematopus.* Tendinous intersections of the muscle belly of the kind described for some Lari by Zusi (1962) were not detected.

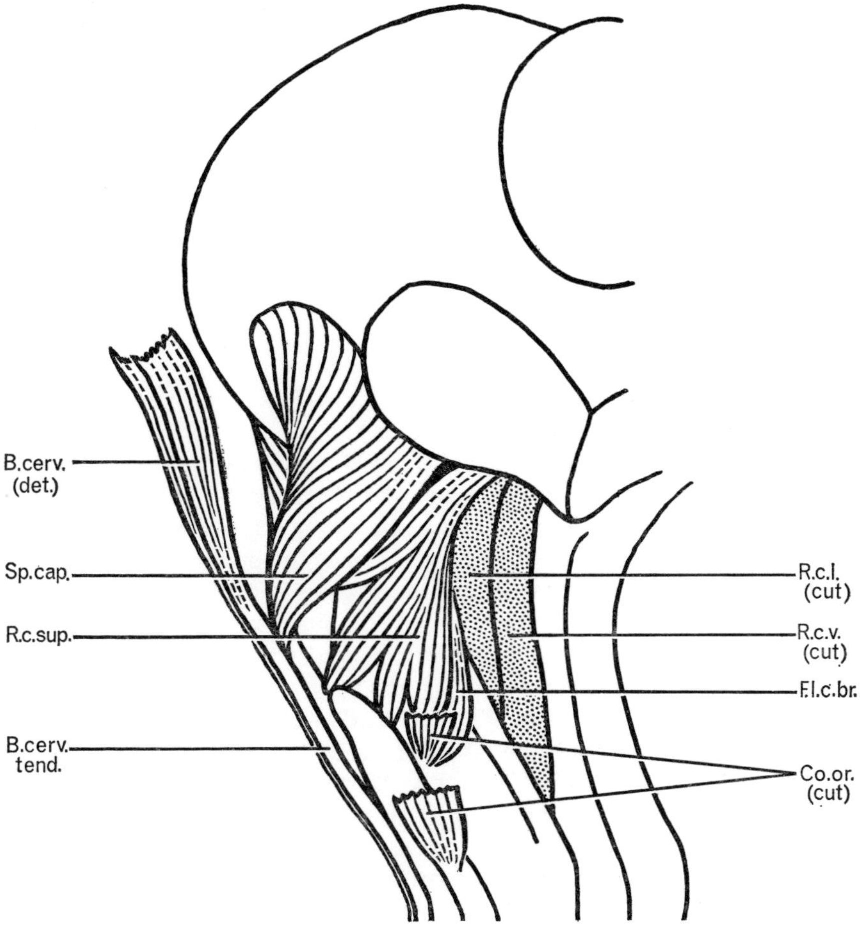

Calidris alpina

Plate 41.
Calidris alpina, cervical muscles inserting on skull. M. flexor colli brevis is also depicted, owing to its close relationship with M. rectus capitis superior.
M. complexus has been removed, leaving only two stumps to indicate its sites of origin, M. biventer cervicis detached from its insertion, and MM. rectus capitis lateralis and ventralis have been largely cut away.

Abbreviations:

B.cerv.(det.) M. biventer cervicis, detached from insertion.
B.cerv.tend. tendon of M. biventer cervicis.
Co.or.(cut) stumps of origins of M. complexus.
Fl.c.br. M. flexor colli brevis.
R.c.l.(cut) M. rectus capitis lateralis, cut surface.
R.c.v.(cut) M. rectus capitis ventralis, cut surface.
R.c.sup. M. rectus capitis superior.
Sp.cap. M. splenius capitis.

Action. Zusi lists the following actions for M. complexus:

a. It tilts the head upward on the atlas.

b. After the head has been fully elevated, further contraction straightens, Section I, and swings it upwards with respect to Section II.

c. Unilateral contraction turns the head and Section I sideways.

He further points out that if the head and Section I are maintained in a constant relative position by the co-operation of synergists (flexors of head, M. splenius capitis, M. splenius colli, M. longus colli ventralis), then the primary action of the muscle would be to raise the head and Section I on Section II.

Since waders, like most of the Lari studied by Zusi, have 5 vertebrae in Section I, M. complexus can only move it relative to Section II if there is origin on 6 or 7. Origin on 7 would be required for it to flex the anterior vertebrae of Section II upwards, a further action suggested by him.

M. complexus must play an important part in directing the movement of the head in feeding actions. For purposes such as seizing mobile prey, or probing, the necessity will arise to move the bill in the straight line which continues its own primary axis of orientation.* To maintain this direction of movement, the neck must be extended as it moves downwards, and the head must be raised with respect to Section I by the action of M. complexus and M. splenius capitis. Synergistic contraction of the head flexors will provide more precise control of this movement. For a bird probing in firm ground, interaction between the bill and the substrate would play an important part in guiding it. M. complexus will act in a similar way to direct the bill as it is extracted from the ground, but with the difference that the posterior part of the muscle will also act to raise Section I. The bill need not conform to such an exact path as the head is raised if prey has only been taken from the surface. In either case, however, powerful contraction of M. complexus will be required if prey is extracted; powerful unilateral action may also be required during probing by some species.

M. biventer cervicis

The muscle arises from the dorsal surface of M. spinalis cervicis; comparative investigation of this origin is not included in the present

* Observation, and analysis of film shows that this does not usually happen when a peck is made at the surface of the ground, the head and bill following a curved trajectory instead.

study. The fibres from this origin insert on the underside of a flat tendon level with 6 or 7, and an anterior group of fibres arise from the dorsal surface of this tendon at about the level of 3. They insert on the ventral side of a short aponeurosis attached to the raised dorsal rim of the occipital, close to the midline. M. complexus lies superficial to this insertion, and M. splenius capitis deep to it. The anterior fleshy portions of the right and left muscles of this name frequently show some degree of fusion in the dorsal midline.

Action. M. biventer cervicis tilts the head upward on the atlas, straightens Sections I and III, flexes II, and swings each section upward. Zusi points out that these effects will be produced simultaneously unless one or more is blocked by other muscles, or environmental forces. In the case of a probing wader extracting its bill from the ground, the effect on the head will be limited by the action of the head flexors and the resistance of the substrate.

M. splenius capitis

This muscle originates from the dorsal and lateral surfaces of the neural spines either of 2 only, or of 2 and 3. Of the 5 representative species, the double origin is shown by *T. totanus*, *N. arquata* and most specimens of *C. alpina*. The muscle is strikingly well developed in some specimens of *N. arquata*, in which the posterior border of the muscle may form a curve extending posterior to the site of origin; a median aponeurosis between 2 and 3 provides a further site for the attachment of fibres. In both *Numenius* and *Haematopus*, the area of insertion is maximal.

There is fleshy insertion near the dorsal border of the occipital, deep to M. biventer cervicis and M. complexus. The lateral edge of the insertion is often slightly aponeurotic.

Action. M. splenius capitis tilts the head upward on its pivot with the atlas, and by unilateral contraction it turns the head sideways. Zusi points out that the part of the muscle arising on 3 will have turning the head as its chief function. He stresses the importance of the muscle for *Rynchops* in resisting lateral environmental forces by synergic action with the MM. intertransversarii.

The muscle inserts on the head at an unfavourable angle compared with M. complexus, owing to its origin close to the pivot, but it will be capable of producing more rapid movements. Since it arises more medially, it would also appear able to move the head laterally through a wider angle. Its role in resisting lateral forces will be of particular importance in vigorous probing.

M. rectus capitis ventralis

M. rectus capitis ventralis arises aponeurotically from the sublateral process of 6; from the medial surface of the aponeurosis attaching M. rectus capitis lateralis to the hypapophyses of 5, 4, 3 and 2; and from the ventral surface of 1. Zusi recognizes medial and lateral parts of this muscle, incompletely separated by the dorsal carotid arteries. Similar structure is seen in waders. Fibres of the medial part diverge to a wide fleshy insertion on the basitemporal plate, while those of the lateral part arise more posteriorly, and converge on an aponeurosis attached to the basitemporal plate immediately anterior to the insertion of the lateral branch of M. rectus capitis superior.

Little variation in structure or siting was observed; the attachment to 6 appears extremely weak in the Phalaropodidae.

Action. M. rectus capitis ventralis is an important flexor of the head and Section I; owing to its more anterior insertion, its mechanical advantage for flexing the head downwards is greater than that of M. rectus capitis superior.

M. rectus capitis lateralis

The muscle arises aponeurotically from the hypapophyses of 5, 4, 3 and 2, and inserts by a narrow aponeurosis on the raised lateral rim of the exoccipital immediately anterior to M. complexus, extending to the tip of the opisthotic process. Little variation in structure was discovered in the specimens examined, but a long area of insertion and prominent opisthotic process indicate hypertrophy in a number of genera, notably *Numenius, Scolopax, Limosa, Limnodromus* and *Haematopus*.

Action. Contraction will tilt the head upwards, and unilateral action will also turn it slightly sideways. However, the site of the muscle, close to the pivot of the head, is inefficient for producing these movements, and a more important action is likely to be that of rotating the head about its longitudinal axis. Simultaneous contraction of head flexors on the same side will be necessary to prevent upward tilting; this task will be performed largely by the lateral parts of M. rectus capitis superior and M. rectus capitis ventralis.

M. rectus capitis superior

In *P. apricaria, N. arquata* and one specimen of *T. totanus*, there is origin on 1 to 5; in other specimens of *T. totanus*, and in *C. alpina* and *G. gallinago*, origin is from 1 to 4 only, a condition shown by the majority of species examined. *Micropalama* is exceptional in having origin only on 1 to 3. The extent of origin for all species is shown in Table X.

The sites of origin are the anterior and ventral surfaces of the diapophysis of 5; the lateral strut and ventral edge of the prezygapophysis of 4; the ventro-lateral surface of the anapophysis, and the lateral surface of 3; the anapophysis of 2, with a few fibres sometimes extending on to its neural arch; and the lateral surface of the neural arch of 1.

Insertion is fleshy and by a strong aponeurosis which is more or less divided into lateral and medial parts in most species. The site of attachment is a transverse ridge on the basitemporal plate, behind the area of insertion of M. rectus capitis ventralis. The ridge is extremely prominent in *Numenius* and *Haematopus*.

Action. M. rectus capitis superior is a flexor of the head and Section I. The synergic role of head flexors during raising and lowering of the head has been discussed under M. complexus. Unilateral contraction of the muscle, together with M. rectus capitis lateralis of the same side, will rotate the head about its long axis, an action which may have to proceed against considerable environmental forces in some probing species.

Other Charadrii

Gross morphology of the jaw muscles has been described for representatives of all superfamilies of the Charadrii except the Dromadoidea by Yudin (1965). This permits brevity in the present account which deals principally with features of structure not discussed by Yudin.

Important aspects of M. adductor externus considered by Yudin are the extent of the external temporal region, and the presence or absence of attachment to the post-orbital process. The external temporal region reaches its greatest development in *Dromas*, the right and left muscles almost meeting in the dorsal midline; skeletal material examined indicates a similar condition in *Esacus* and *Orthorhamphus* (Burhinoidea). Attachment to the post-orbital process is especially prominent in *Dromas*, *Chionis* and *Thinocorus*, and involves a dorsal fork from the caudal end of Ap. 2 in the first two, while in the latter, the post-orbital and zygomatic processes meet and fuse as in, e.g., many Galliformes. The internal structure of the muscle is similar throughout the suborder; the complex, multipinnate architecture based on Aps. N and O is more highly developed than in the Lari and Alcae (see Plates 24 and 25). Part B has a lateral expansion in *Pluvianus* and *Chionis*. In the latter this has taken the place of Part A ventral, which is vestigial; this leads Yudin (1965, fig. 71) to label it, incorrectly as M. adductor externus medialis (=Part A ventral). In fact it is Part B that is subdivided into dorsal and ventral sections. Ap. N makes a bifurcated insertion far rostrally on the mandible, medial to the ventral fibres of Part A. The fibres accompanying Ap. N constitute the dorsal section of Part B, while the ventral section consists of a lobe of fibres fanning out to a wide insertion on the ventral lateral surface of the mandible. Ap. B spreads out over the dorsal surface of this lobe, fading out short of its edges. A bulky but weakly pinnate Ap. D slip is visible in *Dromas*, and an Ap. A[1] slip is present in *Burhinus*, *Chionis* (in which it is nearly concealed by M. pseudotemporalis profundus), *Pluvianus* and *Peltohyas*.

M. pseudotemporalis superficialis has a bipinnate medial slip in all but the Jacanidae, *Thinocorus* and *Peltohyas*. In *Chionis* and *Dromas*, this slip makes a separate insertion on the mandible above N. ramus mandibularis, the main tendon (Ap. M) passing below it to insert. In *Burhinus*, Ap. M is forked near the insertion, a weak dorsal branch inserting above the nerve, while the main tendon inserts below it. In the remainder, the muscle has only one attachment to the mandible, and this is below N. ramus mandibularis in all except *Peltohyas*, in which it passes above as in all Charadrioidea.

M. pseudotemporalis profundus is bulky in *Dromas* and *Chionis*, and its dorsal fibres insert on the aponeurotic dorsal medial surface of M. adductor externus, Part A, forming a bipinnate structure; in *Dromas*, this attachment is made by a distinct superficial slip arising on the caudal lateral side of M. pseudotemporalis profundus. Parts M and O of M. pterygoideus are clearly separated in all but the Jacanidae. N. pterygoideus passes between them, except in *Burhinus*, in which it penetrates Part O, as in the Charadriidae. In *Peltohyas* (Plate 20), the muscle is divided in two places; N. pterygoideus penetrates the more caudal of the two dividing grooves. In *Pluvianus* there is partial division anterior to N. pterygoideus which traverses the main line of division.

M. stylohyoideus inserts on the rostral end of the basihyal (caudally in the Jacanidae and *Chionis*), usually dorsal to M. thyrohyoideus, but lateral to it in *Pluvianus* and *Peltohyas*. It is produced into a flap extending to cover the ventral anterior surface of the ceratohyal in *Dromas*, *Burhinus* and most Glareoloidea. M. geniohyoideus has a lateral origin only in *Thinocorus* and *Peltohyas*. M. genioglossus is present in *Dromas*, *Burhinus* and all the Glareoloidea. Its form in *Burhinus* is distinctive; it is strong, and the right and left muscles are fused for some distance from the origin, which is by a short, strong aponeurosis from the mandibular symphysis (Plate 35). The rostral part of M. ceratoglossus is generally well developed, and in *Chionis* the two sides are fused. M. hyoglossus anterior is absent in *Burhinus*, and the right and left MM. hyoglossi obliqui are fused in all but *Chionis*, *Pluvianus* and *Thinocorus*. In the first two, the muscle is small, and the right and left sides do not even meet in the midline. In *Thinocorus*, M. hyoglossus obliquus is of unusual form, inserting on the midline at the caudal end only of the basihyal, whose ventral and anterior lateral surfaces are occupied by the origin of the very large M. hyoglossus medialis, which is divided into right and left muscles (Plate 34). M. cleidohyoideus shows very variable insertion, as in the Charadrioidea. The other tongue muscles differ little from their condition in the Charadrioidea.

The complement of origin sites for neck muscles inserting on the head is shown in Table X. The salivary glands are particularly well developed in the Glareoloidea and Thinocoroidea. In the latter, Gl. mandibularis 1 is large and ventrally situated, and Gl. mandibularis 2 extends far posterior, medial to the insertion of M. geniohyoideus on the epibranchial and is expanded behind M. depressor.

Table X.
Sites of origin of M. complexus, M. splenius capitis and M. rectus capitis superior. Brackets indicate sites not occupied in all specimens of a species dissected. Asterisks indicate species of which only one specimen was dissected.

SPECIES	***M. complexus***					***M. spl. cap.***		***M. rect. cap. sup.***				
	3	4	5	6	7	2	3	1	2	3	4	5
Actophilornis africana	X	X	X			X		X	X	X	X	X
Irediparra gallinacea	X	X	X			X		X	X	X	X	X
*Hydrophasianus chirurgus**	X	X	X			X		X	X	X	X	X
Jacana spinosa	X	X	X			X		X	X	X	X	X
Rostratula benghalensis		X	X			X		X	X	X	X	
Haematopus ostralegus		X	X	X		X	X	X	X	X	X	X
*Pluvianellus socialis**		X	X	X		X		X	X	X	X	X
Vanellus vanellus		(X)	X	X		X	X	X	X	X	X	
V. armatus		X	X	X		X	X	X	X	X	X	X
*V. spinosus**		X	X	X		X	X	X	X	X	X	X
V. tectus		X	X	X		X	X	X	X	X	X	X
*V. malabaricus**	X	X	X	X		X	X	X	X	X	X	X
V. coronatus		X	X	X		X	X	X	X	X	X	X
*V. senegallus**		X	X	X		X	X	X	X	X	X	X
*V. leucurus**		X	X	X		X	X	X	X	X	X	X
V cayanus		X	X	X		X		X	X	X	X	X
V. chilensis		X	X	X		X	X	X	X	X	X	X
V. indicus		X	X	X		X	X	X	X	X	X	X
V tricolor			X	X		X	X	X	X	X	X	X

SPECIES	*M. complexus*					*M. spl. cap.*		*M. rect. cap. sup.*				
	3	4	5	6	7	2	3	1	2	3	4	5
*V. miles**		X	X	X		X	X	X	X	X	X	X
Pluvialis apricaria		X	X	X		X		X	X	X	X	X
P. dominica		X	X	X		X		X	X	X	X	(X)
P. squatarola		(X)	X	X		X		X	X	X	X	X
Charadrius hiaticula		(X)	X	X		X		X	X	X	X	
C. dubius			X	X		X		X	X	X	X	
C. wilsonia			X	X		X		X	X	X	X	
C. vociferus			X	X		X	(X)	X	X	X	X	
C. pecuarius			X	X		X		X	X	X	X	
C. tricollaris		(X)	X	X		X		X	X	X	X	(X)
C. alexandrinus			X	X		X		X	X	X	X	
*C. peronii**			X	X		X		X	X	X	X	X
*C. bicinctus**		X	X	X		X		X	X	X	X	X
*C. falklandicus**		X	X	X		X		X	X	X	X	
C. mongolus		X	X	X		X	(X)	X	X	X	X	X
*C. leschenaultii**		X	X	X		X		X	X	X	X	
*C. asiaticus**		X	X	X		X		X	X	X	X	X
C. modestus		X	X	X		X		X	X	X	X	(X)
C. melanops			X	X		X		X	X	X	X	
C. cinctus			X	X		X		X	X	X	X	
Eudromias ruficollis		X	X	X		X		X	X	X	X	X
Aechmorhynchus cancellatus		X	X	X		X		X	X	X	X	
Bartramia longicauda		X	X	X		X	X	X	X	X	X	
Numenius phaeopus	(X)	X	X	(X)		X	(X)	X	X	X	X	
N. arquata		X	X	X		X	X	X	X	X	X	X
Tringa erythropus		X	X			X	X	X	X	X	X	
T. totanus		X	X			X	X	X	X	X	X	(X)
T. flavipes		X	X			X	X	X	X	X	X	
T. stagnatilis		X				X	X	X	X	X	X	
T. nebularia		X	X			X	X	X	X	X	X	
*T. melanoleuca**		X	X			X	X	X	X	X	X	
T. ochropus		X	X	X		X	X	X	X	X	X	
*T. solitaria**		X	X			X	X	X	X	X	X	X
T. glareola		X	X	X		X	X	X	X	X	X	
Xenus cinereus		X	X	X		X		X	X	X	X	
Actitis hypoleucos		X	X	X		X		X	X	X	X	
A. macularia		X	X	X		X		X	X	X	X	
*Catoptrophorus semipalmatus**		X	X	X		X	X	X	X	X	X	
Heteroscelus brevipes		X	X	X		X	X	X	X	X	X	
H. incana		X	X	X		X	X	X	X	X	X	
Aphriza virgata		X	X	X		X		X	X	X	X	X
Arenaria interpres			X	X		X		X	X	X	X	
*Gallinago stenura**			X	X		X		X	X	X	X	
G. gallinago			X	X		X		X	X	X	X	
*G. paraguiae**			X	X		X		X	X	X	X	
*Scolopax saturata**			X	X		X		X	X	X	X	
S. rusticola			X	X		X		X	X	X	X	
*Philohela minor**			X	X		X		X	X	X	X	
Lymnocryptes minima		X	X	X		X		X	X	X	X	

SPECIES	*M. complexus*					*M. spl. cap.*		*M. rect. cap. sup.*				
	3	4	5	6	7	2	3	1	2	3	4	5
Limosa limosa		X	X	X		X		X	X	X	X	X
L. haemastica		X	X	X		X		X	X	X	X	X
L. lapponica		X	X	X		X		X	X	X	X	X
Limnodromus griseus			X	X		X		X	X	X	X	X
Crocethia alba			X	X		X	X	X	X	X	X	
Calidris canutus		X	X	X		X		X	X	X	X	
*C. tenuirostris**		X	X	X		X		X	X	X	X	
C. pusilla		X	X	X		X	X	X	X	X	X	
C. ruficollis		X	X	X		X	X	X	X	X	X	
C. minuta		X	X	X		X	X	X	X	X	X	
C. temmincki		X	X	X		X	X	X	X	X	X	
C. subminuta			X	X		X		X	X	X	X	
*C. minutilla**			X	X		X	X	X	X	X	X	
C. fuscicollis		X	X	X		X	X	X	X	X	X	
*C. bairdii**		X	X	X		X	X	X	X	X	X	
C. melanotos		X	X	X		X	X	X	X	X	X	
C. acuminata	(X)	X	X	X		X	X	X	X	X	X	
C. maritima		X	X	X		X	X	X	X	X	X	
C. alpina		(X)	X	X		X	X	X	X	X	X	
C. testacea		X	X	X		X		X	X	X	X	
Limicola falcinellus		X	X	X		X		X	X	X	X	
Micropalama himantopus		X	X	X		X	X	X	X	X		
Tryngites subruficollis		X	X	X	X	X		X	X	X	X	
Philomachus pugnax		X	X	X		X	X	X	X	X	X	
*Ibidorhyncha struthersii**		X	X			X	X	X	X	X	X	
Himantopus himantopus		X	X			X	X	X	X	X	X	X
Recurvirostra avosetta		X	X			X	X	X	X	X	X	X
*R. novae-hollandiae**		X	X			X	X	X	X	X	X	X
Phalaropus fulicarius		X	X			X		X	X	X	X	
Lobipes lobatus		X	X			X		X	X	X	X	
*Steganopus tricolor**		X	X	X		X		X	X	X	X	
Dromas ardeola		X	X	X		X		X	X	X	X	
Burhinus oedicnemus	X	X	X			X		X	X	X	X	
B. capensis	X	X	X			X		X	X	X	X	
B. magnirostris	X	X	X			X		X	X	X	X	
Pluvianus aegyptius		X	X			X	X	X	X	X	X	X
*Cursorius cursor**	X	X	X	X		X		X	X	X	X	X
C. temminckii	X	X	X	X		X		X	X	X	X	X
*C. coromandelicus**	X	X	X	X		X		X	X	X	X	X
*Rhinoptilus africanus**	X	X	X	X		X		X	X	X	X	X
*R. cinctus**		X	X	X		X		X	X	X	X	X
*R. chalcopterus**		X	X	X		X		X	X	X	X	X
Peltohyas australis		X	X	X		X		X	X	X	X	
Stiltia isabella	X	X	X	X		X		X	X	X	X	
*Glareola pratincola**	X	X	X	X		X		X	X	X	X	
G. nuchalis	X	X	X	X		X		X	X	X	X	
Thinocorus orbignyianus		X	X	X		X	(X)	X	X	X	X	X
T. rumicivorus		X	X	X		X		X	X	X	X	
Chionis alba		X	X	X		X		X	X	X	X	X

Conclusions and Discussion

This paper has presented accounts of feeding behaviour and anatomy of the feeding apparatus in the Charadrii. The Charadrioidea have received fullest attention, with special emphasis on five representative species. Observations on behaviour have illustrated the variety of ways in which jaws, neck and tongue may be used, and the environmental forces to which they may be subjected. In the anatomical sections, skull structure has been discussed and reviewed, and detailed descriptions given of jaw muscles, hyoid skeleton and musculature, salivary glands and epidermal features, and cervical muscles inserting on the head. The detailed treatment has revealed numerous differences among the wide range of species examined, which in many cases appear significant when viewed from an adaptive or phylogenetic standpoint. The actions of muscles and functions of other structures examined have already received some attention. It remains to discuss at greater length the relations between behaviour and ecology on the one hand and morphology on the other. The five representative species will be dealt with first, followed by a review of the remaining species, treated systematically. The final discussion draws attention to some points of general significance and outstanding problems.

Comparison of Representative Species

Golden Plovers and Redshanks rely largely on prey captured on or near the surface and detected by visual means. The feeding substrates used by the Golden Plover are relatively hard, especially during frost; its feeding movements include surface pecks and more prolonged excavation. Redshanks feed on softer substrates and take many prey from tidal pools; pecks and "mowing" predominate, but brief probes occur occasionally. Golden Plovers show great mobility, but have the lowest actual feeding rate of the five.

The remaining three species obtain much food by probing, and test probes are used in addition to sight for searching. Curlews in some circumstances take much prey on the surface, but probes are still of major importance. The vigorous probing techniques, the downcurved bill and the firm substrates frequented impose severe demands on the jaw apparatus. The large body side is of basic importance in meeting these needs. Dunlin make extensive use of small surface items such as *Hydrobia;* probing occurs more frequently on softer substrates. Probes are mostly swift, and involve "quivering". The feeding rate is extremely high, as might be expected for a small species feeding on very small prey, and test probes are made in rapid series ("stitching"). Snipe rely almost entirely on probing, and the rate and duration of probes are high. Environmental forces are minimized by the probing techniques, which involve little reorientation of the bill underground, and by the semi-liquid nature of the feeding substrate.

The short bill of the Golden Plover confers a high mechanical advantage on the adductor muscles, but reduces the potential for rapid closing. This apparent disadvantage may be offset by the speed with which the bill can be brought to bear on the prey. A longer bill used in a similar way on hard substrates would require considerable reinforcement, making it more unwieldy. Many of the prey animals on pasture are likely to be visible only very briefly, and in unexpected places, and it is essential that the bill should be aligned quickly. Observation confirms that a high proportion of feeding movements are made to one side, behind, or even on the run. Speed is also essential to the Redshank, as many aquatic prey are capable of rapid darting as an escape movement; a longer bill is possible as prey are taken from soft substrates or from water, but the velocity ratio is thereby reduced. Bill length in the other three species is primarily related to probing. The extremely long bill of the Curlew poses problems in transferring prey from bill tip to mouth, especially as the tongue is too short to aid this action. This may be partly offset by the very low velocity ratio, which facilitates the very rapid mandible movements required for synchronised head jerking and jaw action. In the Dunlin and even more in the Snipe, prey are often partly or entirely consumed without removal of the bill from the ground, reducing the risk of loss or breakage of the prey animal.

Straight bills are efficient both for swift capture and probing, and are possessed by the Golden Plover, the Redshank and the Snipe. The slight hooking at the tip of both jaws in the Redshank reduces the danger of hard-bodied prey slipping from the bird's grasp, while the notched tip of the upper mandible in Snipe aids in grasping worms. The advantage of a straight bill is sacrificed by the Curlew for the ability to explore a wider radius with the bill tip, saving time and energy in firm substrates. The slight decurvature of the Dunlin's bill is less easy to explain, as manoeuvring during probes results mainly in widening the top of the hole rather than exploring at depth. Improved grip, and reduction of the extent of head lowering needed for "stitching" may be significant factors.

The jaw musculature of the Golden Plover and the Redshank is relatively unspecialized; retention of the external temporal region of M. adductor and the caudal lobe of M. pseudotemporalis superficialis contribute to the force and range of movement of the adductors. Strong adduction is important for the Golden Plover when extracting large earthworms, and is further aided by the relatively large absolute size, a bulky M. pseudotemporalis profundus and the high mechanical advantage. The Redshank also requires strong adduction for grasping hard-bodied and active prey, but the mechanical advantage is less; this may be compensated for by the more complex structure of M. adductor, Part A, and the usually well developed Ap. D slip. Protraction against the substrate probably occurs in many of the prolonged feeding movements of Golden Plovers, though there is no evidence of true "gaping"; it is certainly infrequent in the Redshank, and this is reflected in its relatively small orbital process and M. protractor.

The Curlew shows an unmistakable resemblance to other large Tringinae in its jaw muscles, but they are strongly hypertrophied. The very deep mandibular fossa, the sharply incurved dorsal edge of the mandible, and increased area of aponeuroses provide a large extra surface for the insertion of M. adductor, Part A. These features clearly contribute to the need for a strong bill tip grasp despite the low mechanical advantage. The emphasis on Part A may reflect its importance in countering lateral and twisting forces. M. pterygoideus, Part O, shows multiplication of aponeuroses, with corresponding changes in the surface features of the pterygoid; this muscle is essential for support against disarticulation, as well as playing an important part in retraction. Part N of M. pterygoideus possesses an extra raphe, a significant feature in view of its action in bowing the mandibular rami – an essential faculty in the Curlew owing to the large prey, especially crabs, regularly swallowed whole. The quadrate and M. protractor are surprisingly little enlarged, despite the fact that protraction against the resistance of the substrate must regularly occur. The massive M. depressor no doubt aids this action. Its bulk is important also because the retroarticular process shows little enlargement, and the mechanical advantage is thus extremely low; perhaps this is essential to allow rapid jaw movement when prey is being raised up the bill.

Both the Dunlin and the Snipe have lost the external temporal region of M. adductor and the caudal lobe of M. pseudotemporalis superficialis as the result of morphological changes in the skull. Great differences exist in the jaw musculature, however. The adductors are of simple structure in the Dunlin save for the prominent Ap. D slip, which provides efficient adduction over the short distance required for most feeding movements and may be of special value in prey manipulation. In the Snipe, reduction in bulk and range of movement is accompanied by an increase in pinnate structure of both M. adductor and M. pseudotemporalis superficialis, providing sufficient force to grasp even large worms despite the low mechanical advantage. In the Snipe and the Curlew, much variation has been found in the detailed structure of M. adductor; it would be most interesting to see if the variants showed correlation with other features, e.g., bill length, in a longer series of specimens.

M. pterygoideus is well developed in the Snipe and Dunlin, but shows no structural modifications associated with its important role in the manipulative action of the bill. A well developed retroarticular process and pinnate M. depressor are found in both species; the depressor is of particularly complex structure in the Snipe. The capacity to depress the mandible underground is likely to be important, despite the highly rhynchokinetic upper jaw, and M. depressor also supplements the action of M. protractor. The large retroarticular process also provides room for the origin of the bulky M. stylohyoideus and M. serpihyoideus. The enormous M. protractor is a striking feature of the jaw musculature in the Snipe. Other waders with a much smaller M. protractor also protract against the resistance of the substrate, however, and the significant factors are probably the high total of time actually spent probing, and the manner of prey extraction, which requires repeated protraction underground.

Loss of the external jugomandibular ligament has occurred in the Dunlin and the Snipe as in most other highly rhynchokinetic species; the precise significance of this is unclear. The medial brace (see Bock 1960a) is found in the Golden Plover and the Curlew. Its presence in the Golden Plover, as in most other Charadriidae may be related to the generally hard substrates frequented, and it must provide valuable support when "snatching" with wide open jaws occurs. The medial brace in Curlew is required for support against the severe forces arising during its vigorous probing, and is not found in other Scolopacidae. The mandible quadrate articulation is surprisingly loose in Curlew; the quadrate condyles provide little support against backward disarticulation, and the post-orbital ligament shows no reinforcement as in *Haematopus* and some *Vanellus* spp. This perhaps facilitates lateral movement of the mandible, which may be involved in steering large prey items into the mouth. In any case, it is clear that the burden of support against environmental forces is taken by the musculature. The advantages of this type of support in the avian skull are discussed by Bock (1969; see also Spring, 1965).

The ratio of tongue to bill length shows moderate reduction in the Snipe, and great reduction in the Curlew in which reinforcement of the jaws has almost completely occluded the bill lumen for most of its length.

The Golden Plover's tongue resembles that of nearly all other plovers in its entirely cartilaginous entoglossum. Differences in tongue musculature principally concern muscles moving the entoglossum. A distinct M. hyoglossus medialis is found in the Golden Plover, as in most Charadriidae. M. hyoglossus obliquus is of type 2 in Snipe and Dunlin, as in most other highly rhynchokinetic species with well developed tongues, probably providing the rigidity needed for its active role in prey consumption. M. stylohyoideus and M. serpihyoideus also show hypertrophy in these species. The basihyal, and consequently the origin of M. hyoglossus obliquus are very short in the Snipe as in other Scolopacinae; this may be in part due to the reduced space available owing to the form of the skull, though the basihyal remains long in *Limnodromus*.

Of the regions bearing epidermal papillae, most diversity is seen in the lining of the upper jaw. Small and numerous papillae are present in the Snipe, aiding the grasp of large earthworms; papillae are also numerous in the Dunlin. The complement of salivary glands is the same in all five species except for the addition of Gl. palatinae in the Curlew. Marked reduction of glands is evident in the Snipe, probably due to the high proportion of slimy prey taken from wet substrates. Hypertrophy of Gl. mandibularis 1 is seen in Dunlin, as in other Calidridinae, providing sufficient lubrication for the tongue despite the high proportion of dry prey. In chicks of other species examined, the glands were similar in relative development to those of adults.

Several features of the neck muscles studied appear adaptive to feeding methods. Marked hypertrophy is again shown by the Curlew, connected with the vigorous head movements made in all directions while probing. M. splenius capitis has origin on 3 in this species, and also in the Redshank and Dunlin. Since this modification aids lateral turning of the head, it must be of importance for the frequent pecks to one or other side made by the Redshank, and for the side-to-side movement often sustained over long periods in the "mowing" of Redshanks and "stitching" of Dunlin. The absence of M. complexus origin on 5 in the Redshank is also related to feeding behaviour. Because probing is infrequent, and many prey are taken from water, powerful head extension is unnecessary, and repeated movement of segment I on segment II will not normally be required. This feature is paralleled by many other aquatic feeders (see Table X). The Golden Plover possesses an origin complement typical of inland feeding plovers, which differs from most shore plovers by the inclusion of 4 in the origin of M. complexus and 5 in that of M. rectus capitis superior. This arrangement may be expected to aid maintenance of an erect head and neck carriage for adequate visibility in pasture, and efficient capture of prey in awkward situations among grass.

Systematic Review

As this investigation has concentrated upon the superfamily Charadrioidea, the following review deals chiefly with the families which it comprises. The superfamilies Glareoloidea and Burhinoidea deserve special comment, however, and are also included. Additional information revealed by this study about other superfamilies of the Charadrii is consistent with the findings of Yudin (1965).

Rostratulidae

In the structure of the feeding apparatus, as in many other aspects of its morphology, *Rostratula* shows puzzling features. The extremely simple structure of M. adductor, Part B, resembles that of no other member of the Charadrii, while the reduction of Part A ventral, the unusual path of N. pterygoideus, the dorsally situated retroarticular process and the unique bill are all noteworthy. The lack of M. complexus origin on 6 is a feature seen in many other aquatic feeding waders.

Most recent classifications place this group close to the other Charadrioidea, although egg white protein studies give anomalous results (Sibley, 1960), and the patterns of the downy young strongly suggest affinities with the Jacanoidea (Jehl, 1968a). They obviously deserve continued attention, and detailed studies of feeding behaviour and ecology are most desirable.

Haematopodidae

The unique feeding methods entail exceptionally high environmental forces, reflected in many features of the feeding apparatus. The post-orbital ligament has double attachment to the skull, and the jaw muscles show hypertrophy and increased structural complexity. The large M. depressor and long retroarticular process are of obvious use for opening bivalves by gaping. The tongue is short, owing to the structural reinforcement of the lower jaw, while the neck muscles show hypertrophy and a high total of origin sites.

Haematopus resembles the Charadriidae and Recurvirostridae in the course pursued by N. pterygoideus and in the entirely cartilaginous entoglossum.

Charadriidae

Feeding methods and the feeding apparatus show much uniformity throughout the group, and many remarks about the Golden Plover apply to other members. Most frequent relatively hard substrates. The bill is usually short, and is moderately rhynchokinetic except in *Pluvianellus*. The medial brace and external jugomandibular ligament are present throughout. Features distinguishing them from the Scolopacidae include the path of N. pterygoideus, the usual presence of the Ap. A^1 slip, the invariable absence of the Ap. D slip, and the entirely cartilaginous entoglossum of the great majority.

The affinities of several genera to either this family or the Scolopacidae have been disputed. This study supports the current placement of *Arenaria* and *Aphriza* with the latter. *Phegornis mitchelli* has also caused difficulty (see Seebohm, 1888, Lowe, 1931, and Bock, 1958). Recent work, on skeletal features and downy young, gives strong evidence that it is a plover (Storer, Zusi, personal communications). At my request, Dr. Zusi kindly checked some features in an alcoholic specimen of *Phegornis* at the Smithsonian Institution, Washington, and these are consistent with this conclusion; N. pterygoideus passes through Part O, an Ap. A^1 slip is present, and there is no Ap. D slip. *Peltohyas*, also, should be included with the plovers on the evidence of the present study.

Within the Charadriidae, *Vanellus* comprises a well marked group of species. Distinctive features are the large Ap. A^1 slip and the double origin of M. splenius capitis; and in some species, a lateral mandibular expansion of M. adductor, Part B, and a medial slip of M. pseudotemporalis superficialis (both primitive characters), a forked postorbital ligament, M. hyoglossus obliquus of type 2 and an ossified base to the entoglossum. The small *V. cayanus* lacks all these features and appears convergent with *Charadrius* spp. The larger size of a few species of *Charadrius* (the "plains plovers" of Bock, 1958) and of *Eudromias* and *Pluvialis* is evidently adaptive to the steppe, montano or plains areas which they inhabit for at least part of the year. They also possess a distinctive complement of neck muscle origins (see Table X and remarks concerning the Golden Plover).

Pluvianellus possesses M. hyoglossus obliquus of type 2, and a well developed medial slip on M. pseudotemporalis superficialis. Its most distinctive feature, however, is the highly rhynchokinetic upper jaw. Although the possibility of affinity with *Arenaria* has been suggested (e.g., Bock, 1958, and Jehl, 1968a) the course of N. pterygoideus is through Part O, as in all Charadriidae.

Scolopacidae

Features distinguishing this family from the Charadriidae include the path taken by N. pterygoideus, the frequent presence of an Ap. D slip; and the bony base of the entoglossum. M. hyoglossus obliquus is of type 2 in a few Tringinae and nearly all others, and M. genioglossus is found in a few Tringinae. The external jugomandibular ligament is absent in all but the larger Tringinae, and the medial brace has only been found in *Numenius*.

Many possess highly rhynchokinetic jaws, apparently evolved independently in several lines. The findings of the present investigation suggest two main paths of development in the family. One such pathway is represented by typical Calidridinae, small birds taking much of their prey from the surface of soft substrates. Probing is relatively infrequent in many of these species, but their highly rhynchokinetic jaws may also be of great value for efficient seizing and rapid consumption of small prey – important in view of their extremely high feeding rates. (See Recher, 1966, for further discussion of the relation of body size to prey and feeding methods in waders).

The other evolutionary pathway envisaged is one in which adaptation for shallow water feeding has been important, and it is represented by the Tringinae, Scolopacinae, *Limosa* and *Limnodromus*. Most are medium or large sized birds. Many Tringinae exhibit only moderate rhynchokinesis, and capture active swimming prey. Specialization for probing, seen in the remainder, probably arose as a means of exploiting sedentary prey at the bottoms or edges of shallow water. Early stages in this process are represented by *Xenus* and *Catoptrophorus*, while the peak of specialization is reached by the Scolopacinae. Probers in these groups are highly rhynchokinetic, but their strongly reinforced upper jaws contrast with those of the Calidridinae in which lightness is at a premium.

The subfamilies will now be considered individually:

1. Tringinae

The Redshank typifies well the way of life and structure of most Tringinae. "Mowing" appears to be a feeding technique characteristic of the subfamily, though it is used also by *Gallinago* and *Limosa*. Several smaller species taking mainly small swimming invertebrates show weak jaw musculature, of which a feature is the lack of mandible overlap by M. pseudotemporalis profundus. Larger species taking shrimps, small fish, etc., show hypertrophy of jaw muscles, but a reduced tongue/bill ratio. An exception is *Catoptrophorus* which spends more time probing. As in Redshank and shallow water feeders of other groups, M. complexus lacks origin on 6, and in *Tringa stagnatilis*, even origin on 5 is lost.

Bartramia and *Aechmorhynchus* are puzzling aberrant genera. *Bartramia* feeds on grasslands, but its weak jaw muscles and short tongue contrast with those of plovers, which its habits are said to resemble. The rictus lies far back, suggesting frequent wide mouth opening. Perhaps these features are adaptive to a diet of Orthoptera, which figure prominently in gut analyses. The isolated *Aechmorhynchus* parallels the Calidridinae in several features of jaw and tongue musculature.

2. Arenariinae

The interesting feeding methods of *Arenaria* include vigorous excavation, but not true probing; the possible significance of its highly rhynchokinetic upper jaw has already been mentioned. The external jugomandibular ligament and medial brace are absent, but the jaw muscles are hypertrophied, especially M. depressor, correlating with its use of "gaping". M. biventer cervicis must play an important part in maintaining neck attitude while rolling *Enteromorpha*, and it is noticeably enlarged. M. splenius capitis only has a single origin, despite its importance for stone turning; its concentration near the pivot is probably necessary for rapid upward tilting of the head. *Aphriza* has a moderately rhynchokinetic upper jaw and less hypertrophied musculature. Its feeding habits are apparently less specialized.

The position of the Arenariinae relative to the Tringinae and Calidridinae has been debated by a number of investigators. The present investigation provides no strong evidence of greater affinity one way or the other, though several features recall the Calidridinae – the absence of the caudal slip of M. pseudotemporalis superficialis, the absence of an external jugomandibular ligament, the form of M. hyoglossus obliquus and the insertion of M. stylohoideus, and the size and form of Gl. mandibularis 1. *Arenaria* recalls the Tringinae in the structure of M. adductor externus, while *Aphriza* lacks the highly rhynchokinetic jaw seen in all Calidridinae. However, the rather sparse field accounts of *Aphriza* suggest a way of life more resembling that of the Calidridinae. It is thus of considerable interest that Jehl (1968b) has mustered strong evidence for the close affinity of *Aphriza* with *Calidris canutus* and *C. tenuirostris* (though considering *Arenaria* closer to the Tringinae). Close study of this species, especially in the field, should be most rewarding, and may provide valuable information on factors influencing the evolution of the highly rhynchokinetic upper jaw.

3. Scolopacinae

The Scolopacinae generally resemble *G. gallinago* in their extensive use of probing, and show much uniformity of structure. The Woodcocks (*Scolopax* and *Philohela*) have colonized woodland habitats. Damp feeding areas are chosen, but evidently greater environmental forces have to be overcome than by the Snipe, to judge from the larger cranium and more robust skull, even more complex muscle architecture, and large M. depressor and retroarticular process. By contrast, *Lymnocryptes* is smaller than *Gallinago* spp., and shows moderate convergence with the Calidridinae in its size, lighter bill, and less complex structure of the adductor muscles. The highly developed papillae lining the tip of its upper jaw are noteworthy.

4. Calidridinae

C. alpina typifies this subfamily well, though probing more than most. "Stitching" appears to be a feeding technique largely characteristic of this subfamily. The Ap. D slip is prominent in the great majority; those in which it is vestigial or absent have little in common except moderate or large size compared with the rest. The few in which M. splenius capitis lacks origin on 3 also include the largest species, which are those making least use of rapid side-to-side head movements.

Tryngites shows structural modifications associated with its plover-like habits. The jaw and tongue muscles both show hypertrophy, though the jaw muscles retain the simple structure characteristic of the subfamily. Hypertrophy of salivary glands is striking, presumably a consequence of the arid habitats often frequented. M. complexus has origin on 7, a unique feature in waders, perhaps connected with its characteristic crouching posture. *Limicola* also shows jaw and tongue muscle hypertrophy, with a huge Ap. D slip, complex folding of Ap. M, pinnate M. pseudotemporalis superficialis and massive M. depressor. The bill is larger and more strongly reinforced than in *Calidris*. These features show some convergence with the Scolopacinae, perhaps in adaptation to feeding on larger prey, but have been modified from features highly characteristic of the Calidridinae. *Micropalama* closely resembles *Calidris* in jaw muscle structure, and the light construction of its distinctively shaped bill. It appears ill adapted to even moderate environmental forces, but most probing is into very soft, water covered mud. M. rectus capitis superior shows loss of origin on 4, evidently connected with feeding habits.

The association in several classifications between *Micropalama* and *Limnodromus* appears to rest on external characters and some superficial similarity of feeding behaviour. The internal morphology of the feeding apparatus, however, differs extensively, and the similarity is a case of moderate convergence. It should be clear from the preceding descriptions that *Limosa* and *Limnodromus* are sharply dissimilar to the other Calidridinae in many important features of the feeding apparatus. They appear to have evolved along quite a distinct path from the typical Calidridinae, and the evidence of this study suggests strongly that they should be separated from them. Kozlova (1961–62) came to similar conclusions, and revived the Limosinae of earlier workers to accommodate *Numenius*, *Limosa* and *Limnodromus*. *Numenius* certainly shows strong affinities with *Limosa*, but the present study equally supports its association with the Tringinae; it might therefore be simpler to place at least *Numenius* and *Limosa* in the Tringinae. (Jehl, 1968a, suggests this, but proposes dividing the Tringinae into three tribes.)

Lowe (1931) believed that *Limnodromus* should be placed with the Scolopacinae. Few subsequent workers have followed this proposal, but it has recently received strong support from Jehl's work (1968a). The present study confirms the great resemblance between the two groups, but also shows a number of distinct similarities between *Limosa* and *Limnodromus*. Thus, the pattern of minor raphes and branches of aponeuroses revealed in section (Plate 24) shows distinct likenesses. Both *Limosa* and *Limnodromus* have a band of fibres diverging from the dorsal rostral edge of M. adductor, Part A, ventral, and overlapping Part A dorsal – a feature confined to these two genera. The Ap. D slip in both arises from its usual site on the otic process of the quadrate. The proportionate length of the basihyal in *Limnodromus* is much greater than in the Scolopacinae, and the general form of the hyoid resembles *Limosa* (Plate 30).

The resemblance between *Limnodromus* and the Scolopacinae is nevertheless striking. Apart from skull morphology, the jaw muscles show such similarities as a multipinnate arrangement of the dorsal fibres of M. adductor, based on Aps. A^1 and D, dorsally pinnate M. pseudotemporalis superficialis, short narrow M. pseudotemporalis profundus and huge M. protractor. (The latter feature is probably a consequence of changes in skull form – see under M. protractor.) *Limnodromus* is Snipe-like in feeding behaviour, and shows little resemblance to Godwits in this respect. Perhaps *Limnodromus* is best regarded as a rather conservative genus within the Scolopacinae, retaining features which indicate their close affinity to the Tringinae, and perhaps especially to *Limosa*.

Phalaropodidae

The phalaropes have been associated with the Recurvirostridae in several schemes of classification, but differ from them and resemble the Scolopacidae, in the path of N. pterygoideus and the bony base of the entoglossum. The upper jaw is moderately rhynchokinetic. Prey are small, and feeding movements are confined to pecks into the water surface. The jaw muscles are correspondingly weak, with M. adductor of very simple structure, M. pseudotemporalis profundus lacking any mandible overlap, and M. pseudotemporalis superficialis lacking a caudal extension. M. complexus lacks origin on 6 in *Phalaropus* and *Lobipes*, and M. rectus capitis ventralis is very weakly attached to 6. Gl. mandibularis 1 is prominent, despite the aquatic habits, and is evidently important for the action of the well-developed tongue.

Recurvirostridae

The Recurvirostridae resemble the Charadriidae in the path of N. pterygoideus, the presence of the Ap. A^1 slip, and the entirely cartilaginous entoglossum. *Himantopus* appears highly adapted for rapid jaw action; velocity ratio is high, the bill light and tapered, and the adductors bulky enough to ensure adequate acceleration and grip. *Recurvirostra* has a bill form adapted to gathering large numbers of small organisms in a short time from mud or water surfaces. Hypertrophy of M. protractor and the quadrate and of M. depressor and the retroarticular process aid frequently repeated bill opening in water or mud, despite increased resistance due to the flattened bill form. *Ibidorhyncha* has a sharply decurved bill, evidently used for capturing aquatic prey among pebbles. Though it is said sometimes to probe, it is unlikely that the decurvature is exploited as in *Numenius*, since the musculature, though well developed, shows no comparable hypertrophy.

Gl. mandibularis 1 is absent in all three, correlating with the aquatic habits and the short tongue necessitated by the structure of the jaws. M. complexus lacks origin on 6 as in other shallow water feeders, but the importance of lateral head movement is indicated by M. splenius capitis origin on 3.

Glareoloidea

Peters includes *Peltohyas australis* in this superfamily, following Lowe (1931). This course of action has been questioned by several later workers, and Bock (1964b) produces considerable evidence for its inclusion in the Charadriidae. On the other hand, Jehl (1968a) finds further evidence for its retention in the Glareoloidea. The present study supports Bock's recommendation, since the insertion of

M. pseudotemporalis superficialis is single and lies above N. ramus mandibularis, a condition only found in the Charadrioidea.

Peltohyas, nevertheless, shows interesting features. M. pterygoideus shows two lines of division, the posterior one being penetrated by N. pterygoideus (Plate 22), suggesting an intermediate condition in the change from the arrangement found in most Charadrii (including the Glareoloidea) to that found in the Charadriidae. *Peltohyas* also possesses M. genioglossus, which has been found in no other plover.

Yudin (1965) suggests that *Pluvianus* may not be a member of the Charadriiformes at all. The present study neither supports nor weakens this suggestion in the absence of detailed information on the feeding apparatus of other orders. The jaw muscles generally resemble those of the other Glareoloidea examined, though the Ap. A^1 slip and the medial slip of M. pseudotemporalis superficialis are better developed.

Burhinoidea

Yudin (1965) considers that this group should be returned to a position near the Otididae (Gruiformes). It is the only other superfamily investigated in which the relation of N. pterygoideus to M. pterygoideus is the same as in some Charadrioidea (Haematopodidae, Charadriidae and Recurvirostridae). This feature is probably of little taxonomic relevance in this case, however, since it is the ordinal status of the Burhinoidea which is in dispute.

Discussion

The descriptions which have been presented in this account reveal in detail the extent of morphological diversity in the feeding apparatus of the waders and studies of feeding behaviour have given insight into the adaptive value of many features. We may now examine the implications of these findings for an understanding of the process of adaptation, and point out some of the problems that remain.

Attempts to explain morphological features purely in adaptive terms are hazardous; the evolutionary history of the species or group under review must also be taken into account. A valuable theoretical background to this type of problem is provided by Bock (1959, 1963, 1965, 1967) and Bock & Von Wahlert (1965). In this investigation, the problem has been attacked by examining as wide a range of species as possible. By doing so it becomes possible to recognize in many cases the influence of phylogenetic factors. Thus, in the Golden Plover, M. pterygoideus, Part O, is penetrated by N. pterygoideus, while in the other four representative species the nerve passes between Parts M and O. It seems unlikely, however, that comparisons between these five species alone would ever shed much light on this puzzling difference when it is considered that the Golden Plover resembles in this respect all other Charadriidae, as well as the Haematopodidae and Recurvirostridae – groups containing species of very diverse structure and habits. Probably this feature arose early in the history of these groups, and has been integrated successfully into subsequent modifications.

This comparative approach is particularly valuable in dealing with cases of convergence. Thus the Snipe-like external characters of *Limicola* have in the past led to conjecture about its possible relationships with the Scolopacinae. The structure of its jaw muscles, however, shows clearly that it belongs among the Calidridinae; the extra strength required to utilize its large probing bill is obtained by hypertrophy of characteristic features of its subfamily, notably the prominent Ap. D slip. Plover-like members of the Scolopacinae such as *Tryngites*, *Bartramia*, *Arenaria* and *Aphriza* provide further examples.

The evolution of the highly rhynchokinetic upper jaw provides further insight into the relation between adaptive and historical factors. This feature has appeared independently in at least seven lines represented among present-day Charadrioidea, five of them among the Scolopacidae. A further knowledge of the evolutionary history of the Charadrioidea might well reveal more, even among existing species. Thus, if Jehl (1968b) is correct in believing *Aphriza*, *Calidris canutus* and *C. tenuirostris* to be closely related, then the highly rhynchokinetic jaws of the two latter species presumably arose independently of the same feature in other *Calidris* species. This type of situation has been discussed by Bock (1963), who points out that many apparently homologous structures probably arose independently, but within groups possessing a high degree of common genetic potential.*

* Similar structures arising independently, e.g., by parallelism or convergence, would usually be termed analogous. Bock suggests that this term should be used only to denote lack of common origin, without any implications of morphological similarity. He also proposes that the term "homology" should be redefined to allow origin from a group with similar genetic potential to stand as the criterion, rather than origin from a single ancestral species, but points out that a consequence of this would be to remove the present sharp boundary between homology and analogy.

In the Charadrioidea, this genetic potential is at least partly manifested in the moderate rhynchokinesis shown by less specialized genera, and in their general dependence on open marshy or coastal habitats. Closer analysis indicates that the adaptive factors which have evoked the appearance of highly rhynchokinetic jaws differ somewhat in each of the seven lines. Jaws of this type may be regarded as broadly adaptive to any type of feeding which would be facilitated by independent movement of the tip; within this broad category, other factors have played a part. Thus, a highly rhynchokinetic upper jaw is advantageous for probing, since it reduces the length of culmen to be moved against resistance; and it also permits delicate manipulation at the bill tip, facilitating the capture of difficult prey, or large numbers of prey in a short time. It has appeared in adaptation to circumstances requiring different combinations of these factors, falling roughly into two sub-categories – moderate or large birds, probing near or under water, and small birds feeding very rapidly from the mud surface, and occasionally probing just below it.

The value in taxonomy of feeding apparatus characters deserves some general appraisal in the light of this study. The jaw muscles are of special interest, owing to attempts which have been made by previous workers to derive taxonomic or phylogenetic characters from them. The most ambitious of these attempts, that of Beecher (1953), has been severely criticized by Mayr (1955).

The findings of this investigation bear out the need for caution urged by Mayr. It has been possible to recognize the aponeuroses found by Zusi (1962) in four Lari throughout a wide range of Charadrii, and it seems likely that they are present in many other orders. Since these aponeuroses are the basis for the main patterns of pinnate fibre arrangement, it is clear that similar patterns may emerge independently. Thus the pinnate slip on the medial side of M. adductor described in the lark *Eremophila* by Bock (1960b) conforms very closely in situation and structure with the Ap. D slip of many waders.

There is reason, nevertheless, to hope that jaw muscle characters may achieve some taxonomic usefulness on a more modest scale. Starck (1959) has discussed their value for this purpose, and concludes that taxonomic information may be obtained from the jaw musculature, but that much more detailed structural analysis is required than was undertaken by Beecher. In particular, he recommends close attention to innervation. The present study bears out his views. In addition to the presence or absence of pinnate structures such as Aps. A^1 and D, the detailed relations of aponeuroses seen in section, and the relationships of nerves to muscles have been found useful. Features such as the development of the external temporal region of M. adductor, the presence of attachment to the post-orbital process, and the caudal extensions and medial slips of M. pseudotemporalis superficialis may also be helpful, and have been utilized with some success by Yudin (1965) in a general survey of the Charadriiformes.

The remaining systems investigated have received less taxonomic attention with such exceptions as the studies of Sushkin (1927) and Mudge (1903). Certainly, adaptive factors account for many of the modifications of these systems in waders. Some features of tongue anatomy appear useful, such as the presence or absence of bone in the entoglossum; a better understanding of the functional significance of this feature would aid in assessing its taxonomic value. The slips of origin of neck muscles would provide easily scored characters, but whether taxonomic meanings could be discerned from them is doubtful. Those investigated here showed a good deal of intraspecific variation, and clear evidence of strong adaptive influence. Considered as a whole, however, the tongue, salivary glands and neck muscles provide a further insight into feeding adaptations which may well help in reaching correct taxonomic conclusions.

The complex interdependence of modifications adaptive to a particular mode of feeding have been shown very clearly by such studies as those of Bowman (1961) and Zusi (1962). This account provides numerous further instances. Interdependence of adaptations complicates the task of interpreting them, and it is therefore desirable to study as many as possible of the systems directly involved in feeding. The value of this approach may be illustrated by reference to the Curlew. The long bill of this bird is often used for probing in the firm soil of pastures, and thus requires considerable structural reinforcement. This has the effect of largely occluding the bill lumen, and only a short tongue can therefore be accommodated. Gl. mandibularis 1 which provides lubrication for tongue action is consequently reduced. The short tongue and tough substrates prevent prey from being consumed during the course of a probe as in the Snipe; instead they are first extracted, by repeated probing with changes of orientation, aided by bill decurvature. This in turn results in neck muscle hypertrophy, and is also another factor requiring skull and bill reinforcement. The extent of bony reinforcement is minimized by the support given by the jaw muscles, and therefore these also require hypertrophy. The great length of the bill reduces the mechanical advantage of the muscles attached to it, but, increases its capacity for rapid action. This seems to be an advantage, since the retroarticular process remains short although M. depressor is enlarged. Probably this attribute offsets another disadvantage of the long bill and short tongue – the difficulty of moving prey from the bill tip to the mouth.

In conclusion, some important problems which still require investigation may be mentioned. Intraspecific variation (see Berger, 1956) has been encountered in many species, and in all of the systems studied. The possible evolutionary importance of these variations is difficult to assess at present. It would be interesting, for example, to see whether structural variants of M. adductor in Snipe or Curlew showed any correlation with dimensional or other features in a long series of specimens. Body size, only briefly touched on here, is of great importance to a full understanding of the process of adaptation. It will influence morphological features both mechanically and ecologically. The mechanical effects stem from the fact that the strength of components is proportional to their cross-sectional area, and hence increases as the square of linear dimensions, while weight (dependent on volume) increases as the cube. Therefore, proportionally thicker bones and hypertrophied muscles are to be expected in larger species. Since such adjustments add further to weight, they will be progressively less effective as size increases. The adoption of multipinnate muscle structure where feasible would be one way of overcoming this self-defeating process, and this may provide some explanation of the tendency noted in this study for small waders to show not only less bulky jaw muscles than large species, but often simpler ones as well.

Ecologically, also, body size imposes important restrictions, and not merely on the size of prey which can be taken. Since small birds have in general a higher rate of metabolism than larger ones, their rate of food intake must be proportionately higher. Consequently, they can most effectively exploit prey which is not only small, but abundant and easily accessible, so that it can be consumed rapidly and without prolonged searching. Some information on the effects of such limitations on shore feeding waders is given by Recher (1966), but scope remains for extensive investigation of this problem.

Finally, morphological differences between species competing ecologically deserve attention. Where waders are concerned, studies of competition for such major foods as *Hydrobia* and *Nereis* should produce interesting results. Some information of this kind has been obtained in the course of the present study, and will form the basis of future papers.

Summary

1. The thesis presents detailed information on the anatomy of the feeding apparatus in the Charadrii, and assesses, as far as possible, the adaptive significance of its modifications. This assessment has been aided by studies of feeding behaviour, and the results of these studies are also presented. Throughout, emphasis is on the superfamily Charadrioidea, and especially on five species – Golden Plover, Redshank, Curlew, Dunlin and Common Snipe.

2. Feeding methods of the five representative species are described in detail, and the results of analyses of stomach contents are given. Golden Plovers feed on pasture, taking prey at or near the surface; feeding rates are low, but feeding behaviour is characterized by frequent swift runs. Redshanks feed inland or on the shore, often while wading in shallow pools. The majority of feeding actions are surface pecks, but prolonged "sweeping" movements across the mud surface with rapidly vibrating mandible are often used, and swift, brief, probes also occur. Curlews feed on shore and pasture. Feeding actions include pecks, test probes, and deep, vigorous probes with many changes of bill orientation. Film sequences are described which shed light particularly on upper jaw movements. Dunlins use surface pecks, short quivering probes, and extremely rapid series of test probes ("stitching"); very high feeding rates may be achieved. Snipes rely almost entirely on probing in soft substrates. Probes may be prolonged, but involve little reorientation of the bill. Manipulative use of the upper jaw by a captive specimen is described.

3. Information available on the feeding methods of other Charadrioidea is summarized.

4. Materials and methods used in the anatomical investigations are described, and the specimens dissected are listed; there are 311 of these, representing 118 species.

5. Environmental forces acting on the skull and jaws, especially during probing, are analysed. Cranial kinesis is reviewed, and the occurrence and functions of various types are discussed. The movements of the lower jaw, and their relation to those of the upper are examined. Trends in the orientation of the bill axis relative to the cranium, and the principal modifications of bill form are reviewed. Seven ligaments of the skull are described; presence or absence of L. jugomandibulare externus is the most significant variation.

6. Detailed descriptions of jaw musculature are given, and the actions of muscles and their components are discussed. M. adductor externus is of complex structure, and exhibits numerous modifications in the siting and architecture of its constituent parts; the presence or absence of two bipinnate slips are of particular interest. M. pseudotemporalis superficialis varies in extent of pinnate structure, and the presence or absence of a lateral caudal extension. M. pseudotemporalis profundus is of simple structure in most species. M. pterygoideus exhibits two alternative structural types in relation to the point of entry of N. pterygoideus, and also some variations in architecture. M. protractor is parallel fibred, but varies considerably in size. M. depressor also varies in relative bulk, and may possess raphes arising in three distinct situations.

7. The hyoid skeleton is described; variations in the relative extent of bone and cartilage in the entoglossum are of special interest. The length of the tongue relative to that of the bill is considered, and the relevance of this relationship to feeding methods is examined.

The hyoid muscles are described and their actions analysed. Principal variations are the position of insertion of M. stylohoideus, the extent of fusion between right and left M. hyoglossi obliqui, and the presence or absence of M. hyoglossus anterior, M. hyoglossus medialis and M. genioglossus.

8. Epidermal papillae are found on the palate, lining the upper jaw, at the base of the tongue and at the posterior end of the larynx. Variations in their density and siting are described and discussed.

Four paired and one median salivary glands are commonly present. Of these, Gl. palatinae is absent in many species and Gl. mandibularis 1 in a few. Considerable variations in the relative size of the paired glands are encountered among the species examined. These variations are examined in relation to prey and feeding methods.

9. Six cervical muscles (not including dermal muscles) inserting on the skull are described, and their actions discussed. M. complexus, M. splenius capitis and M. rectus capitis superior show significant variations in the number and siting of slips of origin.

10. Structural modifications of the feeding apparatus in Charadrii of other superfamilies are reviewed. A particularly interesting feature of the jaw musculature is the structure of M. pseudotemporalis superficialis, and especially its sites of insertion relative to N. ramus mandibularis. Of the two structural types of M. pterygoideus, one occurs only in the Burhinoidea, with an intermediate condition in *Peltohyas*. Most variations in tongue structure have counterparts among the Charadrioidea, with the exception of the unusual condition of M. hyoglossus medialis in the Thinocoroidea. Variations in occurrence and development of salivary glands are mentioned. Numbers and sites of origins for cervical muscles inserting on the skull are tabulated with those for the Charadrioidea.

11. Adaptive features in the representative species are surveyed. The upper jaw is highly rhynchokinetic in Curlew, Snipe and Dunlin, and strongly reinforced in the first two. Jaw muscles are well developed, but relatively unspecialized in Golden Plover. Those attached to the mandible have a high mechanical advantage owing to the relatively short bill, an arrangement combining power and manœuvrability. They are also well developed in Redshank with some additional structural complexity seen also in other large Tringinae, ensuring power to deal with relatively large prey despite a lower mechanical advantage. They are basically similar in Curlew, but much hypertrophied, compensating for bill length, and providing power for resisting environmental forces. The adductors are simple and reduced in Dunlin, though the Ap. D slip is prominent. M. protractor and M. depressor are well developed, reflecting their use during probing. The latter features are greatly emphasized in the predominantly probing Snipe. Skull morphology in the latter reduces the space available for the adductors, and sufficient power for prey up to large earthworm size is ensured by intricate pinnate structure.

The tongue musculature is similar in Golden Plover, Redshank and Curlew. M. hyoglossus obliquus is of type 2, and M. stylohyoideus enlarged in Snipe and

Dunlin, reflecting use of the tongue during probing in conjunction with the highly rhynchokinetic upper jaw. By contrast the tongue is very short in the Curlew, probably on account of the bony reinforcement of the jaws; this necessitates removal of prey before consumption. The salivary glands appear most prominent in Dunlin, especially Gl. mandibularis 1 which may be important for tongue action. They are reduced in the Snipe which obtains slimy food in wet substrates. The neck muscles show a complement of origin slips in the Golden Plover resembling that of other pasture feeding plovers, presumably adaptive to foraging among grass. The Redshank has an abbreviated M. complexus like many other waders which feed extensively in shallow water. The neck muscles of the Curlew show much hypertrophy adaptive to its vigorous probing techniques.

12. Remaining species of Charadrii are surveyed from adaptive and taxonomic view points. Points of special importance include the anomalous features of *Rostratula;* evidence supporting the assignment of *Pluvianellus* and *Phegornis* to the Charadriidae and *Aphriza* and *Arenaria* to the Scolopacidae; factors affecting the evolution of the highly rhynchokinetic upper jaw in the Scolopacidae; the subfamilial affinities of several genera of Scolopacidae; the affinities of the Phalaropodidae; and the systematic position of *Peltohyas.*

13. The problem of discriminating between adaptive and phylogenetic aspects of morphological features is discussed. Examples of convergence, and of the independent origin of similar features among waders are examined. An assessment is made of the taxonomic value of the various features investigated. The extent of interdependence between the adaptations studied is illustrated. Outstanding problems are pointed out.

References

Alexander, R. McN. 1968. *Animal Mechanics.* London.

American Ornithologists' Union. 1957. *The A.O.U. Check-list of North American Birds.* 5th Ed. Baltimore.

Antony, M. 1920. Uber die Speicheldrusen der Vogel. *Zool. Jb. Abt. Anat. u. Out. der Tiere,* **41** : 545–660.

Barnikol, A. 1951. Uber einige Gesetzmassigkeiten im Aufbau der motorischen Trigeminusäste bei Vögeln. *Anat. Anz.,* **98** : 217–223.

——— 1953a. Zur Morphologie des Nervus trigeminus der Vogel unter besonderer Berucksichtigung der Accipitres, Cathartidae, Striges und Anseriformes. *Z. wiss. Zool.,* **157** : 285–332.

——— 1953b. Vergleichend anatomische und taxonomisch phylogenetisch Studien am Kopf der Opisthocomiformes, Musophagidae, Galli, Columbae und Cuouli. Ein Beitrag zum *Opisthocomus* Problem. *Zool. Jb., Abt. Syst., Ok. u. Geog. der Tiere.,* **81** : 488–526.

Beecher, W. J. 1953. A phylogeny of the oscines. *Auk,* **70** : 270–333.

——— 1962. The bio-mechanics of the bird skull. *Bull. Chicago Acad. Sci.,* **11** : 10–33.

Bent, A. C. 1927. Life histories of North American Shore Birds. Part I. *Bull. U.S. natn. Mus.,* **142** : ix + 420 pp.

——— 1929. Life histories of North American Shore Birds. Part II. *Bull. U.S. natn. Mus.,* **146** : ix + 412 pp.

Berger, A. J. 1956. Anatomical variation and avian anatomy. *Condor,* **58** : 433–441

Beven, G. 1946 Food washing of Whimbrel. *Br. Birds.,* **39** : 249–250.

Boas, J. E. V. 1929. Biologisch-anatomische Studien uber den Hals der Vogel. *K. danske Vidensk. Selsk. Skr., Naturvidenskab. Math. Afdel.,* Ser. 9, **1** : 102–222.

Bock, W. J. 1958. A generic review of the plovers (Charadriinae, Aves). *Bull. Mus. comp. Zool. Harv.,* **118** : 27–97.

——— 1959. Preadaptation and multiple evolutionary pathways. *Evolution,* **13** : 194–211.

——— 1960a. Secondary articulation of the avian mandible. *Auk,* **77** : 19–55.

——— 1960b. The palatine process of the premaxilla in the Passeres. *Bull. Mus. comp. Zool. Harv.,* **122** : 361–488.

——— 1963. Evolution and phylogeny in morphologically uniform groups. *Am. Nat.,* **97** : 265–285.

——— 1964a. Kinetics of the avian skull. *J. Morph.,* **114** : 1–41.

——— 1964b. The systematic position of the Australian Dotterel, *Peltohyas australis.* Emu, **63** : 383–403.

——— 1965. The role of adaptive mechanisms in the origin of higher levels of organization. *Syst. Zool.,* **14** : 272–287.

——— 1966. An approach to the functional analysis of bill shape. *Auk,* **83** : 10–51.

——— 1967. The use of adaptive characters in avian classification. *Proc. XIV. Int. Orn. Cong.,* pp. 61–74.

——— & Von Wahlert, G. 1965. Adaptation and the form-function complex. *Evolution,* **19** : 269–299.

Bowman, R. I. 1961. Morphological Differentiation and Adaptation in the Galapagos finches. *Univ. Calif. Publs. Zool.,* **58** : vii + 326 pp.

Browne, P. W. P. 1952. Food and habitat of Jack Snipe. *Br. Birds,* **45**: 222–223.
Cholodkowsky, N. 1892. Zur Kenntnis der Speicheldrusen der Vogel. *Zool. Anz.,* **15**: 205–254.
Crawshay, R. 1907. *The birds of Tierra del Fuego.* London, xl + 158 pp.
Dewar, J. M. 1908. Notes on the Oystercatcher (*Haematopus ostralegus*) with reference to its habit of feeding on the mussel (*Mytilus edulis*). *Zoologist,* **12**: 201–212.
——— **1909.** Notes on the feeding behaviour of the Dunlin (*Tringa alpina*). *Zoologist,* **13**: 1–14.
——— **1910.** A preliminary note on the manner in which the Oystercatcher (*Haematopus ostralegus*) attacks the purple shell (*Purpurus lapillus*). *Zoologist,* **14**: 109–112.
——— **1913.** Further observations on the feeding habits of the Oystercatcher (*Haematopus ostralegus*). *Zoologist,* **17**: 41–56.
——— **1915.** The relation of the Oystercatcher to its natural environment. *Zoologist,* **19**: 281–291.
Dittberner, W. 1966. Zum Nahrungserwerb des Grunschenkels (*Tringa nebularia L.*). *Beitr. Vogelk.* **12**: 209–211.
Drinnan, R. E. 1957. The winter feeding of the Oystercatcher (*Haematopus ostralegus*) on the cockle (*Cardium edule*). *J. Anim. Ecol.,* **26**: 441–469.
——— **1958a.** Winter feeding of the Oystercatcher on the edible mussel in the Conway estuary. *Fishery Invest., London,* Ser. 2, **22**: 1–15.
——— **1958b.** Observations on the feeding of the Oystercatcher in captivity. *Br. Birds,* **51**: 139–149.
Edgeworth, F. H. 1935. *The Cranial Muscles of Vertebrates.* Cambridge.
Ehlert, W. 1964. Zur Okologie und Biologie der Ernahrung einiger Limikolen – Arten. *J. Orn.,* **105**: 1–53.
Engels, W. L. 1938. Tongue musculature of passerine birds. *Auk.,* **55**: 642–650.
Fallet, M. 1962. Uber Bodenvogel und ihre terricolen Beutetiere. Technik der Nahrungssuch – Population dynamik. *Zool. Anz.,* **168**: 187–212.
Farner, D. S. 1960. Digestion and the Digestive System. In *Biology and Comparative Physiology of Birds,* Vol. I, edited by A. J. Marshall. London, xii + 518 pp.
Feare, C. J. 1966. The winter feeding of the Purple Sandpiper. *Br. Birds,* **59**: 165–179.
Feninger, O. 1937. *Anatomische und funktionelle Untersuchungen an Schädeln der Limicolae.* Unpubl. diss., Vienna.
Fenton, J. T. 1953. Curlew eating winkles. *Br. Birds,* **46**: 410.
Fiedler, W. 1951. Beitrage zur Morphologie der Kiefermuskulatur des Oscines. *Zool. Jb. Abt. Anat. u. Opt. Tier,* **71**: 235–288.
Fisher, H. I. 1955. Some aspects of the kinetics in the jaws of birds. *Wilson Bull.,* **67**: 175–188.
——— **& Goodman, D. C. 1955a.** An apparatus for measuring kinesis in avian skulls. *Wilson Bull.,* **67**: 18–24.
——— **& Goodman, D. C. 1955b.** The myology of the Whooping Crane, *Grus americana. Illinois biol. Monogr.,* **24 (2)**: 127 pp.
Fürbringer, M. 1922. Das Zungenbein der Wirbelthiere insbesondere der Reptilien und Vogel. *Abh. heidelb. Akad. Wiss.,* Abt. ii, xii + 164 pp.
Gadow, H. & Selenka, E. 1891. Aves. In Bronn's *Klassen und Ordnungen des Thier-Reichs, in Wort und Bild.,* Vol. 6, Leipzig.
Gans, C. & Bock, W. J. 1965. The functional significance of muscle architecture, a theoretical analysis. *Ergebn. Anat. EntwGesch.,* **38**: 115–142.
George, J. C. & Berger, A. J. 1966. *Avian myology.* London & N. York.

Gibb, J. 1956. Food, feeding habits and territory of the Rock Pipit, *Anthus spinoletta*. *Ibis*, **98**: 506–530.

Goodall, J. D., Johnson, A. W. & Phillippi, R. A. 1951. *Las aves de Chile.* Buenos Aires.

Goodman, D. C. & Fisher, H. I. 1962. *Functional anatomy of the feeding apparatus in waterfowl.* Carbondale, Illinois.

Goss-Custard, J. D. 1967. The winter predation of *Corophium volutator* by Redshank (abstract). *Ibis*, **109**: 475.

Greenway, J. C. 1958. *Extinct and vanishing birds of the world.* American Committee for International Wildlife Protection, Special Publication No. 13, New York.

Greschik, E. 1913. Histologische untersuchungen der Unterkieferdruse (*Glandula mandibularis*) der Vogel. Ein Betrag zur Kenntnis der Mucinbildung. *Aquila*, **20**: 331–374.

Hartley, P. H. T. 1948. The assessment of the food of birds. *Ibis*, **90**: 361–381.

Heppner, F. 1965. Sensory mechanisms and environmental clues used by the American Robin in locating earthworms. *Condor*, **67**: 247–256.

Hofer, H. 1950. Zur Morphologie der Kiefermuskulatur der Vogel. *Zool. Jb., Abt. Anat. u. Ont. der Tiere*, **70**: 427–600.

Holmes, R. T. 1966. Feeding ecology of the red-backed sandpiper (*Calidris alpina*) in Arctic Alaska. *Ecology*, **47**: 32–45.

Holting, H. 1912. *Uber den mikroskopischen Bau der Speicheldrusen einiger Vogel.* Inaug. Diss., Giessen, 39 pp., Hanover.

Jehl, J. R. 1968a. Relationships in the Charadrii (shorebirds) : a taxonomic study based on colour patterns of the downy young. *Mem. San Diego Soc. Nat. Hist.*, 3, 54 pp.

——— **1968b.** The systematic position of the surfbird, *Aphriza virgata*. *Condor*, **70**: 206–210.

Johnson, A. W. 1964. Notes on Mitchell's plover *Phegornis mitchellii*. *Ibis*, **106**: 249–251.

Jollie, M. 1957. The head skeleton of the chicken and remarks on the anatomy of this region in other birds. *J. Morph.*, **100**: 389–436.

Kautz, H. 1931. *Die Muskulatur der Vogelzunge.* Unpubl. diss., Vienna.

Kobayashi, H. 1954. Observations of the Painted-Snipe *Rostratula bengalensis* (1), *Tori*, **13 (64)**: 31–39. In Japanese.

Kozlova, E. V. 1961. (Waders). *Fauna SSSR. Nov. Ser.*, 80, Moscow-Leningrad. In Russian.

——— **1962.** (Waders). *Fauna SSSR. Nov. Ser.* 81, Moscow-Leningrad. In Russian.

Lakjer, T. 1926. *Studien uber die Trigeminus-versorgte Kaumuskulatur de Sauropsiden.* Copenhagen.

Larson, S. 1957. The suborder Charadrii in Arctic and Boreal areas during the Tertiary and Pleistocene. A zoogeographic study. *Acta vertebr.*, **1**: 1–84.

Lebedinsky, N. G. 1918. Untersuchungen zur Morphologie und Entwicklungs geschichte der Unterkiefers der Vogel. *Revue suisse Zool.*, **26**: 129–146.

——— **1920.** Beiträge zur Morphologie und Entwicklungsgeschichte des Unterkiefers der Võgel. *Verh. naturf. Ges Basel.*, **31**: 39–112.

——— **1921.** Zur syndesmologie der Vogel. *Anat. Anz.*, **54**: 8–15.

Lowe, P. R. 1931. An anatomical review of the "waders" (Telmatomorphae), with special reference to the families, subfamilies and genera within the suborders Limicolae, Grui-Limicolae and Lari-Limicolae. *Ibis*, 721–771.

Marinelli, W. 1928. Uber den Schadel der Sohnepfe. Versuch einer funktionellen Analyse des Kieferapparats. *Palaeobiologica*, **1**: 135–160.

Mayr, E. 1955. Comments on some recent studies of song bird phylogeny. *Wilson Bull.*, **67**: 33–44.

Milne, B. S. 1956. A report on the bird population of Beddington Sewage Farm, 1954–55. *London Bird Report*, **20**: 39–54.

Moller, W. 1931. Uber die Schnabel-und Zungenmechanik blutenbesuchender Vogel. II. *Biol. Gen.*, **7**: 99–154.

Mudge, G. P. 1903. On the myology of the tongue of parrots with a classification of the order, based upon the structure of the tongue. *Trans. zool. Soc. London*, **16**: 211–278.

Norton-Griffiths, M. 1967. Some ecological aspects of the feeding behaviour of the Oystercatcher *Haematopus ostralegus* on the edible mussel *Mytilus edulis*. *Ibis*, **109**: 412–424.

Peters, J. L. 1934. *Check-list of Birds of the World.* Vol. 2. Cambridge, Mass.

Recher, H. F. 1966. Some aspects of the ecology of migrant shorebirds. *Ecology*, **47**: 393–407.

Säve-Söderbergh, G. 1944. Notes on the Trigeminal musculature in Non-Mammalian tetrapods. *Nova Acta R. Soc. Scient. upsal.*, Ser. 4, 13.

Schumacher, S. 1929. Zur mechanik und verwendungsart des Schnepfenschabels. *Z. f. Morphol. u. Okol. d. Tiere.*, **15**: 90–108.

Seebohm, H. 1888. *The geographical distribution of the family Charadriidae, or the plovers, sandpipers, snipes and their allies.* London.

Sibley, C. G. 1960. The electrophoretic patterns of avian egg-white proteins as taxonomic characters. *Ibis*, **102**: 215–284.

Simmons, K. E. L. 1951. Feeding habits of the Greenshank. *Br. Birds*, **44**: 179.

——— 1961. Foot-movements in plovers and other birds. *Br. Birds*, **54**: 34–39.

Simonetta, A. M. 1963. Cinesie morfologia del cranio negli uccelli non passeriformi. Studio su varie tandenze evolutive. Parte Ia *Archo. zool. ital.*, **48**: 53–135.

Simpson, G. G. 1953. *The Major Features of Evolution.* Columbia, New York.

Sims, R. W. 1955. The morphology of the head of the hawfinch. (*Coccothraustes coccothraustes.*) *Bull. Br. Mus. nat. Hist.* (Zool.), **2**: 369–393.

Spencer, K. G. 1953. *The Lapwing in Britain. Some account of its distribution and behaviour, and of its role in dialect, folk lore and literature.* London and Hull.

Sperry, C. C. 1940. Food habits of a group of shorebirds, woodcock, snipe, knot and dowitcher. *Wildl. Res. Bull.*, **1**: 1–37.

Spring, L. W. 1965. Climbing and pecking adaptations in some North American woodpeckers. *Condor*, **67**: 457–488.

Starck, D. 1959. Neuere Ergebnisse der vergleichenden Anatomie und ihre Bedeutung fur die Taxonomie erlautert an der Trigeminus-Muskulatur der Vogel. *J. Orn.*, **100**: 47–59.

——— & Barnikol, A. 1954. Beitrage zur Morphologie der Trigeminus muskulatur der Vogel (besonders der Accipitres, Cathartidae, Striges und Anseres). *Morphol. Jb.*, **94**: 1–64.

Stout, G. D. (editor). 1967. *The shorebirds of North America.* New York.

Streefkerk, C. J. 1960. *Verslag van het vergelijkend onderzoek naar de wijze van voedsel zoeken van enige soorten steltlopers.* Uitgegeven door de Christelijke Jeugdbond van Natuurvrienden. Amsterdam.

Sushkin, P. P. 1927. On the anatomy and classification of the Weaver-birds. *Bull. Amer. Mus. nat. Hist.*, **57**: 1–32.

Thomson, A. L. (editor). 1964. *A New Dictionary of Birds.* London and New York.

Tinbergen, N. & Norton-Griffiths, M. 1964. Oystercatchers and Mussels. *Br. Birds*, **57**: 64–70.

Tomkins, I. R. 1947. The Oystercatcher of the Atlantic coast of North America and its relation to Oysters. *Wilson Bull.*, **59**: 204–208.

Van der Klaaim, C. J. 1963. Projections, deepenings and undulations of the surface of the skull in relation to the attachment of muscles. *Verh. K. ned. Akad. Wet. Afd. natuurkunde.* 2 reeks, **55**: 246 pp.

Von Kripp, D. 1933a. Der Oberschnabel-Mechanismus der Vogel (Nach den Methoden der graphischen Statik bearbeitet). *Morphol. Jb.,* **71** : 469–544.

———— **1933b.** Beitrage zur mechanischen Analyse des Schnabel-mechanismus. *Morphol. Jb.,* **72**: 541–566.

———— **1935.** Die mechanische Analyse der Schnabelkrummung und ihre Bedeutung fur die Anpass forschung. *Morphol. Jb.,* **76**: 448–494.

Weymouth, R. D., Lasiewski, R. C. & Berger, A. J. 1964. The tongue apparatus in hummingbirds. *Acta Anat.,* **58**: 252–270.

Wilkinson, D. H. 1951. Unusual feeding activity in the Spotted Redshank. *Br. Birds.,* **44**: 285–286.

Witherby, H. F., Jourdain, F. C. R., Ticehurst, N. F. & Tucker, B. W. 1943. *The Handbook of British Birds.* Vol. 4, revised, London.

Wormald, H. 1909. A tame Snipe and its habits. *Br. Birds.,* **2**: 249–258.

Yudin, K. A. 1961. (On the mechanism of the jaw in the Charadriiformes, Procellariiformes and some other birds.) *Trudy. zool. Inst. Leningr.,* **29**: 257–302. In Russian.

———— **1965.** (The phylogeny and classification of the Charadriiformes.) *Fauna SSR. Nov. Ser.* 91. Moscow-Leningrad. In Russian.

Zusi, R. L. 1962. Structural adaptations of the head and neck in the black skimmer *Rynchops nigra* Linnaeus. *Publs. Nuttall orn. Club.,* 3, vii + 101 pp.

———— **1967.** The role of the Depressor Mandibulae Muscle in Kinesis of the Avian Skull. *Proc. U.S. Nat. Mus.,* **123 (3607)** : 28 pp.

———— **& Storer, R. W. 1969.** Osteology and Myology of the head and neck of the Pied-billed Grebes (*Podilymbus*). *Misc. Publs. Mus. Zool. Univ. Mich.,* No. 139, 49 pp.

Also personal communications from the following:

Prof. R. W. Storer, University of Michigan.
Sheila S. White, Dept. of Veterinary Anatomy, University of Liverpool.
Dr. R. L. Zusi, Smithsonian Institution, Washington, D.C.